*Soviet and Western Perspectives
in Social Psychology*

Other Pergamon titles of interest

K. DANZIGER
Interpersonal Communication

O. K. GARNICA AND M. L. KING
Language, Children and Society

M. S. MIRON AND A. P. GOLDSTEIN
Hostage

J. MONAHAN
Community Mental Health and the
Criminal Justice System

M. SHERMAN
Personality: Inquiry and Application

I. SILVERMAN
The Human Subject in the Psychological
Laboratory

J. SYDNEY-SMITH AND L. G. KILOH
Psychosurgery and Society

D. N. WEISTUB
Law and Psychiatry

Soviet and Western Perspectives in Social Psychology

Edited by

LLOYD H. STRICKLAND

Carleton University

PERGAMON PRESS

OXFORD · NEW YORK · TORONTO · SYDNEY · PARIS · FRANKFURT

U.K.	Pergamon Press Ltd., Headington Hill Hall, Oxford OX3 0BW, England
U.S.A.	Pergamon Press Inc., Maxwell House, Fairview Park, Elmsford, New York 10523, U.S.A.
CANADA	Pergamon of Canada, Suite 104, 150 Consumers Road, Willowdale, Ontario M2J 1P9, Canada
AUSTRALIA	Pergamon Press (Aust.) Pty. Ltd., P.O. Box 544, Potts Point, N.S.W. 2011, Australia
FRANCE	Pergamon Press SARL, 24 rue des Ecoles, 75240 Paris, Cedex 05, France
FEDERAL REPUBLIC OF GERMANY	Pergamon Press GmbH, 6242 Kronberg-Taunus, Pferdstrasse 1, Federal Republic of Germany

First edition 1979

British Library Cataloguing in Publication Data

Paradigms and Priorities for Social Psychology II *(Conference), Carleton University, 1977*
Soviet and Western perspectives in social psychology.
1. Social psychology — Congresses
I. Title II. Strickland, L H
301.1   HM251   79—40311

ISBN 0—08—023389—9

Printed and bound at William Clowes & Sons Limited Beccles and London

Contents

Part III Theory and Research: Reciprocal Implications   209

Part IV Assessment   317

Name Index   325

Subject Index   333

Conference Participants

Aboud, Frances E. Assistant Professor, McGill University

Andreeva, Galina M. Head of Chair of Social Psychology, Moscow State University

Barefoot, John C. Associate Professor, Carleton University

Berry, John W. Professor, Queen's University

Bodalev, Alexei A. Secretary, Psychology and Age Physiology Division, Academy of Pedagogical Sciences of the USSR

Bueva, Lyudmilla P. Deputy Director, Institute of Philosophy, Academy of Sciences of the USSR

Dale, Jill Executive Secretary, The Paterson Centre, Carleton University

Dutton, Donald G. Associate Professor, University of British Columbia

Gribanov, Dmitri P. Senior Scientist, Academy of Sciences of the USSR

Holmes, John G. Associate Professor, University of Waterloo

Kiesler, Charles A. Executive Officer, American Psychological Association

Lomov, Boris F. Director, Institute of Psychology, Academy of Sciences of the USSR

Marshall, Marilyn E. Chairman, Department of Psychology, Carleton University

Morawski, Jill G. Graduate Student, Carleton University

Myers, C. Roger Executive Officer, Canadian Psychological Association

Nosulenko, Valeriy N. Senior Scientist, Academy of Sciences of the USSR

Pollenetsky, Elisabeth Medical Officer, Department of Veterans' Affairs, Government of Canada

Segalowitz, Norman Chairman and Associate Professor, Concordia University

Shorokhova, Ekaterina V. Deputy Director, Institute of Psychology, Academy of Sciences of the USSR

Strickland, Lloyd H. Professor, Carleton University

Stroebe, Wolfgang Professor, University of Marburg

Swingle, Paul G. Professor, University of Ottawa

Thorngate, Warren Associate Professor, University of Alberta

Zajonc, Robert B. Professor, University of Michigan

Introduction

LLOYD H. STRICKLAND

This book is one tangible outcome of an occasion marked by great dedication and effort on the part of social psychologists from North America and Continental Europe. It differs greatly from any previous, comparable endeavours, in that the majority of contributions are from Canada and Soviet Russia, and not the United States and Western Europe. Its *raison d'être* is to demonstrate how the spokesmen for what might be construed as two emerging social psychologies described their disciplines to each other. This "acquaintance process" was one which crossed hemispheric lines of territory, history, ideology, economics, language and philosophy; it is therefore remarkable that such a brief meeting should have been as fruitful and spontaneous as it turned out to be. Its success is, as the reader will finally observe, testimony to the idea that certain problems involving man and his social relations are considered important by people of vastly different heritages.

It would be gratifying to be able to declare at the outset that the symposium which generated these papers and discussions was the product of initial scholarly contemplation of these different backgrounds, that sober reflection then led to derivation of competing sets of social psychological theories and hypotheses, which finally met in planned confrontation in the academic arena. This would be a misleading indulgence. Rather than

1

attempt to impose an image of planned coherence on the symposium's events and issues, I shall instead invoke one of the basic principles of Soviet social psychology, i.e., that all social phenomena must be viewed in their temporal/historical context. Some informal history is therefore in order.

During 1974 and 1975, a young social psychologist from the University of Leningrad, Vladimir P. Trusov, visited the Social Psychology Laboratories at Carlton University. He had come to study certain aspects of Western social psychology, particularly the effects of some contemporary "methodological problems" (demand characteristics, experimenter effects, effects of deception, etc.) on experimental social psychology. An informed reader, recalling the above date, would correctly note that these issues were *not* then current, although the work of Orne (1962), Rosenberg (1965), Rosenthal (1966) and others had had an unquestionable impact on the field. The time lag, which led to Trusov's disconfirmed expectations, and which characterizes much scientific exchange between East and West, was a primary reason for the conference. It may be three, four or even five years before a completed piece of interesting research finds its way through a competitive Western publication process to colleagues in the USSR (if, indeed, one knows who they might be); it takes longer, if formal translation is necessary. Likewise, it will be clear from perusal of an issue of *Soviet Psychology* that we in the West must wait at least as long for developments from the USSR, and unless we read Russian, we have very few other potential sources of such information. It is probably also true that we have not sought it very aggressively.

So, the seeds for the conference were sown by Trusov and myself, largely in response to the delay in our exchange of scientific information — available printed words are, to put it simply, too few and far between. Trusov had arrived to study a slightly dated topic — the social psychology of the experiment; what he found was that Western social psychology had progressed well into what is generally termed its "crisis", and, indeed, had shown some signs of emerging from it, possibly slightly the better for wear. Instead of observing or running experiments concerned with, say, role-playing as a substitute for manipulation of naive subjects, Trusov found himself wading through drafts of various papers for a 1974 conference, some of which were subsequently published (Strickland, Aboud, and Gergen, 1976). The symposium which had spawned that collection had apparently been a success; it therefore seemed natural to ask if a Soviet-Western meeting would be of equal value, were it even possible to arrange one.

This question was the immediate stimulus for subsequent efforts expended by many people from either inside or outside social psychology; but of course the collective endeavours had their basis in more than an academic's interest in writing or assessing theoretical papers.

It is hard to believe that most of us, particularly in North America, are so nearly ignorant of developments in social psychology in the USSR as we appear, a point discussed elsewhere by Krauss (1972). To be sure, there are recent signs of an increasing interest in these developments (McLeish, 1975; Corson, 1976). In the West a Marxist approach to social psychology is beginning to be bruited about (e.g., Armistead, 1974), and West European social psychologists have begun formal contacts with colleagues from East Europe and the USSR. Elsewhere, social psychology probably lags behind the other divisions of psychology, both clinical and experimental, in its acquaintance with developments in the Soviet Union. Indeed, many Western colleagues have expressed surprise that there should even exist a Soviet *social* psychology, as though the fact that the discipline would of necessity be very young somehow made it less deserving of acknowledgement. Possibly this unfamiliarity stems from our recent preoccupation with ourselves, our past and our future, but whatever its reason, it is not defensible to let our ignorance continue.

While it obviously shares much with the United States, Canada is, in many important ways (its expanse, its geography, its multi-cultural nature, etc.) very similar to the USSR. As Canadian social psychologies emerge, comparison with developments in the Soviet Union is obviously to be desired. Psychologists in the United States, where, perhaps, most of the significant developments in modern social psychology have occurred, definitely seem interested in more immediate knowledge of research and theory from a country which itself represents one of the most significant large-scale social experiments in history. This seems to have been acknowledged by the American Psychological Association, among what White (1976) 'has called the "safe" areas of psychology. Regarding Soviet interests, the following statements should convince the Western reader that his ideas and research will have an eager audience in the USSR.

> The tasks facing social psychology call for energetic elaboration of its theories and research methods from the Marxist viewpoint.
> It is perfectly clear that the principles, methods, and conceptual apparatus developed in bourgeois social psychology bear the stamp of bourgeois ideology. The problems of social psychology reflect the contrast in approaches to society and man between the psychology of capitalist countries and Soviet psychology. Therefore, the elaboration of Marxist social psychology requires a critical analysis of everything being done in the capitalist countries (Lomov, 1972, p. 342).
> Social psychology is an indispensable component of any scientific study of socioeconomic, political, legal, or ideological problems, However, we cannot say that the problems, approaches, and methods in this field have been defined with adequate clarity. Psychological and concrete social investigations are often interchanged. The development, from a Marxist perspective, of the concepts and categories of social psychology has been delayed. Occasionally, conceptions from bourgeois social psychology are uncritically adopted.
> Yet, in contrast to psychophysiology, neurophysiology, and engineering psychology, in which there is a broad area of tasks common to Soviet and foreign science, social psychology is the subject of an intense ideological struggle. Therefore, the achievements in this area of psychology in different countries cannot be directly compared: they must be evaluated from a class perspective. In this context, critical analysis of the concepts, approaches, and methods developed in capitalist countries assumes paramount importance. A necessary condition for solving this task is the further development of a general theory of psychology and, above all, of its methodological problems Lomov, 1972, p. 350).
> Thus, if we now return to consideration of the overall tasks of social psychology, we find that a basis does exist for the conclusion that it is clearly inadvisable to reject various notions in social psychology just because they are employed in capitalist-oriented scholarship. Soviet psychologists must purify them of much theoretical overlay that is foreign to us, and if these notions are based on psychological phenomena that do objectively exist, must

give them a correct philosophical interpretation. In so doing, of course, one must not confine oneself to giving a theoretical interpretation of experimental data already accumulated abroad. It is necessary to mount our own experimental research, based on Marxist-Leninist psychological concepts of the individual and the collective. Only thus will we gain the opportunity to engage in constructive, fundamental and persuasive criticism of capitalist-oriented social psychology and to advance Soviet social psychology (Petrovsky, 1971, p. 395).

To recapitulate, the conference and the book were stimulated by a year's contact between a Soviet and a Canadian social psychologist in the first instance; in the second, they were the result of different sets of academic and cultural concerns. However, in the third, the collective and individual efforts of (mainly) two groups of people to work hard to understand one another and to make themselves understandable provided the real force behind the entire production.

Organizations of the Meetings

It is not appropriate to dwell at length on the complexities of organizing an "East-West Scientific Exchange". Anyone who has been involved in such planning will remember the problems vividly; one who has not may tempt his imagination with such pertinent items of information as these: the first invitations to Soviet participants were dated the third of February 1976, the first affirmation of ultimate Soviet interest was dated the tenth of October 1976, a panel of Soviet participants proposed by Russian officials was dated the seventh of February 1977, and visa requests for Soviet participants were dated the nineteenth of April 1977. As a staff member from the Soviet Embassy in Ottawa said at the beginning, "These things take time". These data are offered not to elicit sympathy for the organizer, Carleton University, or the Canada Council; neither are they cited to cast aspersions on those aspects of the Soviet Union's administrative system responsible for such matters. They simply document the degree of uncertainty in such endeavours, and thereby testify to the commitment of the social psychologists from Canada to the idea of such an exchange.

Selection of participants was, at the same time, easy and

difficult. It was easy to compile a list of Canadians[1] from whom
to select those who could be depended upon to deliver a good
paper. Further, they had to be willing to gamble — it was
acknowledged from the start by all parties that the first such
social psychology conference might not, at the end, take
place, or that it might suddenly be postponed. It was difficult,
however, to stop extending invitations — everyone approached
in Canada accepted immediately, and promised to prepare a
paper regardless of the risks involved. Consequently, many
deserving colleagues were *not* approached. Several other psychologists from the United States and Europe were invited to take
part, but because of uncertainty of the ultimate outcome of the
planning, they were given the option of serving as discussants or
giving a formal paper. As it eventuated, Wolfgang Stroebe
prepared such a paper, which is included in this book; R.B.
Zajonc from the University of Michigan gave a less formal talk,
summarizing recent research reported in detail elsewhere
(Zajonc, 1975), and he commented extensively on certain
formal papers; Charles A. Kiesler of the American Psychological
Association chaired a number of paper sessions and served as a
discussant at others. While a number of different social psychologists from the USSR were invited initially (some of these
were among the Soviet participants) or listed as alternates, the
ultimate membership of the delegation was determined by their
own officials, principally within the Academy of Sciences of the
USSR.

The order of papers given during the conference itself was
determined alphabetically. Until their arrival, it was not known
(a) who would *finally* form the Soviet delegation, or (b) what
their preferred paper topics would be. In the interest of both
simplicity and democracy, participants from each delegation
were scheduled in alphabetical order of last names, but "trades"
of time slots were encouraged when they seemed appropriate.

(1) "Canadian" refers here to participants living in Canada, and does not have necessary
implications for citizenship. Of course no citizenship data figured in any invitations.
However, the issue is of some interest (see the Discussion after John Berry's paper),
and the label "North American" seems somehow more awkward and circuitous
than "Canadian" does imperialistic.

Oddly enough, this rather *ad hoc* arrangement had a number of important effects. It avoided the labelling of sessions or days in a way that would limit paper content and, consequently, the subsequent discussion — that is, there was no *a priori* imposition of contexts (e.g., "General Theory in Social Psychology"). This is important, because it may be more confidently inferred that the topics which *did* turn up repeatedly were important ones for the process of East-West exchanges. Also, the schedule avoided direct infliction of "seniority effects" on the proceedings. If more established voices seemed to be heard more frequently by the week's end, it was because they had earned the recognition of all the participants.

All prospective participants had been asked to consider theoretical and/or professional issues that bore on the area of their particular research interest. Even the few departures from this proposed format had an "instructional" orientation (e.g. "what we have done", or "what we must do") that was compatible with the more empirical orientation of other papers. Indeed, some papers assumed both orientations.

Organization of the Book

For a time, it was proposed to try to represent the conference as the significant social episode it was, presenting the papers in the order in which they were given, tying them together with the transcripts of the recorded discussion, etc. However, the symposium was not construed primarily as an experiment; without the necessary (but entirely inappropriate) "pre- and post-" measures, a complex presentation and discussion of the week's dynamics would have been interesting, but very long and protracted. It was a relatively straightforward task to re-group the papers in terms of their general foci, so as to highlight both the similarities and the differences in the approaches — epistemological, theoretical, and empirical — between and within the delegations.

The reader may question how, with the obvious cultural and professional differences augmented by language discrepancies,

8 *Lloyd H. Strickland*

the conference yielded the coherent papers and discussions assembled and edited herein. The sessions were conducted primarily in English, through an interpreter when necessary, and all of the sessions were tape-recorded. For those papers not presented in English, what follows are edited versions of translations. Likewise, reprinted discussions are edited versions of the post-paper interchanges. With the latter, it has been attempted to include passages which highlight differences in East-West orientations, while excising that interaction primarily concerned with technical aspects of a preceding paper. The reader should not suppose that methodological problems, for example, were ignored — it is rather that in the interest of space, continuity, and focus on the purpose of the conference, details of these more technical aspects have been generally omitted. Where necessary, and particularly at those points where there seemed to be effortful explanations of basic episte-mological, theoretical and conceptual positions, consultation with colleagues familiar with both social psychology and the French, German, or Russian language has been sought. I have attempted to edit a given passage delivered, say, originally in Russian in a way to make it as clear as possible, without transforming Russian thoughts into English thoughts, and thereby destroying the essence of the former. I have felt that the violence done to an original conceptualization by such a conversion is a greater sin than leaving the reader to grapple with, say, a cumbersome sentence or paragraph — particularly when the writing concerns ideas. The following chapters will betoken our success or failure with this strategy.

I. Theory, History, and Social Structure

Jill Morawski (The Structure of Social Psychological Com-munities: A Framework for Examining the Sociology of Social Psychology) argues that a concern for the history and sociology of social psychology has been an important omission in the West. She submits that it is overdue for our social psychology to attain a scholarly grasp of its own past and present social structure. This understanding will be useful because (a) it will make us aware of the socio-cultural factors that have shaped us, (b) it may help us focus our attention on more appropriate theories, and (c) it will enable us to alter effectively psychology's structure and its system of information distribution. Morawski considers three contexts in which a sociological and/or historical orientation would help clarify issues about which there has been much debate: a recent controversy between certain Europeans and Americans about conflict research; the assertion that the course of western social psychology has been charted by an "elite"; and the misleading nature of the "histories" of our discipline that presently exist.

In the subsequent discussion, four points are proposed. Andreeva implies that a historical/sociological analysis of social psychology concerned with "social structure" would take a different course in the USSR. It would focus on factors outside, not inside, the discipline (e.g., see Lubrano, 1976). Kiesler proposes that analysis like Morawski's might also help clarify social psychology's position with respect to other sciences and the public. Thorngate seems to question the value of historical/sociological analysis and submits that our field has other weaknesses that are more important than those which Morawski has considered.

Galina Andreeva provides, in an analysis of the type urged by Morawski, a valuable treatment of the historical development of social psychology in the USSR, considering the problems of its relationship with general experimental psychology, and its progress toward becoming a legitimate field in its own right. She also describes the different "levels of methodology" that are considered in Soviet psychology, and after designating the several major areas of interest within the field, she finally indicates the applied areas into which most of their students progress. The most important aim of the paper, however, is to locate current developments in their Marxist historical/cultural context. One might indeed debate just when to begin dating one's history, especially when it is about ideas; however, it is clear that the social psychologist in the Soviet Union is at least concerned with the question of where his science comes from, and what its present priorities represent.

II. Theory, Methodology, and the Subject Matter of Social Psychology

This section is comprised of nine papers and edited excerpts from the subsequent discussions. The papers each make particular recommendations for progress, whether they focus on theory construction (Berry, Stroebe, Bueva), on content areas (animal behaviour — Barefoot; social perception — Bodalev; personality — Shorokhova; intergroup relations — Holmes), or on methodological problems (Gribanov, Swingle).

The first three papers in this section are concerned with general social psychological theory. John Berry (Comparative Social Psychology: Societal Roots and Universal Goals) argues that social psychology should search for its role as a "universal science", but that different societies *must* develop their own social psychologies, if only because "local" social psychologies are likely to be more accurate theoretically and more useful in their application. The universal social psychology should emerge from the use of comparative methods, focusing on more abstract and general processes. In the course of the discussion, Andreeva tries to clarify "general", and she and Berry develop a schema which will handle two dimensions of theoretical generality. The effects on Canadian social science of US "domination" are reviewed, and proposed solutions for this are assessed with respect to Berry's general proposals.

Stroebe (The Level of Social Psychological Analysis: A Plea for a More Social Social Psychology, examines the most important causes of social psychology's recent period of self-doubt. He notes that many preferred solutions for our problems have involved proposals for methodological improvement, and argues that, instead, we must have a *theoretical* re-orientation — one in which we study the individual (who seems to have become our most important unit of analysis) in his social context. We should, in effect, consider the importance of those variables normally of interest to the sociologist. As an appropriate model for our development he proposes Tajfel's theory of intergroup relations.

Kiesler argues that sociology has not had any more success than social psychology in establishing an understanding of social behaviour — he would accept more balance between sociological and individual emphases, but not an over-balance of the former. Stroebe agrees that social psychology must somehow overlap the two disciplines, and to Lomov's question of how this can be done, Berry proposes, and illustrates, the employment of variables "between" the classic choices of psychology (e.g. the F scale) and sociology (e.g. socio-economic status). Lomov argues that each social science should have its own area, and Zajonc, disagreeing with Lomov, finally exemplifies how we can use both sociological and psychological variables in our research without being eclectic.

Bueva (The Unity of Activity and Social Relations in the Construction of General Theory in Social Psychology) discusses philosophical problems related to how the social structure of society shapes social psychology. Because social behaviour takes widely different forms in society's different groups, it may sometimes seem doubtful that there can be any useful general principles which will emerge. She argues the importance of the Marxist conception of *activity*, maintaining that man's *activity* and his *social relations* are inseparably linked with one another. She comments on the consequences of this unity for research practice and explanation, and deliberates on the problems and directions such a conception will propose for social psychology. After this talk there is an intense episode in which Western social psychologists again try earnestly to comprehend basic terminology of the group from the USSR, involving, in this instance, the concept *activity*. Zajonc finally proposes a conception of this term which seems to be generally acceptable and understandable.

The next subset of papers is concerned with theory in standard "content" areas of social psychology. John Barefoot (The Role of Nonhuman Behaviour in North American Social Psychology) examines reasons why systematic attention to other species has

not, generally, been seen as worthwhile. Because much social
psychology has had an applied orientation, because critics
feel one "drags down" humans in comparing them with animals,
and for other reasons, we may miss the opportunities that
animal studies offer us for cross-species generalization, for gain-
ing an evolutionary perspective on our subject and, thus, for clarifying our problems. Barefoot considers how one result of this
neglect has been over-reliance on and over-interpretation of the
few "classics of the literature of animal social behaviour by
social psychologists. He does this with particular respect to the
research on crowding, offering an alternative, "coping" model
for interpreting this research; he argues that, if we view animal
behaviour as more complex than we have in the past, we may
better estimate the useful implications that animal and human
social behaviour have for each other.

The discussion which followed was particularly intense, with
both criticism and endorsement of certain of Barefoot's arguments by Zajonc, and an expression of deep concern for
caution in cross-species generalization by Lomov.

Alexei Bodalev's paper (On the Study of Some Cognitive
Processes in Soviet Social Psychology) was unorthodox in
comparison with other symposium papers, but it prompted one
of the most productive discussions. In an attempt to "short-
circuit" the delays of the usual publication process, discussed
above as a major reason for the conference, Bodalev acknowledged the difficulty that any Western researchers would have
if they were to try to locate colleagues in the Soviet Union.
He identified social psychologists actively concerned with
cognitive aspects of the communication process, including:
(1) the formation of awareness of social situations from verbal
contacts among participants; (2) developments in person-
perception among communicating individuals as a function of
bodily characteristics and behaviour; (3) the psychological
characteristics of perceivers, and (4) the role of emotional
states and of spatio-temporal factors as determinants of person-
perception and communicative behaviour. He argues that most
work in the person-perception area is interesting theoretically

but that it is of limited value in itself; we should be focusing on the relationship between these processes and the communication situation.

In response to questions concerned with the nature of specific research projects, Bodalev describes instances of work in real situations (physicians-patients, teachers-schoolchildren, managers-subordinates, etc.), and details an experiment on other- and self-perception of wrestling opponents. He also describes studies on conflict and of the identification of certain psychotic states on the basis of non-verbal behaviour.

The arguments of John Holmes and Peter Grant (Ethnocentric Reactions to Social Threat) are based on their discontent with the social psychological "principle" that intergroup conflict leads to ingroup cohesion and outgroup hostility, and on the observation that the evidence for this "principle" is really rather doubtful. They review the relevant literature, considering experimental manipulations and their results, and propose an integration of this material based on systems theory. They clarify why motivation of group members must be considered in a successful analysis of the relationship between conflict, external hostility and ingroup cohesiveness.

The following discussion highlights the concern among the Soviets about what constitutes real conflict, as opposed to perceived conflict, and the importance of this distinction.

Ekaterina Shorokhova (The Socio-psychological Approach to Personality) attempted to explicate the place of "personality" in Soviet social psychology. This role cannot be delineated with the often arbitrary clarity that those of us in the West might be able to summon with respect to our own discipline, since from the Marxist position almost *everything* significantly personal is socially determined. Accordingly, social psychology *must* be concerned with motives, interests, etc. Furthermore, the role of social science must be to help "arrange" social life so that each person may combine social significance with realization of the potential of his unique characteristics. She reviews the effects of the constant social intercourse between the person and his society; she illustrates why one must consider *persona-*

lity and the *collective* as united and inseparable, and examines the emergence of a "communal" type of personality. She discusses the effects of mass media on the development of personality, and shows the paramount importance of personal and cultural *values* as key components of personality. In the ensuing discussion, basic differences between Soviet and Western conceptions of personality are etched, as questions are voiced about the difference between "personality" and "character" in Soviet social psychology, about trans-situational stability of personality, and about the degree of predictive success with Marxist conceptions of personality. Great success is claimed by Bodalev for studies where the basis of prediction is the person's value orientation. Andreeva describes Jadov's currently important "dispositional conception of regulators of social behaviour", in terms of the need level implicit in a given disposition (e.g. "attitude") and the situation in which it is likely to be prepotent. The question of the relationship between "subjective" and "objective" aspects, which must be sharply drawn in Soviet psychology, leads to a discussion of the role of the *activity* of the person in shaping his personality and what he "knows" about the world.

The last two papers in this section involve specific priorities for research practice in social psychology. Paul Swingle (Damned if We Do — Damned if We Don't) discusses the ease with which business and government seem to have come to terms with the principles of behavioural technology and its related equipment (e.g. surveillance hardware, "subliminal stimulation" devices). He contrasts this with the difficulty psychologists have had in deciding whether to use that technology and knowledge themselves to study social behaviour. The latter group, even when it is not in a paralytic state of self-doubt, and even when it proclaims the necessity for study in the field instead of the lab, seems to be unable to decide what is ethical and what is not. Swingle insists that it is our obligation to find out the effects of such "secret" devices or strategies, and to communicate our knowledge to the public.

After Swingle's arguments and observations concerning

Western social psychology, Segalowitz asks about the status of research ethics, including the importance of deception and informed consent, in the USSR, to which there is detailed response by Andreeva.

Dmitri Gribanov, after listening to several of the Western papers and their ensuing discussions, abandoned his intended topic, to explain and argue for the Soviet approach to problems of methodology in social psychology. He criticizes Western science for its attempts to explain complex phenomena in terms of "simpler" approaches – applying explanatory notions from biology to an analysis of society, using the computer as a model for man, etc. Gribanov asserts that dialectical materialism offers a way to avoid these tendencies by defining the appropriateness of scientific endeavour in terms of its match with the particular level of "motion of matter" (mechanical, physical, chemical, biological, or social). Man may be most profitably viewed at the biological or social level; however, since higher levels include lower ones, we must study these also to get a complete understanding of man (e.g., we must be aware of biochemical bases of social behaviour). We should never make the mistake of transferring straight-forwardly the strategies appropriate for one level to another. The different forms or levels of movement interact, but laws should not be transferred from one level to another.

Gribanov's brief . . . and admittedly abstract, argument provokes a number of specific rejoinders. Zajonc, Gribanov and Lomov try to establish where a concept important in social psychology, "information processing", fits in the scheme of "levels of motion", and again, Gribanov and Lomov try to demonstrate how this Marxist approach affects actual research practice, in response to doubts expressed by Kiesler.

III. Theory, Research, and Their Implications for One Another

In this section are grouped the papers that dealt most directly with empirical research, primarily experimental social psychology. It includes four Canadian and two Soviet papers. Those of Lomov and Nosulenko illustrate the basic importance of concepts which have, in previous pages, provoked such searching discussion, such as the centrality of *communication,* the importance of shared *activity,* etc. They also point the way to some exciting possibilities for a "social psychophysics". The papers by Aboud, Dutton, Segalowitz and Thorngate individually propose future research in areas that have both theoretical and "real world" significance; collectively, they reflect the varied theoretical and empirical approach to such problems that typify the development of social psychology in Canada. In doing so, they contrast most clearly with the Soviet social psychological research considered at this conference, both in formal papers and in post-paper discussions.

Lomov's starting point is a familiar one — the notion that the nature of mental processes is determined by the person's *activity,* particularly when the activity involves communication. He describes results from several sets of exploratory studies, wherein he has examined different strategies for the solution of three different types of task, under conditions of individual or joint effort. He considers different stages in the problem-solving process.

Subsequent questions about variations in experimental procedure lead to discussions of the priority of statistical analysis in social psychological research, and exploration is begun for the reason for the differences observed under conditions of communication. Segalowitz proposes that such factors as motivation, or sensitivity to feed-back, or changes in criteria all might be affected in the "social" situation and Aboud hypothesizes the existence and relevance of different kinds of thought processes.

Valeriy Nosulenko (The Estimation of Sound Intensity when Subjects Communicate) begins with the observation that, in Soviet psychology, the concept of communication has become of great interest not only to the social psychologists, but also to the general-experimental psychologist. Sensory scaling obviously a fundamental psychological process — is affected by a great many things, and one of the principal ones is communication. Comparing subjective loudness scales of subjects tested either alone or after communication about their judgements with partners, Nosulenko demonstrates, with results from several experiments, certain major changes in the very nature of such scales and in the stability of individual estimates.

In the following discussion, it becomes clear that communication may modify not only decision-making and information processing, but possibly the basic sensory unit, as well. The "educative" role of communication is, indeed, an important one for the development of a "social psychophysics".

Frances Aboud (Self: An identity, a Concept, or a Sense?) claims that social psychologists, through their use of statistics and "stereotypes" (e.g., "the average subject") have overlooked certain possibly important roles which we should play. First we could provide a model of how to deal with individuals as individuals, not as group members, and, second, we could exhibit, and thus possibly present, the possibility of alternative behaviours which one may perform in a given situation. We are, she says, simply doing what "naive" persons do, i.e., comparing people to standards, and judging them accordingly. Aboud argues that we should at least entertain the alternative possibility of comparing people with ideals, not averages, and she considers consequences of this. This line of thought has implications for social psychologists interested in self-development and self-evaluation, with particular reference to notions of internal consistency, personal uniqueness, and stability of self. Kiesler voices doubts about the worth of some of our current data on the topic. Andreeva raises the question of the importance of the individual's *activity* on the development of his self-concept, and Bueva examines how the value of the individual depends on the particular social structure and educational system.

Donald Dutton (Social Psychology and Community Psychology: The Case of the Police) argues that attempts to bring our social psychological theories to bear in applied settings might help indicate areas of theoretical strength and weakness.

He claims that police organizations offer ideal instances of many of the behaviours that social psychologists wish to study; however, police are *not* studied, primarily because of the negative image of them held by most people. He describes and documents five areas where we might study police: (1) police-subject interaction, proxemics, and non-verbal communication; (2) police attribution of crime causation; (3) the consequences of the ambiguous role of police for their own attitudinal and stereotypic processes; (4) inter-group behaviour and solidarity, and (5) the variety of responses to violence. Dutton feels that social psychology has a lot to contribute to community groups, and that in its attempt to make this contribution, the discipline will itself be strengthened.

This argument raises in Andreeva the question of differences between social psychology and sociology, and she questions whether or not Dutton's interests would be better served by sociology. After some debate on this point, Bodalev describes and discusses an instance of research on police and policing in the USSR. After the question of whose province should include such studies is raised again, Zajonc urges that we focus instead on problems on which all forms of knowledge must converge.

Norman Segalowitz and Micheline Favreau (The Social Psychology of Second Language Communication) review recent research in four related areas: (1) language choice and intergroup relations; (2) effects on communication of variations in dialect; (3) the relationship between social motivation and second-language learning, and (4) cross-language skills and problems of social adjustment. They point out that social psychology has progressed a long way since language problems were linked to problems of intergroup perception, and that we may now approach the study of second-language communication as we would any person-task interaction, one which would be studied by systematic variation in the task parameters.

Excerpts from the discussion touch on social and theoretical significance of inter-ethnic-group communication. The value of these cross-language studies is considered and Bodalev offers an hypothesis about reliance on verbal and non-verbal cues and its possible relation to Pavlov's distinction between first and second signal systems.

Warren Thorngate (Memory, Cognition and Social Performance) urges social psychology's consideration of a new paradigm, one based, on the one hand, on a formal approach to information processing and decision making, and on the other, on introspection and experiment. He sees this scheme as more useful than the traditional approaches which have dominated our discussions of social behaviour and cognition — those based on "attitudes" or "attributions". Thorngate argues for the importance of *familiarity* as a basis for our cataloguing social interactions. He considers how these interactions may be stored in, and retrieved from, memory, and how we select appropriate responses. He argues that traditional social psychology may not have considered such an approach because it has been too tradition-bound.

Acknowledgements

Acknowledgements are due to many people and agencies for the success of the conference and for the appearance of this book. We are indebted to two officials of the Academy of Sciences of the USSR, I.V. Milovidov and Alexandre Kulakov. Similarly, we owe much to the Canada Council, represented in this instance by an indefatigable Jules Pelletier. Many at Carleton University helped smooth the path of the conference and the book, principally Phillip E. Uren, Director of the Norman Paterson Institute for International Affairs, and R.A. Wendt, Dean of Social Sciences.

It must be acknowledged, however, that the energetic sponsorships of supporting officials and intellectual strivings of delegates would have been far less effective were it not for the unflagging efforts of two of the participants. Dr. Elizabeth Pollenetsky was a dazzling interpreter, becoming mistress of the most subtle nuances of social psychological parlance in so short a time, and with such effectiveness, that participants and observers marvelled. Mrs. Jill Dale, of the Paterson Centre, arranged people, rooms, meals, books, money, photocopying and countless other details with such an unobtrusive efficiency that there was not an instance during the conference when interruption of the proceedings by administrative distractions seemed imminent. These two were the only really inexpendable participants.

Subsequent to the conference, my own work and that of various helpers on the preparation of this book have been made possible by a Canada Council Leave Fellowship and a year's tenure in the Department of Experimental Psychology at Oxford. Michael Argyle has been supportive of my editorial and research activities, and tolerant of my erratic absences from meetings of the social psychology group. Wolfson College has provided excellent facilities and occasions for quiet thought as well as for Russian lessons, between my bouts with audiotapes, manuscript drafts, etc. Members of the secretarial and typing staff at the Department of Experimental Psychology have been the most skilled, the most rapid, and the most kindly forgiving I have known in academia. My wife Pat, and numerous colleagues here and at other British universities have provided me with insights into Soviet social psychology that I could never have gained on my own, through many question and answer sessions, at comfortable pubs and after university seminars. Finally, my daughter Jennifer, who turned my scrawled transcripts into typescripts, my tortured sentences into more peaceful ones, and my stack of xeroxed journal pages into neatly abstracted articles, provided a cheerful momentum which made the entire project more fun than an editor really deserves to have.

References

Armistead, N. (Ed.), *Reconstructing Social Psychology,* Harmondsworth, Middlesex: Penguin, 1974.
Corson, S.A. (Ed.), *Psychology and Psychiatry in the USSR,* New York: Plenum, 1976.

Krauss, R.M., Social psychology in the Soviet Union, *Soviet Psychology*, 1972, *11*, 4-7.

Lubrano, L.L., *Soviet Sociology of Science*, Columbus, Ohio: American Association for the Advancement of Slavic Studies, 1976.

Lomov, B., Present status and future development of psychology in the USSR in the light of decisions of the 24th Congress of the Communist Party of the Soviet Union, *Soviet Psychology*, 1972, *11*, 329-58.

McLeish, J., *Soviet Psychology: History, Theory and Content*, London: Methuen, 1975.

Orne, M., On the social psychology of the psychological experiment: with particular reference to demand characteristics and their implications, *American Psychologist*, 1962, *17*, 776-83.

Petrovsky, A.V., Some problems of research in social psychology, *Soviet Psychology*, 1971, *10*, 382-98.

Rosenberg, M., When dissonance fails: On eliminating evaluation apprehension from attitude measurement, *Journal of Personality and Social Psychology*, 1965, *1*, 28-42.

Rosenthal, R., *Experimenter Effects in Behavioural Research*, New York: Appleton-Century-Crofts, 1966.

Strickland, L.H., Aboud, F.E. and Gergen, K.J., *Social Psychology in Transition*, New York: Plenum, 1976.

White, W., To Russia with hope, *A.P.A. Monitor*, 1976, *7*, 1.

Zajonc, R.B. and Markus, G.B., Birth order and intellectual development, *Psychological Review*, 1975, *82*, 74-88.

PART I

History, Social Structure
and the Development
of Social Psychology

The Structure of Social Psychological Communities: A Framework for Examining the Sociology of Social Psychology

JILL G. MORAWSKI

I wonder if poets are cognizant of their impact on scientific discourse; literary excerpts provide the scientific discussant with analogy, description, metaphor, and even wit. Occasionally, the user of poetic phrases even "out-metaphors" the author's original configurations. And in succumbing to the artist's words, I at least feel secure in knowing that I am in good company. Therefore, in this tradition I would like to offer a word from William Butler Yeats:

> Though the great song return no more
> There's keen delight in what we have:
> The rattle of pebbles on the shore
> Under the receding wave.
> (from *The Nineteenth Century and After,* 1932)

The phase represents Yeats's persistent fear — that of imminent death. Borrowing these lines for their applicability to social psychology, one may image the whirl of criticism that proceeded social psychology's youth and picture the quiet motion of the discipline's demise. Several years ago, with the surge of criticism known as the "crisis" in social psychology, that image may have been appropriate. Today it would no longer fit. The phrase cannot represent the final ascent of social psychology with its resonance of critical murmurings. The only wave in the discipline appears to have been nothing more than a momentary indulgence in self-criticism. Social psychology's movement seems to be more enduring for there remain only a few who persist to question the discipline's authenticity (see Gergen, 1976). In other words, just as Yeats's lines may also describe the termination of a fine century, the nineteenth, the analogy for social psychology can be that of a temporary critical period rather than the end of a social scientific discipline.

And yet, the solutions offered to the problems raised in the "crisis" have been neither sufficient nor conclusive. Debates ensuing from Gergen's (1973) thesis on social psychology's cultural determinism are politely continued (but in a less established journal); [1] claims of ideological biases and the neglect of critical historical assessment are pursued by a few interested followers; and criticisms of methodology and of the discipline's position as a natural or social science have yet to affect the products of our research as evidenced in the relatively unaffected contents of established journals. While all these aspects of social psychology, and the apparent resistance to change or challenge them, deserve attention, my present concern rests with one of these issues: the degree to which our scientific enterprise is influenced by extra-scientific factors. Essentially, it is the question of the extent to which the growth of social psychological knowledge is dependent upon social and historical conditions. The primary objective of this paper is to review the claims for social psychology's dependency on or susceptibility to non-scientific influences. From this point, models for the sociology of social psychological knowledge are offered and possible directions for empirical investigations are outlined. It should be noted that this paper contains a theoretical analysis and, therefore, falls err to a cogent criticism which has been addressed to most studies in this area: the lack of empirical verification (Merton, 1961, 1973; Gurvitch, 1971).

Therefore, I will discuss three cases from the sociology of social psychological knowledge that have been subjected to preliminary analyses. However, initial clarification of major

(1) A series of articles concerning Gergen's thesis appeared in *Personality and Social Psychology Bulletin, 2*, 1976.

issues and a prospective on the models available for viewing these issues are essential prerequisites for research. But before embarking on these tasks, it is imperative to heed the specific claims for critical self-reflection of social psychology as well as the major reservations about such self-reflective activities.

On the Indulgence of Self-reflection

Contained in the so-called "crisis" literature are a number of criticisms aimed precisely at disclosing the relation between social psychological knowledge and the social structure within which that knowledge is developed and communicated. Numerous social psychologists have commented on the manner in which theories mirror societal conditions. For instance, Moscovici (1972) perceived bargaining theory as a distinct product of North American economics; Apfelbaum and Lubek (1976) and Plon (1974) criticized the predominant mode of conflict research as illustrative of political and ideological concepts. Historians have discussed the antecedents of the positivist myth, the distorted belief in a value-free science (Samelson, 1974; cf. Buss, 1975, 1976a; Franks, 1975). Others have delineated the relationship between social psychological research and the society or agencies which support that research (Steiner, 1974; Zuniga, 1975). As documented in the case of small group research, institutional and federal funding policies have been shown to influence the scope of the research area as well as the methodologies employed (McGrath and Altman, 1966). These criticisms relate to the contention that social psychological research is susceptible to fads (Steiner, 1974; Cartwright, 1973; Lubek, 1976a). Finally, there is Gergen's (1973) now classic statement that social psychological theories are culturally and historically dependent.

Although these criticisms were all voiced within a relatively short period and in impressive numbers, they are not unique to social psychology. Buss (1975) recently summarized the need for a sociology of psychological knowledge, and in so doing documented the requests for such analyses which appeared within the psychological literature. Buss's article outlined the instances where psychological theories/constructs are explicable only if the social context of that research is made apparent; it documented the emergence of and necessity for a sociology of psychological knowledge. Buss clearly recognized what must follow his statement: the development of a systematic and theoretical framework. Furthermore, he sensed a task that must precede empirical investigations: the *justification* for a sociology of psychological knowledge that exceeds the amusement of heuristics.

Investigation into the sociology of social psychology can be viewed as mere self-indulgence, a squandering of research energies. Statements about the discipline's social structure may elicit a skeptical "So what — what difference will such knowledge make?" The question itself is valid but must be first addressed in terms of the underlying intentions of the doubting Thomases who possess it. A dubious attitude toward such research reflects either a denial of extra-scientific and non-intellectual influences on psychological knowledge — a denial that is not foreign to the sociology of science in general (Crane, 1972) — or repudiation of its importance for the pursuit of social psychological knowledge (see Eysenck's (1976) reply to Buss's article). While the latter attitude implies recognition of the social bases of scientific knowledge, the social influences are considered either to be treated adequately by retrospections of the discipline's elder statesmen or to be a known and perhaps immutable factor of whose prescience cannot or does not guide developments in psychological knowledge. The latter rationale, a recognition yet dismissal of extra-scientific conditions, is common among social psychologists. Consider the comments of a leading North American social psychologist who noted how cultural factors restrict the usefulness of a certain European text of social psychology: "From an American perspective the culture gap displayed is so great that the book is unlikely to be very influential on our own attempts to come to grips with the crisis in the field" (Smith, 1973, p. 610). Aside from discernible ethnocentrism, the statement depicts an awareness of social and historical factors yet implies that such speculation is sufficient; additional analyses appear unnecessary. Such treatment will lead the social psychologist no further than it has led many sociologists; both disciplines are beset with a wealth of theory and speculation yet marked by a conspicuous absence of methodology and empirical applications (Crane, 1967; Merton, 1973; Gurvitch, 1971). Thus, it is essential to address the "so whats", the questions of to what ends is this information valuable. While sociologists of science have prepared a multiplicity of replies, the fundamental arguments for a sociology of social psychological knowledge can be summarized in three points.

(1) *Recognition of the socio-historical factors which affect our knowledge.* As mentioned, not all psychologists recognize the extra-scientific bases of psychological knowledge and even for many who do, the nature of this interdependence is either vaguely understood or not appreciated. As Samelson (1974) has demonstrated, most social psychologists perceive their history as one stemming from the methodological rigor of positivism but without the value-laden aspects of positivistic doctrines. Therefore, the first asset of a sociology of social psychological knowledge would entail the awareness of the extra-scientific influences on social psychology and the consequences that these influences would have on any proposed philosophic or scientific conceptualization of man. This in turn will foster a better understanding of social psychological theories: "One of the practical aims of a sociology of psychological knowledge would be to emphasize the relationship between fact and value within psychology and thereby help to make psychologists more self-conscious of the implications their research has with respect to creating a specific kind of description and knowledge" (Buss, 1975, p. 991).

(2) *An approach to revised and more appropriate social psychological theories.* Recognition of the conditions contributing to the nature of social psychological knowledge can proceed to application to the construction of new modes of thought. First, as Buss (1975) has suggested, such awareness "may serve the purpose of explicitly adopting nontraditional

epistemological criteria of truth" (p. 1000). Several individuals
have presented models for social psychology that are grounded
on ·what may be termed "enlightened" epistemologies. Israel
(1972) has called for a "critical social science" that would
apply critical analyses and self-reflection to empirical social
theories by accommodation of extra-scientific values, social
interests, and stipulations on the nature of man. Israel's suggestions are based in part on the work of Habermas who has devised
methods for the critical analysis of scientific epistemologies
(cf. Habermas, 1968, 1971). Rommetveit (1976) has proposed
an "emancipatory social psychology" that includes an
explication of philosophical norms implicit in social psychological research. Thus, the explicit discussion of "personal
versus impersonal causality, of crime versus sickness, and of
the nature of social reality will lead to a better understanding of
the indeterminacy of our science as well as 'emancipatory
self-understanding', a picture of man as a creature, capable of
transforming part of his subjectivity into states of intersubjecti-
vity" (Rommetveit, 1976, p. 17).

Similar advances have been made by those investigating the
prospects for a dialectical psychology; such a model accounts
for the relationships not only between the individual and society,
but between the scientist and society (Riegal, 1975, 1976;
Wozniak, 1975). In this sense a "scientific dialectics leads to
developmental and historical awareness which is expressed,
for example, in the understanding of the struggle between
different scientific theories" (Riegal, 1976, p. 697). Related
to these objectives are the proposals for reflexive psychological
research, that is, the idea that a "self consciousness includes
the psychologist's awareness of his relationship to and with his
subject matter and the awareness of his own role with respect
to his inquiry. The knowledge that derives from such reflexi-
vity is a tripartite knowledge — about the subject, about the
researcher, and about the knowledge itself" (Gadlin and Ingle,
1975, p. 1008).

These examples should suffice as illustrations of the creative
effects which a critical self-understanding may foster at the

epistemological and metatheoretical levels of social psychology.

(3) *The potential to constructively alter the discipline's structure and dissemination of information.* The proposals that incorporate the sociological and historical aspects of scientific knowledge are designed for the achievement of a better understanding of social psychology as well as the social nature of man. Additionally, we may also achieve a better understanding of our discipline and the ways in which knowledge is enunciated and disseminated. Such understanding may be advantageous to the processes of communicating information and coordinating programs. One obvious condition that would receive clarification is the scarcity of interdisciplinary communications; the social and historical factors which have determined the structure and division of disciplines have already received preliminary attention by Campbell (1969). The existing networks and the future possibilities for transnational communications between social psychologists may be similarly examined. Further research may lead to the elimination of obsolete structures and a constructive interdependence between social scientific fields as well as measures for international communication systems.

Models from the Sociology of Science

As an outgrowth of the sociology of knowledge, the sociology of science has been developed to extend upon and confirm the principal thesis presented by Mannheim that "there are modes of thought which cannot be adequately understood as long as their social origins are obscured" (Mannheim, 1936, p. 2). Numerous aspects of social psychology can be considered within this context; however, the sociology of science encompasses various theoretical and methodological approaches and it is necessary to ascertain the adequacy of these in terms of the special conditions of and objectives for social psychological knowledge.

Merton (1961) has presented a three-fold description of the methodological approaches in the sociology of science: the historical development of ideas, the relations between the discipline and society, and the social structure of the discipline as it affects intellectual activities. While Merton's taxonomy incorporates the major trends it overlooks two important dimensions in such research. First, sociologies of science can be differentiated by the *source* of influence on science which they attend to. Basically, this is the question of whether the influence on any science is external or internal to the discipline. Second, sociologies of science may focus on certain *types* of scientific thought: intellectual or social. Regarding these dimensions, Cole and Cole (1973) have prepared a typology of sociologies of science which incorporates the possible combinations ensuing from the emphases on particular types and sources of influences on science. This typology can be utilized to briefly sketch the basic models available for analysis of social psychology and evaluate the adequacy of each (see Table 1 in the Appendix).

The first model comprises the investigation of the intellectual sources of scientific development which appear internally – within the science or discipline. In this case, the influence of intellectual ideas becomes the primary focus and social factors are either denied or neglected. Within social psychology, this model has been frequently employed albeit without being explicitly defined as a sociology of scientific knowledge. These analyses have been developed primarily from the work of Thomas Kuhn (1963): the notions of "paradigm", "normal science", and "scientific revolutions". While Kuhn recognized the importance of social factors his chief concern has been with existing scientific ideas and their relations to new ones (Cole and Cole, 1973). Within social psychology the Kuhnian paradigm has been used to explain the growth of a particular issue, such as risky shift research (Cartwright, 1973) and interpersonal attraction research (Triandis, 1975). Similarly, it has been employed prescriptively, i.e., to outline the epistemological directions of research or theory development (cf. articles in Strickland, Gergen and Aboud, 1976). For social psychology, this model presents several difficulties. In its emphasis on

intellectual factors there also appears a necessity to consider
epistemologies and assumptions of scientific proof. This not only
happens in social psychology but has also been found to cause
insurmountable problems for the sociologist of science, regardless of his scientific speciality (Crane, 1972). Second, attending
only to intellectual factors perpetuates the notion that enters
into many Kuhnian-oriented papers; that is, there may be a
continued neglect of internal and external social influences.
Further, a reliance on the paradigm concept has not ensured a
comprehension of Kuhn's arguments; in general usage, confusion
or misinterpretation of Kuhn's ideas has become problematic
(Masterman, 1970; Briskman, 1972; Samelson, 1973).

The second theme found in the sociology of science entails
attention to the external influences of intellectual activities.
Included in this category are studies which trace the transference of ideas between disciplines or specialities, studies which
could be appropriately designated as histories of ideas (see
Lovejoy, 1936; Bynum, 1975). Since the communication and
acceptance of intellectual ideas requires considerable time,
most research of this type would be retrospective or historical.
Few such studies on social psychology are available with the
exception of those tracing the influence of biological research
on nineteenth century social theories (Semmel, 1960; Phillips,
1970; Mandelbaum, 1971). Inherent in this approach is the
neglect of social conditions and problems of epistemology.

Another methodology consists of examining the external
influences on a science, but it focuses on the manner in which
external variables interact with social conditions of that science.
This position is closely related to the original tenets of the sociology of knowledge: the influence of societal conditions and
social structure on the growth of knowledge. Social psychologists have discussed this influence on their discipline (cf.
Moscovici, 1972; Zuniga, 1975); for instance, Steiner (1974)
claimed that the popularity of group research has been dependent
upon social and political conditions in the United States.
However, such a position falls err to the same problems which
arose in earlier formulations in the sociology of knowledge:

a vagueness of ideas regarding societal intervention and political influence and extreme difficulties in conducting empirical tests of these propositions (Crane, 1972). This approach is also susceptible to an under-evaluation of intellectual ideas and unique social surroundings within the science or discipline.

Finally, the sociology of science can be directed toward the concern for the social factors operating within that science; the internal organization of science is studied in terms of its influence on scientific knowledge. This technique has the advantage of suspending epistemological judgements, avoiding vagueness of the greater society/science assumptions and incorporating feasible empirical investigations (Crane, 1972). It has been shown that through the research on a science's social structure, one can investigate a community's cognitive norms (Crane, 1972; Whitely, 1974; Van Nossum, 1974), communication patterns (Hagstrom, 1965; Crane, 1972), stratification (Cole and Cole, 1973; Mulkay, 1972), and specific relationships between disciplines and government (Blume, 1974; Mulkay, 1976).

In summary, this final approach to the sociology of social scientific disciplines appears to be a feasible and promising one. In addition, there are at least three ways in which social psychology is particularly suited for such an approach. First, as mentioned, there is awareness among social psychologists that the discipline's social structure somehow influences intellectual and theoretical developments (i.e., Cartwright, 1973; Steiner, 1974). Yet little has been done to ascertain the nature and extent of these influences. Second, controversies and issues have occasionally been explained in terms of ideological, community or national differences among social psychologists (i.e., Smith, 1973; Shaver, 1974) but these comments have received little attention. Finally, some have argued that the social structure of social psychology is controlled by a chosen few who are able to exert considerable influence on the discipline's growth and operation (i.e., see Strickland *et al.*, 1976; Lubek, 1976b). All of these points relate directly to the question of how the internal social structure affects social psychological knowledge.

Furthermore, until these questions are addressed, many of the commentaries regarding the political, societal, and ideological implications of social psychological research can receive only tentative and superficial treatment.

Lest my comments have appeared only reflective of the despondent attitude of disgruntled individuals who finally abandoned the criticisms found originally in the "crisis" literature and, hence, if they sound much like an echo of another pebble, the remainder of my paper is devoted to more constructive issues. Thus far, I have attempted to answer the "what fors" which have served as replies to the claims for a sociology of social psychological knowledge, and to present a sketch of the available models for empirical research. In conclusion, I wish to discuss three issues within social psychology that could benefit from critical socio-historical examinations. It should be remembered that these issues are offered as preliminary case studies; ultimately, further analysis is required but at this point they may be used to elucidate the potential methods and approaches to a sociology of social psychological knowledge.

I. Controversies in Social Psychology: A Case Study

Historians and sociologists alike have found that the analyses of scientific controversies or disputes offer valuable insight into the nature of a discipline's development. Historians of psychology have illustrated how the analysis of controversies between individuals or groups may uncover the psychological, emotional and cognitive components of a controversy as well as its intellectual perimeters which affect the final resolution or consequent development of the issue (Pongratz, 1967, 1975; Krantz, 1969; Henle, 1973).

Within the sociology of science, the nature of intellectual controversies has received various interpretations. Originally, Merton (1973) explained such conflicts as either a normal manifestation of scientific ethos, an organized skepticism toward innovations and discrepant interpretations, or a conflict between individuals which arises from ethnocentrism and cast mores. More recently, controversies have been explained not only through scientific ethos and ethnocentrism but also through the existence of divergent "cognitive norms" or professional ideo logies (Farrell, 1975; Hagstrom, 1965; Robbins and Johnston 1976). Accordingly, research groups are seen to operate within the norms of theory, methodology, and research techniques which may differ from those norms of another group. In these cases, the groups' mutual involvements with the same issue/problem result in a conflict that may be unresolvable.

The notion of "cognitive norms" within scientific communities is usually presented through the Kuhnian framework (1963) of a paradigm: the shared exemplars of one group may differ significantly from the other, and inevitably a conflict over some issue arises (Farrell, 1975; Robbins and Johnston, 1976). However, reliance on the debatable (and certainly exploited) ideas of a paradigm is not essential to acceptance of the notion of "Cognitive norms". Others have explained how a research community can reach a consensus on the definition of pheno-mena, technical applications, and interpretations of findings (Whitely, 1974). Regardless of the epistemological explanation for "cognitive norms" or consensus, there is agreement on the high probability of eventual conflicts between relatively inde-pendent research communities. There is also agreement on the importance of such controversies; whether they result in crisis or revolution, controversies frequently represent a major development in the history of the scientific discipline. However, controversies may spawn alienation, fragmentation and the formation of "deviant" specialities which depart from the discipline (Hagstrom, 1965; Crane, 1972; Farrell, 1975; Robbins and Johnston, 1976).

This lengthy introduction to the research on scientific controversies is intended to provide a framework from which to review a recent controversy within social psychology. This particular controversy has been conducted in conference papers and journal discussions. It has been concerned with the nature of conflict research and is represented, on one side by a North American, Morton Deutsch, and on the other side by several

European social psychologists, notably of two supposedly divergent ideologies that separate North American and European ideals for social psychology (Nemeth, 1974; Chadwick-Jones, 1976). Before the insufficiencies of this explanation are discussed, a brief history of the "Deutsch versus Europe" debate is in order.

The criticism of North American conflict research was formally presented on three separate occasions; each statement focused extensively on the work of Morton Deutsch. Apfelbaum and Lubek (1976) argued that North American conflict research (1) was ideologically and financially tied to the American perception of the Cold War; (2) was based on a particular economic conception of man as illustrated in gaming theories; and (3) failed to account for all forms of conflict, specifically those of whom they identified as "invisible groups". Deutsch (1976) replied that North American research on conflict had a history that predated Cold War politics and was developed in conjunction with many forms of conflicts, including those of minorities. The second episode, published in a European journal, consisted of an equally critical essay on conflict research in which Plon (1974) singled out Deutsch's research as the subject of his critique. Plon argued that North American conflict research (1) was rooted in Cold War events; (2) reflected political discourse while presenting itself as apolitical, i.e., it represented a reductionist model of interpersonal exchange — an economic process among individuals; (3) assumed a process of resolution that arose from dominant North American ideology; and (4) these biases were reflected in gaming research. Deutsch (1974) again replied that North American conflict research (1) began much earlier than the Cold War; (2) recognized more than a single dimension of conflict; (3) required a theory of society only in regards to the *application* of research; and (4) other models of society, besides a Marxist one, are conceivable. A similar, although less hostile, debate occurred between Deutsch (1975) and a reviewer, Billig (1975), of Deutsch's latest volume on conflict research.

The published commentaries on this controversy provide

negligible enlightenment on the nature of the dispute. Nemeth (1974), while agreeing with Plon's attack on the ideology implicit in North American conflict studies, criticized Plon for neglecting his own ideological ploys and forcing a one dimensional view of North American research. Likewise, Chadwick-Jones (1976), in agreeing with some of Plon's comments, also argued that Plon's views were equally parochial, implied reductionism (upward reduction to a sociological level), and overlooked much North American research (primarily field studies) which attends to the social structure of a conflict situation.

Not only are these commentaries on the conflict research controversy devoid of suggestions to solve the apparent puzzles resulting from the discrepant explanations, but they also fail to examine, or even to describe, the nature of the disagreements. In other words, they omit analyses of significant sociological and psychological processes within that situation. The controversy may be more clearly understood in view of the aforementioned research on scientific disputes. Three points taken from this literature demonstrate the value of such cognitive and sociological analyses. First, scientific controversies in which the two sides hold divergent cognitive norms usually exhibit an inability to communicate efficiently; the protagonists tend to "talk through" each other (Robbins and Johnston, 1976). For instance, Deutsch insisted on his own "marxism" in a fashion that betrayed his deafness to Plon's statements on Marxist analysis. In his retort regarding the necessity for a theory of society, Plon apparently missed some of the same points which had eluded Deutsch.

Second, scientific disputes involving variant cognitive strategies can be distinguished by the wholesale dismissal of the opponent's arguments and a determined reinstatement of one's own paradigm (Robbins and Johnston, 1976). And while empirical evidence is rarely used in such exchanges, its appearance is marked by a certain vulnerability. In such a manner Deutsch rejected the criticisms aimed at game theory and reinforced his own conceptions about the model as useful in theoretical endeavors. Where both sides supported their contentions with empirical evidence they placed themselves in vulnerable, if not dangerous, positions. Apfelbaum, Plon, and Deutsch all backed their arguments about the origins of North American conflict research with historical examples. Yet, all three err in their perception of historical events.[2]

Finally, scientific controversies may indicate roles manifested through professional and social group identity. In turn, divergence from these professional roles frequently results in the exploitation of certain authorities and denial of others; essentially, further alienation between groups ensues (Farrell, 1975; Robbins and Johnston, 1976). Indeed, such activities comprised a major portion of the conflict debates. The exchanges included a significant amount of personal comments ranging from questioning an individual's linguistic skills to their professional competency.

When the issue over conflict research is reviewed in terms of its social and cognitive perimeters, the controversy can be identified, not so much as an empirical debate over theory, but as a series of communications structured by non-empirical conditions. It becomes obvious that future interactions on this problem must attend to these social and cognitive factors if the controversy is to be understood. The consequence of ignoring these factors may resemble the conclusions to similar controversies in other scientific communities: alienation, greater fragmen-

(2) In an analysis of the historical statements made by Apfelbaum and Lubek (1976) and Deutsch (1976) I found that neither could support their positions with historical evidence. For instance, Apfelbaum and Lubek dated the beginning of conflict research with the Cold War and post-World War II international politics. Deutsch believes such research originated from the emergence of social psychology and concomitantly, international strife in the 1930s. From a review of historical conditions it becomes obvious that both international turmoil and inter-American unrest existed prior to either the 1930s or 1940s; further, support for conflict situations could be found at almost any chosen date. The history of a scientific discipline cannot rest entirely on political history; the records of the discipline's activities must be of some importance. Deutsch and Apfelbaum and Lubek would have discovered a wealth of pre-1920 conflict research had they consulted psychological texts and annals. For example, studies in eugenics, instincts, evolution, and psychoanalysis often dealt with the subject of conflict (cf. Bagehot, 1873; Trotter, 1916; Semmel, 1960).

tation, and restricted communications (Hagstrom, 1965; Crane, 1972; Robbins and Johnston, 1976; Farrell, 1975).

II. Elites in Social Psychology

The second case for a socio-historical examination constitutes the idea of power and prestige and its distribution within the social structure of scientific disciplines. Although social psychologists have suggested the existence of a disciplinary power structure, no formal or systematic investigation of the phenomenon has been initiated. While the issue of such a power structure received considerable attention at a recent conference, there was not even consensus on whether any power structure actually existed (cf. Strickland *et al.,* 1976). Indeed, those who recognized such a structure within the discipline disagreed about its influence on theoretical or experimental research. Accordingly, the "power" was thought to comprise either an "interlocking directorate in social psychology in the United States which controls the journal space" (Gergen), a consequence of our ambiguous criteria for judging excellence (Zajonc), or it was a meaningless concept since it was thought to be widely diffused among numerous groups including government agencies and research review panels (Secord). In a synopsis of the power discussion it was even suggested that the discussion itself was in various ways determined by the power structure among the discussants (Lubek, 1976b, 1976c).

As this particular discussion illustrates, the question of a power hierarchy or elites within social psychology will merely continue as intuitive vocalizations until two problematic issues are confronted: (1) an explication of what constitutes a power structure, hierarchy, or elite and how these phenomena influence social psychological knowledge, and (2) the empirical examination of these concepts in the functioning of social psychology. The first issue can be approached initially through the literature on the social structure of scientific disciplines. The second can only be realized through systematic investigations. Ultimately, judgements on the power structure must await empirical analysis;

yet, these analyses can be prompted by similar research on other scientific disciplines.

As mentioned earlier, more researchers are finding that internal analysis of a science — its structure, networks and communications — provide fruitful insights into the discipline's acquisition of knowledge. Analysis of the social systems and cognitive structures of scientific communities avoids assumptions about scientific proofs (i.e., positivism and values) (Crane, 1972; Hagstrom, 1965). Utilizing this approach, many scientific communities have been found to contain an elite, a powerful subgroup within the field. *The Oxford Dictionary* defines elite as "the choice part" and within the sociology of science it has been used to refer to those scientists who belong to the apex of the discipline's hierarchy (Cole and Cole, 1973) — a small number of individuals who, by virtue of achieved status, have come to hold positions of prestige and power. The presence of elites is evidenced through three distinct conditions: rewards and facilities are distributed unequally; there is a small network of social ties among the members; control and direction of the activities of others are associated with the elite, and members influence further recruitment into the elite (Cole and Cole, 1973; Mulkay, 1976). Sociological studies on specific communities have disclosed interesting findings on the functioning of elites. While social and economic backgrounds appear to have negligible influence on an individual's later recognition or membership in a prestigious network, the institution where an individual received training as well as that of his current affiliation are highly relevant (cf. Crane, 1967; Merton and Zuckerman, 1973; Mulkay, 1976). One study found that scientific recognition is more likely to come from the individual's affiliation with a prestigious university than his/her level of productivity (Crane, 1967). Other studies have discovered that acceptance of research for journal publication is highly related to the author's and reviewer's institutional affiliation (Crane, 1967; Yotopoulos, 1961). Informal communication networks between eminent scientists, fostered by concentrations of such individuals at select institutions, has been shown to bear significant weight in the recruitment, training, and rewards of younger members (Mulkay, 1976). These findings relate to Merton's (1968) notion of the Matthew Effect: the greater one's eminence or prestige, the more credit he will receive for any contribution. Essentially, these findings support the notion of elite groups within scientific communities.

There is also considerable evidence for the influence of these elites in activities of other scientists and interactions between the scientific community and government. Elites exert control over or guide the research of others through their domination of research groups and committees which review programs and allocate funds (Blume, 1974; Mulkay, 1976). Further, they usually represent the links between governmental bodies and the scientific community and, therefore, are involved in advisory committees for research and funding (Mulkay, 1976).

Investigations such as these, applied to social psychology, would provide far better awareness than informal discussions and complaints concerning a "power structure". The existence of an elite, or elites, and the evidence from other disciplines that elites are influential both in internal and external functions of the discipline, not only suggest that similar affairs predominate social psychology but also that they can be systematically investigated.

To further test for the presence or absence of an elite among social psychologists would be a relatively straightforward procedure. A preliminary examination of journal referees (editors and editorial staff) and a prestigious social psychological society suggested that there is some type of influential subgroup of social psychologists. To assess this possibility, the membership in a restricted society, i.e., one with membership granted by peer nomination alone (Society for Experimental Social Psychology — SESP), was compared to editorial involvement in two major North American social psychological journals (Perlman, 1977), *Journal of Experimental Social Psychology (JESP)* and *Journal of Personality and Social Psychology (JPSP)*, for a five year period (1971-1975). During this time, 61% or more of the combined editorial board members belonged to the society. At any time, between 6% and 11% of the editorial members held positions in *both JPSP* and *JESP* as well as their membership in SESP. Regarding the number of individuals involved it was found that a total of 104 individuals occupied 319 positions between 1971 and 1975 (see Table 2 in the Appendix).

From these limited data the existence of a small group which shares a significant portion of editorial positions is apparent. But these data suffice only as indicators and require comparison with a larger sample of North American social psychologists. The findings are further restricted by a problem that complicates most analyses of elites: the difficulty with discrimination between prestige and power achieved primarily from quality of productivity and such status achieved through other means (cf. Mulkay, 1976). One possible solution to this problem will come from the use of citation and publication analyses which enable a quantitative assessment of productivity and recognition. Although these analyses are not without drawbacks (Cole and Cole, 1973; Buss, 1976b, 1976c), they can support other methods of investigating the hierarchy of disciplinary social structures (see Xhignesse and Osgood, 1967; Myers, 1970; Buss, 1976b; Perlman, 1977). In summary, the initial findings do suggest that prestige is shared by a small number and that it is related to a means of control over disciplinary activities.

The present case also contains geographical limitations: this examination has concentrated on North American journals and hence, primarily on North American social psychologists. While some sociologists of science argue that intellectual ideas are free from national boundaries (cf. Merton, 1961), these data indicate that geography or language plays some role in determining memberships of social networks (only two European social psychologists were on either editorial board). However, nationality does not clearly define social structure, or even elites; for instance, close examination of Canadian social psychologists would provide an excellent case for studying transnational and multi-lingual networks (in the present analysis only five social psychologists working in Canada were editorial board members although a larger number belonged to SESP). Canadian psychology has thus far only received minor historical (cf. Camfield, 1969) and sociological (cf. Buss, 1976b) consideration. The situation is not limited to the Canadian example; the history and organization of social psychology in other areas also deserve examination from the point of internal social structure and transnational relations.

III. On the History of Social Psychology

Finally, I would like to consider a third case for analysis: the emergence of historical inquiries into social psychology. If interest in history is an indication of a discipline's maturity — and there is evidence that it is (Hagstrom, 1965) — then it may be said that social psychology is coming of age: the recent attention that social psychologists have accorded their history would attest to this developmental process. Concern for the history of social psychology has been expressed in special sessions of conferences, critical articles (Buss, 1975, 1976a; Baumgardner, 1976; Samelson, 1973, 1974), and in a newsletter devoted entirely to historical research.[3] However, this interest is not shared unanimously. In a recent survey on the history of sociology, the subgroup of social psychologists replied negatively to questions of the value of historical research (Jones and Kronus, 1976).

Regardless of the current attitude toward the history of social psychology, it is evident that in the last fifty years social psychologists have exhibited minimal concern about their past (Baumgardner, 1976). Hendrick (1976) has attributed this tendency to the ahistorical nature of Kurt Lewin's work, the ideas which Hendrick believes significantly shaped social psychology in the United States. This disinterest in history has also been attributed to (a) the appearance of research interests such as interpersonal relations, structure of small groups, and decision

(3) This newsletter is now appended to the newsletter of the Society for the Advancement of Social Psychology.

making processes which have no nineteenth century counter-parts (Lipset, 1968; Jones and Kronus, 1976), or (b) the obser-vation that the more a researcher is devoted to "scientism" the less importance he attaches to his discipline's history (Stocking, 1965; Jones and Kronus, 1976).

These interpretations of social psychology's ahistoricity relate to two historiographical emphases: Whiggish history or *presentism* where only those events of the past which support present conditions are studied and *inductive* history where history entails the chronological documentation of facts in a black and white fashion — a record of those events which are considered correct according to current science (cf. Agassi, 1963, for a discussion of these trends in the history of science). In the USSR, Yaroshevskii (1973), in Europe, Van Hoorn (1972) and in North America, Stocking (1965) have documen-ted the limitations which presentism and antiquarianism place on any historical studies of psychology. Within this framework, the history of social psychology is construed either as non-existent, since there appear to be no antecedents to most current research, or the history of social psychology is viewed as a chronicle of those correct/white events which apprehended current scientific enterprises. The former case accounts for the lack of historical studies and the latter explains the existence of a restrictive and general body of historical information. For instance, most histories of social psychology tend to be inductive accounts of the emergence of positivism and scientific metho-dology (Samelson, 1974). The standard history of the discipline, by Gordon Allport (1968), exemplifies this pattern. Other histories consist of either biographies or evolutionary histories of particular social psychological ideas (Morawski, 1976).

The lack of historical scholarship and the consistent bias in those studies which have been completed can be understood in terms of the historian's adherence to certain historiographies. In turn, these historiographical biases reflect a specific epis-temology of social psychology: social psychological knowledge is perceived as resulting primarily from cumulative scientific achievements. Extra-scientific factors — both intellectual and non-intellectual — are *not* acknowledged. Therefore, when social psychologists investigate their discipline's past they look for a specific social psychology, possibly a social psychology that never existed or existed only among a particular group. But if it is acknowledged that current social psychology is tentative — it is neither committed to nor certain of its scientific position and functions (cf. Gergen, 1973; McGuire, 1973; Thorngate, 1976) — then it should be recognized that social psychology's history may be as volatile. And if it is recognized that social psychological knowledge is influenced by extra-scientific variables, then its history can be reviewed within a similar context. In effect, historical research has been conditioned by prevalent views about the nature of social psychological knowledge and, in turn, has supported those perceptions in whatever historical reports were compiled. Consequently, adequate historical research is related to the development of a sociological analysis of social psychological knowledge.

Potentially, a contextual history — investigations that attend to social, political, and economic conditions — may serve to clarify contemporary issues. Historical studies may delineate or supplement knowledge of social psychology. One pertinent issue is the relative independence or interdependence of North American and European social psychology. While some claim that European social psychology is identified with its North American counterpart (Taft, 1976; Moscovici, 1972), others perceive distinct differences between the two communities (Shaver, 1974; Smith, 1973; Faucheux 1976; Triandis, 1976). These arguments contain respective assertions as to either shared or independent historical precursors. While the debate is intriguing in its own right, it has become pertinent to a current theoretical problem; in a recent discussion on the proper directions for cross-cultural research the question of cultural relativism in social psychology is integral to the adequacy of each position. On the one hand, European and North American social psychology, since they presumedly developed within independent societal and academic traditions, are considered ethnocentric sciences (Faucheux, 1976; Triandis, 1976). Therefore, it is recommended that precautions be taken when using or comparing research from the other community. On the other hand, such ethnocentrism was denied; it is argued that social psychological problems and techniques are universal since "The scientific approach to the study of human behavior is peculiarly 'western', not only in its orientation, but in its very existence" (Taft, 1976, p. 327). Thus, the issue of the social context and history of social psychology is paramount to one's position regarding cross-cultural research strategies.

Historical research into the development of social psychology and the possible communities within the discipline can clarify contemporary issues in cases such as that of cross-cultural investigations. This particular issue is a complex one and certainly will not be resolved from any single piece of research. But historical studies can contribute; there is already evidence of distinct intellectual influences between the European and North American traditions. In the past, social scientific communities were not exposed to the same literature; isolation of ideas has resulted primarily from the absence of translations, restricted communications, and limited publications. For example, the social psychological works of several mid-nineteenth century Germans (Wundt, Steinthal, and Lazarus, as well as a journal founded by the latter two) have never appeared in English or French translations. Thus, this literature has been confined to a restricted audience. In one of the earliest histories of social psychology, the notion of distinct "national" communities and restricted communications was shown to be of considerable influence (Karpf, 1932). Also related to the situation where ideas may be isolated is the effect which contrasting academic and educational systems may have had on a community's exposure to specific works or ideas. For instance, Hegel was not widely known in England until a secondary source on his work was published in 1865. This publication signalled the onset of an idealist trend among British psychologists and social theorists (Hearnshaw, 1964, pp. 126-8), a trend that had materialized forty years earlier in Germany. However, it has also been suggested that, more recently, European social psycho-

48 *Jill G. Morawski*

logy has assimilated the problems and research of North American social psychology (Moscovici, 1972). This implication of "Americanization" of European research also deserves attention and the historian of more contemporary events could readily approach the issues through methodologies from the sociology of science — network analyses, citation analyses, and investigation of communication patterns.

In summary, historical analyses of social psychology, when approached within a contextual framework (cf. Van Hoorn, 1972) will function not only to elucidate the extra-scientific dimensions of the discipline's development but also may be beneficial to understanding contemporary conditions. If the social structure and communication networks of the past are investigated in terms of their impact on social psychological knowledge, then the creation and development of that knowledge will receive the comprehensive study that is necessary.

Conclusion

The three cases considered here — the conflict controversy, cross-cultural research and cultural relativism, and power structures — do not typify comprehensive studies. Rather, they are preliminary explorations into the socio-historical aspects of social psychological knowledge. They must be followed by systematic investigations that incorporate other factors, intellectual as well as extra-scientific. In other words, these cases have been offered as examples — prospectives — of the type of research necessary to confront the underlying facets of social psychological knowledge.

Furthermore, these examples reflect the strategical and theoretical preferences which were outlined earlier in the paper. They support the suggestion that, while the sociology of science seeks to understand scientific knowledge in its various interrelations with socio-historical conditions, the examination of the science's internal functioning (in this instance, social psychology) is functionally more promising as an initial venture. As noted, this approach allows one to suspend judgement and avoid assumptions about epistemologies and the correct processes of scientific proof. The investigation of the internal social structure and communications accommodates the possibility of unique scientific ethos within a discipline and can incorporate consideration of cognitive structure and processes.

This paper has, for the most part, emphasized the ideas of investigating the social structure — hierarchy, communications, and cognitive norms — of social psychology. And, although alternate models from the sociology of science are available and applicable, concentration on the social structure of social psychology is, at present, the most promising.

While president of the Social Science Research Council, Pendelton Herring noted a recurrent tendency among social scientific disciplines which has since been labeled "Herring's Law". Herring stated that "Every discipline does worst that which is at the putative center of its field" (Herring quoted in Selvin, 1976, p. 49). Economists fail to balance their own budgets and historians forget their own past (Selvin, 1976). In keeping with the points addressed in this paper it may be added that social psychologists have neglected to review their own social relations.

References

Agassi, J., Toward an historiography of science, *History and Theory*, 1963, 2.

Allport, G., The historical background of modern social psychology. In G. Lindzey & A. Aronson (Eds.), *The Handbook of Social Psychology*, Vol. 1, Reading, Mass.: Addison-Wesley, 1968.

Apfelbaum, E. and Lubek, I., Resolution versus revolution: The theory of conflicts in question. In L.H. Strickland, K.J. Gergen, & F.E. Aboud (Eds.), *Social Psychology in Transition*, New York: Plenum, 1976.

Bagehot, W., *Physics and Politics*, New York: Alfred A. Knopf, 1873.

Baumgardner, S.R., Critical history and social psychology's "crisis", *Personality and Social Psychology Bulletin*, 1976, 2, 460-5.

Billig, M., Review of "The resolution of conflict" by Morton Deutsch, *European Journal of Social Psychology*, 1975, 5(3), 409-14.

Blume, S.S., *Toward a Political Sociology of Science*, New York: The Free Press, 1974.

Briskman, L.B., Is a Kuhnian analysis applicable to psychology? *Science Studies*, 1972, 2, 87-97.

50   Jill G. Morawski

Buss, A.R., The emerging field of the sociology of psychological knowledge, *American Psychologist*, 1975, *30*, 988-1002.

Buss, A.R., Galton and the birth of differential psychology and eugenics: Social, political, and economic forces, *Journal of the History of the Behavioral Sciences*, 1976, *12*, 47-58 (a).

Buss, A.R., Evaluation of Canadian psychology departments based upon citation and publication counts, *Canadian Psychological Review*, 1976, *17*(2), 143-50 (b).

Buss, A.R., Comment on my critics, *Canadian Psychological Review*, 1976 *17*(4), 305-7 (c).

Bynum, W.F., The great chain of being after forty years: An appraisal, *History of Science*, 1975, *13*, 1-28.

Camfield, T.M., Psychologists at war: The history of American psychology and the first world war, Ph.D. dissertation, The University of Texas at Austin, 1969.

Campbell, D.T., Ethnocentrism of disciplines and the fish-scale model of omniscience. In M. Sherif & C.W. Sherif (Eds.), *Interdisciplinary Relationships in the Social Sciences*, Chicago: Aldine, 1969.

Cartwright, D., Determinants of scientific progress: The case of research on the risky shift, *American Psychologist*, 1973, *28*, 222-31.

Chadwick-Jones, J., The debate between Michel Plon and Morton Deutsch: Some related comments, *European Journal of Social Psychology*, 1976, *6*, 128-36.

Cole, J.R. and Cole, S., *Social Stratification in Science*, Chicago: University of Chicago Press, 1973.

Crane, D., The gatekeepers of science: Some factors affecting the selection of articles for scientific journals, *American Sociologist*, 1967, *12*, 195-201.

Crane, D., *Invisible Colleges*, Chicago: University of Chicago Press, 1972.

Deutsch, M., The social-psychological study of conflict: Rejoinder to a critique, *European Journal of Social Psychology*, 1974, *4*, 441-56.

Deutsch, M., A reply to Billig, *European Journal of Social Psychology*, 1975, *5*, 415-18.

Deutsch, M., Discussion of E. Apfelbaum's "Conflicts: resolution or revolution?" In L.H. Strickland, K.J. Gergen, & F.E. Aboud (Eds.), *Social Psychology in Transition*, New York: Plenum, 1976.

Eysenck, H.J., Ideology run wild, *American Psychologist*, 1976, *31*, 311-12.

Farrell, L.A., Controversy and conflict in science: A case study — The English biometric school and Mendel's laws, *Social Studies of Science*, 1975, *5*(3), 269-302.

Faucheux, C., Cross-cultural research in experimental social psychology, *European Journal of Social Psychology*, 1976, *6*(3), 269-322.

Franks, P.E., A social history of American social psychology up to the second world war, Ph.D. dissertation, State University of New York at Stony Brook, 1975.

Gadlin, H. and Ingle, G., Through a one-way mirror: The limits of experimental self reflection, *American Psychologist*, 1975, *30*, 1003-10.

Gergen, K.J., Social psychology as history, *Journal of Personality and Social Psychology*, 1973, *26*, 309-20.

Gergen, K.J., Social psychology, science and history, *Personality and Social Psychology Bulletin*, 1976, *2*, 373-83.

Gurvitch, G., *The Social Frameworks of Knowledge* (Trans. by M.A. Thompson and K.A. Thompson), New York: Harper & Row, 1971.

Habermas, J., *Towards a Rational Society: Student Protest, Science and Politics* (Trans. by J.J. Shapiro), Boston: Beacon, 1968.

Habermas, J., *Knowledge and Human Interests* (Trans. by J.J. Shapiro), Boston: Beacon, 1971.

Hagstrom, W.O., *The Scientific Community,* New York: Basic Books, 1965.

Hearnshaw, L.S., *A Short History of British Psychology: 1840-1940,* London: Methuen, 1964.

Hendrick, C., A comment on the lack of historical study of experimental social psychology, *Newsletter of the History of Social Psychology Group,* 1976, *3,* 3.

Henle, M., On controversy and its resolution. In M. Henle, J. Jaynes & J. Sullivan (Eds.), *Historical Conceptions of Psychology,* New York: Springer, 1973.

Israel, J., Stipulations and construction in the social sciences. In Israel, J. and Tajfel, H., *The Context of Social Psychology: A Critical Assessment,* London: Academic Press, 1972.

Jones, R.A. and Kronus, S., Professional sociologists and the history of sociology, *Journal of the History of the Behavioral Sciences,* 1976, *12,* 3-13.

Karpf, F.B., *American Social Psychology: Its Origins, Development, and European Background,* New York: McGraw-Hill, 1932.

Krantz, D.L., The Baldwin-Titchener controversy: A case study in the functioning of schools. In D.L. Krantz (Ed.), *Schools of Psychology: A Symposium,* New York: Appleton-Century-Crofts, 1969.

Kuhn, T.S., *The Structure of Scientific Revolutions,* Chicago: University of Chicago Press, 1963.

Lipset, S.M., History and sociology. In S.M. Lipset & F. Hofstadter (Eds.), *Sociology and History,* New York: Basic Books, 1968.

Lovejoy, A.O., *The Great Chain of Being,* Cambridge: Harvard University Press, 1936.

Lubek, I., An historical and social psychological analysis of research on aggression: Some shocking truths (and deceptions). Paper presented at the annual meeting of Cheiron, Washington, D.C., 1976 (a).

Lubek, I., A note on the power and structure in social psychology, *Representative Research in Social Psychology,* 1976, *7,* 87-8 (b).

Lubek, I., Some tentative suggestions for analyzing and neutralizing the power structure in social psychology. In L.H. Strickland, K.J. Gergen, & F.E. Aboud (Eds.), *Social Psychology in Transition,* New York: Plenum, 1976 (c).

Mandelbaum, M., *History, Man and Reason,* Baltimore: The Johns Hopkins Press, 1971.

Mannheim, K. *Ideology and Utopia: An Introduction to the Sociology of Knowledge,* London: Routledge & Kegan Paul, 1936.

Masterman, M., The nature of a paradigm. In I. Lakatos & A. Musgrave (Eds.), *Criticism and the Growth of Knowledge,* Cambridge: Cambridge University Press, 1970.

McGrath, J.E. and Altman, I., *Small Group Research, A Synthesis and Critique of the Field,* New York: Holt, Rinehart & Winston, 1966.

McGuire, W., The yin and yang of progress in social psychology, *Journal of Personality and Social Psychology,* 1973, *26,* 446-56.

Merton, R.K., Social conflict over styles of sociological work. Fourth World Congress of Sociology, *Transactions,* Louvain, Belgium: International Sociological Association, 1961, *3,* 21-46.

Merton, R.K., The Matthew effect in science, *Science,* 1968, *159,* 56-63.

Merton, R.K., *The Sociology of Science: Theoretical and Empirical Investigations,* Chicago: University of Chicago Press, 1973.

Merton, R.K. & Zuckerman, H., Institutionalized patterns of evaluation in science. In R.K. Merton, *The Sociology of Science: Theoretical and Empirical Investigations,* Chicago: University of Chicago Press, 1973.

Morawski, J., Approaching a historiography of social psychology: Some tentative thoughts on its current position, unpublished manuscript, Carleton Universtiy, Ottawa, 1976.

Moscovici, S., Society and theory in social psychology. In J. Israel & H. Tajfel (Eds.), *The Context of Social Psychology: A Critical Assessment,* New York: Academic Press, 1972.

Mulkay, M.J., *The Social Process of Innovation,* London: Macmillan, 1972.

Mulkay, M., The mediating role of the scientific elite, *Social Studies of Science,* 1976, *6,* 445-70.

Myers, C.R., Journal citations and scientific eminence in contemporary psychology, *American Psychologist,* 1970, *25,* 1041-8.

Nemeth, C., Whose ideology? A rejoinder to M. Plon, *European Journal of Social Psychology,* 1974, *4,* 437-40.

Perlman, D., Rating journals: Citations count, *Society for the Advancement of Social Psychology Newsletter,* 1977, *3,* 1, 8-9.

Phillips, D.C., Organicism in the late nineteenth and early twentieth centuries, *Journal of the History of Ideas,* 1970, *31,* 413-32.

Plon, M., On the meaning of the notion of conflict and its study in social psychology, *European Journal of Social Psychology,* 1974, *4,* 389-436.

Pongratz, L.J., *Problem-geschichte der Psychologie,* Bern: Francke Verlag, 1967.

Pongratz, L.J., The problem- or issue-centered approach to the history of psychology, Workshop presented at the annual meeting of Cheiron, Ottawa, 1975.

Riegal, K., Toward a dialectical theory of development, Unpublished manuscript, University of Michigan, 1975.

Riegal, K., The dialectics of human development, *American Psychologist,* 1976, *31,* 689-700.

Robbins, D. and Johnston, R., The role of cognitive and occupational differentiation in scientific controversies, *Social Studies of Science,* 1976, *6,* 349-68.

Rommetveit, R., On "emancipatory" social psychology. In L.H. Strickland, K.J. Gergen, & F.E. Aboud (Eds.), *Social Psychology in Transition,* New York: Plenum, 1976.

Samelson, F., Paradigms, labels, and historical analysis, *American Psychologist,* 1973, *28,* 1141-3.

Samelson, F., History, origin, myth, and ideology: Comte's "discovery" of social psychology, *Journal for the Theory of Social Behavior,* 1974, *4,* 217-31.

Semmel, B., *Imperialism and Social Reform,* Cambridge: Cambridge University Press, 1960.

Selvin, H.C., Durkheim, Booth and Yule: The non-diffusion of an intellectual innovation, *European Journal of Sociology,* 1976, *17,* 39-51.

Shaver, P., European perspectives on the crisis in social psychology, *Contemporary Psychology,* 1974, *18,* 356-9.

Smith, M.B., Criticism of a social science, *Science,* 1973, *180,* 610-12.

Steiner, I.D., Whatever happened to the group in social psychology? *Journal of Experimental Social Psychology,* 1974, *10,* 94-108.

Stocking, G., On the limits of "presentism" and "historicism" in the historiography of the behavioral sciences, *Journal of the History of the Behavioral Sciences,* 1965, *1,* 211-19.

Strickland, L.H., Gergen, K.J. & Aboud, F.E. (Eds), *Social Psychology in Transition,* New York: Plenum, 1976.

Strickland, L.H. *et al.,* The "power structure" in social psychology, *Representative Research in Social Psychology,* 1976, *7,* 79-86.

Taft, R., Cross-cultural psychology as a social science: Comments on Faucheux's paper, *European Journal of Social Psychology,* 1976, *6,* 323-30.

Thorngate, W., Possible limits on a science of social behaviour. In L.H. Strickland, K.J. Gergen, & F.E. Aboud (Eds), *Social Psychology in Transition,* New York: Plenum, 1976.

Triandis, H., Toward a paradigm for research in interpersonal behavior, Unpublished manuscript, University of Illinois, Urbana-Champaign, 1975.

Triandis, H., On the value of cross-cultural research in social psychology: Reactions to Faucheux's paper, *European Journal of Social Psychology,* 1976, *6,* 331-42.

Trotter, W., *Instincts of the Herd in Peace and War,* New York: Macmillan, 1916.

Van Hoorn, W., *As Images Unwind,* Amsterdam: University Press, 1972.

Van Nossum, W., The development of sociology in the Netherlands: A network analysis of the editorial board of the *Sociologische Gids.* In R. Whitely (Ed.), *Social Processes of Scientific Development,* London: Routledge & Kegan Paul, 1974.

Whitely, R., Cognitive and social institutionalization of scientific specialities and research areas. In R. Whitely (Ed.), *Social Processes of Scientific Development,* London: Routledge & Kegan Paul, 1974.

Wozniak, R.H., A dialectical paradigm for psychological research, unpublished manuscript, University of Minnesota, 1975.

Xhignesse, L.V. and Osgood, C.E., Bibliographical citation characteristics of the psychological journal network in 1950 and 1960, *American Psychologist,* 1967, *22,* 778-91.

Yaroshevskii, M.G., Categorical analysis of the evolution of psychology as an independent body of knowledge, *Soviet Psychology,* 1973, *12,* 23-52.

Yotopoulos, P.A., Institutional affiliation of the contributors to three professional journals, *American Economic Review,* 1961, *51,* 665-70.

Zuniga, R.B., The experimenting society and radical social reform, *American Psychologist,* 1975, *30,* 99-115.

Appendix

Table 1. Typology of influences on scientific development for studies in the sociology of science (from Cole and Cole, 1973, p. 3)

	Source of influence on science	
Type of influence	Internal to the institution of science	External to the institution of science
Intellectual	TYPE I	TYPE II
Social	TYPE III	TYPE IV

Jill G. Morawski

Table 2

Ind. involved in	Editorial board membership				
	1971	1972	1973	1974	1975
JPSP, JESP, & SESP*	3(6)**	6(11)	5(10)	5(6)	6(7)
JESP & SESP	16(53)	16(57)	14(54)	14(52)	19(59)
JPSP & SESP	13(62)	18(67)	17(65)	31(63)	33(62)
JESP & EAESP	1	0	0	0	0
JPSP & EAESP	0	0	0	0	0
JPSP & *JESP*	1	1	1	1	2

	Number of editorial positions				
	1971	1972	1973	1974	1975
JPSP	21	27	26	49	53
JESP	30	28	26	27	32
Total	51	55	52	76	85

* Numbers in parentheses represent percent of annual editorial membership.
** Based on SESP membership list of 1976; total membership = 216.

Discussion

ANDREEVA: Are you sure that the notion "social structure" in relation to social psychology is relevant, as you have discussed problems of communication of hierarchies or cognitive norms within this science? It seems to me you are discussing not the social structure of social psychology; rather, you have given us an analysis of social psychology from the point of view of "science of science". If you speak about social structure, it seems to me you have to connect these problems with the social structure of society, but I don't see that you did this.

MORAWSKI: I've chosen to look at what we would call the internal social structure — one may speak of external social structure and internal social structure. People who have attempted the sociology of science in Western countries, who have attempted to look at the relationship between society as a whole and a particular discipline, often can't handle the problem. A good example is Steiner's argument when he talks about the demise of small group research. He attributed this to several factors, but overall he said it was due to political change. But this is hard to document, It's *very* difficult to document. I've argued here that internal analysis would at first help us understand ourselves.

ANDREEVA: In our country we call such an analysis "science of science". This is a new term, and an important one in our investigations.

KIESLER: You seem to have emphasized the social acceptability of traditional social psychology. I've learned that this internal acceptability often doesn't dovetail very well with two other kinds of roles that scientists play, either implicitly or explicitly. One is the role with respect to the public's knowledge. In interaction with people from magazines or newspapers, "explicitly" means to be called the author of something, or appearing personally on some television or radio show; "implicitly" means that your work or ideas have directly influenced the person who *is* writing the article. "Internal acceptability" often doesn't fit with these roles. Then there's another role which has to do with national science, as seen by quite a different group of people, the non-psychological scientists — the people who serve on powerful scientific committees which have impact on legislation, on Federal policy, on the President's policy and so forth. Those two sets of people, the ones who are the national science ingroup and the ones who are the public informants, do *not* match up very well in social psychology and other branches of psychology with the sort of "social acceptability" you have talked about, that determines an ingroup.

MORAWSKI: There's some evidence that it does match up, not in social sciences but in the hard sciences; in physics, chemistry, it does match up.

KIESLER: Yes, I'm sure it does there.

THORNGATE: Let me exaggerate your arguments a little bit, to make a point. It strikes me that, in the extreme, you are saying that we could do more or less anything we wanted, were it not for the social structure of our discipline. My particular bias is that the discipline is limited primarily by its statistical sophistication, which is awful, and its research techniques, which are abysmal.

MORAWSKI: But those problems are already discussed in our "crisis" literature; I'm not arguing that our internal structure is *the* problem with social psychology, but that it's an issue we should be looking at.

THORNGATE: Do you see then that by understanding the sociology of our discipline we will do better research?

MORAWSKI: Yes. It won't solve all our problems, but I feel we'll do better research, because I feel, as I mentioned, with respect to Israel's proposals, that by incorporating these we can come to a better understanding of the social nature of man. Without that understanding, we are hindered in some way by the structure of our own discipline.

THORNGATE: But will that increase be larger than the increase that we might attain by concentrating our efforts on improving our statistical practice and research techniques?

MORAWSKI: I'm not a prophet — I really think that's a difficult question to answer, because they're interdependent.

ZAJONC: I would like to ask you to consider Israel, who has been critical of our situation, who obviously has a deep understanding of social structure, and doubtless of elites; has all this knowledge and wisdom of Israel's helped him do any research in the last twenty years? Has he produced anything of interest?

MORAWSKI: I think his 1972 model is of interest. It may be twenty years old — I don't know — is it?

ZAJONC: Well, he's been criticizing for twenty years.

MORAWSKI: I think that he has in some sense enlightened people on the relationship between the social context and stipulations on the nature of man. It's not that North American social psychologists haven't considered these things, but we haven't utilized them or thought about utilizing them in our theoretical work. So in that sense, I think he has contributed.

THORNGATE: He also hasn't cluttered the literature with more data.

ZAJONC: That's certainly true.

The Development of Social Psychology in the U S S R

GALINA M. ANDREEVA

At the outset, I want to stress that our social psychology is a young science because our society is itself young — this year we shall celebrate its sixtieth anniversary. The most interesting and dramatic events in social psychology occurred after the great October Socialist Revolution when all of our science was reconstructed under the new Marxist orientation. Over the years, all of psychology came to accept Marxist philosophy, the Marxist ideological outlook, etc., but while this process was smooth with general psychology, it was most difficult with social psychology, because its subject matter is closely connected with acute social, political and ideological problems.

Professor Chelpanov, Head of the Department of Psychology and Logic at Moscow State University, proposed the division of psychology into two parts. The first was to be experimental psychology, and the second, social psychology. Only social psychology would necessarily have to accept a Marxist basis, in his view, while experimental psychology had to be independent of any ideological, philosophical, or social orientation. This proposal would have had the effect of acknowledging social psychology as an independent part of science; however, because it implied the exclusion of Marxism from other aspects of psychology, Chelpanov's proposal aroused much opposition. The unfortunate outcome of this was that, with the rejection of Chelpanov's position, the right of an independent existence for social psychology was also rejected. Hence, for some time, social psychology developed not as an independent part of psychology, or even sociology, but only within other subfields of psychological science. It developed particularly within pedagogical science, where it was concerned with problems of the "collective".

A second reason for opposition to social psychology was a faulty comprehension of its subject matter. In the 1920s among the Soviet scientists there were two conceptions of this subject matter. The first was that the field should be responsible for the study of the social determinants of mental processes. The second was that social psychology was the science concerned with specific "socio-psychological phenomena": groups, individuals in groups, communication, etc. If the first point of view had prevailed every one could have said, "We don't need a specific branch of psychology called social psychology. *All* psychology becomes social psychology, because from the Marxist point of view *all* mental processes are explained in terms of their social determinants". Many forgot during that period that social psychology also had the second meaning; but, as it happened, society itself demanded answers to many of these questions, involving problems of the socio-psychological aspects of the development of socialist industrial production, or of the functioning of the system of mass communication, or of the struggle against anti-social or deviant behavior.

Through the late 50s and early 60s it became accepted that social psychology had to exist as an independent branch of science. Since then have come more discussions about the nature of its subject matter, because all is not yet clear. There remains some ambiguity about the relationship between social psychology and general psychology on the one hand, and between social psychology and sociology on the other. Of course, you are aware that this is a problem for social psychology in general, but in our own discussions since the late 1950s, we have considered perhaps three points of view on the matter.

The first was that social psychology's main research focus should be on the behaviour of individuals within groups, the effects of the group on personality — there are different shades of meaning here. This point of view, arising predominantly among sociologically trained social psychologists, was that social psychology deals primarily with socio-psychological aspects of class, ethnic, and professional group memberships. In a way, this is the psychology of large groups — what kinds of groups is another question which I shall discuss later.

The third point of view, which was a sort of compromise between the first two, and which seems to have prevailed, construes social psychology as responsible for studying the individual in his group context as well as for the psychological problems of large social groups. I believe that this view is shared by most of my colleagues, and I can now try to show how it relates to fundamental Marxist philosophical statements.

I will begin with a discussion of some of our methodological problems. Indeed, I see as a methodological problem the issue of the place of social psychology within the system of science, which I have discussed. To explain my point of view, I must consider our understanding of the word "methodology", because it may be a difficult point in our discussions. In English, you have the one word, "methodology" and this term assumes both the technical aspects of investigation along with some more general issues of the logical foundations of science. In our language, we use different words for different levels of methodological analysis.

It will be illustrative to distinguish three levels of methodology, with reference to the Marxist tradition of investigating cognitive processes. First, there is the *general* methodology of scientific knowledge, usually represented by a definite philosophical method. In Marxism, this is the method of dialectical materialism. The second level, I would call a "special" methodology for each separate field of knowledge — the methodology of general psychology, the methodology of social psychology, and so on. This level is represented by the concrete forms of the more general philosophical methods, when they are applied to the given field. At this second level, the basis for analysing a given subject matter is developed from the general principles contained in the general method adopted. For example, I might say that one special, second-level methodological principle developed by Soviet psychology is the *principle of activity*. There are many difficulties with the interpretation and translation of this term, which I shall not discuss right now — it's not the traditional use of the word "activity", but it is the activity of real social man, activity that has a goal. Colleagues from England have suggested that I borrow an old term from McDougall, "goal-directed behaviour". I am not sure that this is good enough, but I mean something like it. At any rate, Soviet social psychology used the notion of "activity" as an important concept with broad explanatory uses. Another principle is the *principle of cultural-historical conditioning* of mental processes. This implies that the basic content of the epistemological problem — for example, the interrelationship between the subject and the object of knowledge — is revealed through the analysis of the social/historical determinants; and of course here, man is both subject and object of social relations. I must stress here that this principle is incorporated into socio-psychological research as a principle of interpretation and explanation. How to do it is not an easy problem, but we accept that it is an important task to incorporate the general philosophical principles of Marxism into the body of social psychology.

The third methodological level is, in our terminology, "methodics". It refers to the means and techniques of research; this corresponds to the traditional English comprehension of methods, procedures or techniques. It is important to say here that we believe that this third level cannot be interpreted without reference to those described previously; it is obvious that if we employ, say, some particular scale of measurement, we imply in the process of construction some philosophical or "special" principles of research methodology.

So, these methodological concerns form the basis of research and it seems that our main task now is the construction of the body of science on those principles. This task is not finished — we will need much time to complete it — but we will all do our best. Toward this end, one methodological development that is important for us now is the contruction of so-called "middle-range" theories. We don't use this term in Russian. We speak instead of "special socio-psychological theories". I feel that these special theories provide the framework into which we can incorporate the philosophical principles, and adopt them into the body of research.

Another methodological problem discussed presently in Soviet social psychology involves the technical equipment of socio-psychological research. Of course, we use many of the devices and techniques that are traditional for Western social psychology — structured and unstructured observation, different scales and questionnaires, experiments, etc. But if we accept that social psychology includes the investigation of two aspects of social reality, we must use not only techniques that are relevant for individual psychological research, but techniques from other branches of science, from anthropology, history, sociology, and so on. How to combine these two technical orientations is a primary problem; it is not usual for psychologically trained social psychologists to use sociological or cross-cultural methods, and it is often impossible for sociologically trained social psychologists to use the laboratory experiments which are traditional for psychologists.

I would like to make one point about the status of laboratory experiments in social psychology. This area has been a problem for you, too, as I see by the endless discussion about the "crisis" in Western social psychology. We agree with those who see the limitations of laboratory experiments — but then what? If we recognize that field experimentation and observation is more relevant for social psychology, this means that our focus must be on real social groups, not laboratory groups. This is in agreement with the Marxist point of view that man must be studied in real, natural settings. So we turn our research away from laboratory experiments and toward real social groups. But here, too, we meet some problems, because subjects for research in natural settings are not, in a strict sense, the same subjects as they are studied in the laboratory — we can have some difficult contacts with our clients in production or in the system of mass communication. Perhaps some of these methodological problems we are discussing now will be more clear if I try to describe the content of social psychology, as we understand it in the Soviet Union.

This will not be just my own point of view — I'm a university professor, and I teach the basic course of social psychology with its special curriculum, which represents the situation within the science. The first part of this course is the historical introduction, where I speak about historical bases, methodological problems, etc., as I have just done here. Then I try to describe the content of social psychology in four blocks:

Social psychology

Introduction	"Obshcheniye" (Communication; Interaction; Person perception)	Groups Large Small	Personality	Applied problems

First are the general problems of social and interpersonal relations, and the role of communication, interaction and social perception *within* the system of social and interpersonal relations. This part involves the general regularities, or perhaps "laws" of communication, interaction, etc. But I must immediately introduce another difficulty by using a new notion. In Russian, we speak here of *obshcheniye* — and this word has no English equivalent! We in the Soviet Union think the word most nearly equivalent to "obshcheniye" is the German word "Verkehr". But we do not have a good translation of "Verkehr" into English, either, so we are just where we were before. But I shall try to show you what we mean.

We interpret this word as *communication* — not communication in the narrow sense, but in its broadest sense. We conceive of "communication" or "communicative processes" as the reality of social and interpersonal relations, and we include the "social context" within this communication system. I can say that one aspect of "obshcheniye" involves communication in the traditional sense (verbal or non-verbal between people, as a kind of exchange of ideas, or beliefs, or knowledges, etc. So we may use the word "communication" if we keep this in mind. But the second aspect of this "communication in the broad sense" involves *interaction*. We interpret interaction as referring not only to the immediate relations between people but to their social relations — interaction involves the exchange of different kinds of activity, because people have exchanged not only ideas, etc., but actions as well. We see, behind the immediate interaction of people, the entire system of social activity, the entire system of the division of labour in society, etc. This is the way we include the social context in the system of interaction. A third aspect of this "obshcheniye", this "communication in the broad sense", is what I would provisionally term "social perception". Here, I mean perception not only of other individuals, but perception of other groups, perception of other communities, and so on. A new approach, which we are trying to elaborate now, is to interpret *group* not only as a possible object of perception, but as a possible subject of the process of perception. Groups can perceive — indeed, in every-day language we use the phrase "the group perceives another group", etc.

To repeat, in this part of social psychology, we include consideration of the social context in our research on different aspects of communication. Of course we are concerned with different kinds of interaction — about cooperation, about competition — but we also try to find some new forms of interaction which stem from the system of social relations within our society. For example, what I think of as competitive activity is not what is traditionally thought of; rather, it is competition in a new sense, which exists in socialist society. Each labour group has a very interesting system of competition in which there are no winners who are just winners, but where everybody tries to contribute something new to the entire group's task. Indeed, this example seems a good vehicle to help one understand how the social context of society modifies the traditional processes which are described in any system of social psychology. In a way, it must help answer one question posed for this conference — that is, whether it is possible to have a social psychology which will be general for different kinds of society. I appreciate that different kinds of socio-economic systems within different societies give us different problems to solve; we in the socialist countries have our problems, you have yours, and so on. But it seems to me that we can speak about social psychology as a science, because we have in different kinds of societies the same socio-psychological processes — interaction is interaction, you have interaction, and we do too. It is the *content* of these particular processes that is derived from the particular social reality.

The next block in this general schema of social psychology I have called "groups". I divide "groups" into two parts, and I shall first consider problems of large social groups. We are concerned with the psychological characteristics of large social groups. At first look, this is not new; but what should be remembered is that the *content* of our analysis of groups, both large and small, stems from Marxist social/philosophical principles. We recognize, of course, that small groups are important units of human life, and we interpret them as frameworks and mechanisms for imparting social norms, ideals, etc. But these norms and ideals are not themselves elaborated within those small groups; their content is better interpreted as the product of large social groups — not unstructured groups, like publics, for example, but definite, lasting groups within society. In the Marxist tradition, we would here consider social classes or different ethnic groups, maybe professional groups or different age groups. In recent years, for example, we have discussed not only problems of youth, but problems of old age, as well, since this latter group make up a large part of the structure of our society. The content of attitudes, our beliefs, our norms begins in large groups, not in small groups, so we must study both of these social units. I know that my attitudes are born within certain small groups during the process of my socialization, but why this and not that attitude? Why do people in general choose this instead of that pattern of behavior?

Why do I accept this and not that norm? What I do is not only
a function of my immediate, small-group environment — it is
rooted in large social units.

What about our interest in small groups? We study all the
problems of group dynamics too, but when I speak of "group
dynamics" I don't employ the term in the sense of Lewin's
tradition. I refer to the dynamic processes within groups —
leadership, attraction, interaction, problem-solving, etc. —
interpreted in a way consistent with the Marxist outlook.

One important distinguishing characteristic of Soviet social
psychology in this context of groups is the notion of "collective". We have a new impetus to study levels of group development, and we interpret "collective" as the highest level of this
development. Professor Strickland was right, when he said
that it is a very old notion in our history, but I disagree with
his suggestion that its roots must be searched for in the hundreds
of years before our revolution. "Collective" has great importance
for us because of the *new* system of social relationships,
because of the *new* economic basis of our society, because
of the *new* organization of the whole of social life. Only in
this context is it possible to understand the notion of "collective" in our sciences — not only in social psychology, because
our historians and sociologists study collectives, too.

An authority on the concept of "collective" is A.V. Petrovsky.
Unfortunately, Professor Petrovsky is absent, but I will try to
outline the main feature of his conception. In brief, he speaks
of the "stratametric conception of group activity". By "stratametric" he means that, instead of relying on sociometry, one
may use complex methods which permit the study of *more than
immediate interpersonal relations*. Imagine that one were to
represent a group with three concentric circles. The external
layer or circle would represent interpersonal relations as they
have been studied traditionally. It would involve emotionally
based relations, the basis being feelings of sympathy or antipathy.
Sociometry is useful for measurement and description only at
this level of intergroup relations.

Petrovsky's idea is that if a small group is developing, and if common performance is the integrative factor in the life of this group, then the next layer of the group structure becomes important. This level involves what Petrovsky terms "unity of value orientation" — it means that we will find the unity among group members not in terms of their emotions, but in the similarity of their value orientations. This involves not only their general value orientation about different questions, but first of all the more specific value orientation concerning group performance. If members begin to share the same values, it means that the group has reached the next level of development.

The third and central aspect of this representation involves the most essential relationships within the group. If *all* the members of the group share the same goals for the group's activities, this means that the feeling of *collectivism* is the dominant feeling. Petrovsky has shown that this new — what I would call — "group work outlook", or collectivism, is inconsistent with the traditional division of groups along a dimension of conformity and non-conformity. He stresses a third possibility: one can be neither a conformist nor a non-conformist — one can be a collectivist, meaning that one consciously shares all the goals of his group concerning its activity.

All this does not mean that we stress only the group context, that we neglect the differences between individuals, or the value of individuals. Rather, it means that only the genuine collective orientation in a group will allow each member to find his own value, to show his own capacities and abilities. I do not want to paint a terrible picture involving the neglect of the traits of the individual.

The next block in my schema is called "personality" — the socio-psychological problems of personality. More will be said about this by Professor Schorokhova, so I will only mention how we stress the problem of socialization and the problem of attitudes. We feel that these two areas are the most "socio-psychological" of the problems of personality. The study of attitudes has a solid tradition in our country. Perhaps you know that Professor Usnadze from our school of psychology in

Georgia made an important contribution in the development of the world's psychology through the introduction of the notion of "set". Set is not the same as attitude, but we study it because it is a basis for the comprehension of attitudes.

With each of the subjects in the blocks I have drawn, we always try to include consideration of the social context in every study. And this brings me back to the main points of this talk: we have society — a definite system of social relations; these are relations not between individuals, but between social groups, as we now speak, between social roles. For example, Marx wrote long ago that when a capitalist and a worker meet, they meet not only as two personalities, but as representatives of two social groups. The actual existence of these social relations is in terms of interpersonal relations, because each person playing his social role retains individual traits. These interpersonal relations may in turn be described as communication, or interaction, or social perception, but *none of these exist without their group context.* These processes take place in large social groups and in small social groups, and they all have an effect on personality — it is in this way that society influences personality. Our practice of including consideration of the social context first with respect to the group, and finally with respect to behavior and personality, represents our attempt to adopt the general statements of Marxist philosophy into socio-psychological research.

With respect to methodological principles of general psychology, what can be said? Many outstanding Soviet psychologists have made contributions here: for example, Vygotsky was the first to write on *social/cultural determinants of mental processes*; Rubenstein and Leontiev wrote on the *principle of activity*; Ananiev was the first to stress the *complex approach to man,* to the inner person. We need time for the task of incorporating these principles into the body of our research, but it is our aim to do so.

I have discussed problems of theory and methodology in the development of our social psychology; I should mention that we also have many important applied problems. Our social psychology is spread throughout different parts of our national life. First of all, we are involved in industry. Many of our graduates go into industry, where they may be responsible for improving the system of interpersonal relations within labour collectives, for example. The second area of society in which we work is the system of mass communication. A third is the police system — many of our graduates go to help in the struggle against anti-social behavior: and so on.

Professor Strickland is right. Social psychology in the Soviet Union is developing very rapidly; but I am sure that we do not yet know the answers to all the interesting questions of human life. But I hope that our successful development will help us find answers to such complex questions.

PART II

*Theory, Methodology and
the Subject Matter
of Social Psychology*

A. THEORY DEVELOPMENT

Comparative Social Psychology: Societal Roots and Universal Goals [1]

J. W. BERRY

A Proposition

Like all social science, social psychology is rooted in a societal system. It is both *desirable* and *possible* to: (a) make these societal bases explicit in order to better match the science with the reality, and (b) analyse commonalities comparatively in order to generate a more universal science of human behaviour.

This proposition is obvious to some, ridiculous to a few and a challenge to others. It is obvious to those who study the development of behaviour cross-culturally; most complex behaviours are culturally patterned, and there is no reason to exclude scientific behaviour from this. It is ridiculous to those who assume that social psychology already constitutes a set of universal principles. And it is a challenge to those who wish to specify these societal bases, and to discover how they may fit together into a wider-based (perhaps even a universally-based) discipline.

Of course, some of these arguments are not being raised here for the first time. In the context of European social psychology, Faucheux (1976), Moscovici (1972) and Ingleby (1974) have all

(1) This chapter is a revision of the paper originally presented at the Carleton conference, and a further revision of Berry (1978a).

71

considered the impact that a society has on the social psychology it does. The arguments of Moscovici (1972) in particular established the point of view that "the social psychology that we ought to create must have an origin in our own reality" (p. 23). He observed that social psychology was largely developed in one society (the USA), which took "for its theme of research and for the contents of its theories the issues of *its own* society" (p. 19). He argued that social psychologists elsewhere "have the choice between building a social psychology appropriate to their society and culture, or to rest content with the application to their teaching and research of a model from elsewhere which is highly restricted" (p. 19). His choice for Europeans was clearly to "turn toward our own reality" on which to build one's own social psychology.

Further afield, Bhatnagar (1975) and others (e.g., Ho, 1975; Okonji, 1975; Patel, 1975; and Trimble, 1975) have all attempted to bring traditional thought systems and ideologies to bear on the analysis of individual behaviour. And internationally, Lyons (1973) has analysed the likely consequences of unicultural dominance in many of the social sciences.

In the context of social psychology in Canada, there has been one attempt to outline some societal features which may require special theoretical and empirical attention (Berry and Wilde, 1971, 1972; Berry, Kalin and Wilde, 1973; Berry, 1974a). These statements were made in the wider context of an increasing self-awareness of both Canadian general psychology (CPA, 1971; Gibson, 1974; Myers, 1970; Weyant, 1974; Wright, 1974) and other Canadian social sciences.[2]

Why Desirable?

We may legitimately ask: why should we try to specify societal

---

[2] Chief among these latter writings are the first two volumes of the Symons Commission on Canadian studies *To Know Ourselves* (Symons, 1975). Other useful sources are: Cairns (1975), Clark (1973), Felt (1975), Gurstein (1972), Jarvie (1976), Kornberg and Tharp (1972), Smiley (1974), Smith (1975), Stoltzman and Gamberg (1975), Sweet (1976).

bases at all? Won't this further fragment an already disorganized science? And in any case, is not the second part (the search for universals) logically contradictory to the first part? These criticisms can best be answered in the light of a later discussion on the "evolution" of a discipline in terms of the differentiation and integration of available knowledge. In the interim, let us consider four positive assertions which may be made.

The first two relate to the initial part of our proposition — the desirability of exploring societal bases to develop local social psychologies. A distinction may be drawn between *what* we study and *how* we study it (Berry, 1976a; Felt, 1975); in other terms, the distinction is between the empirical content and the theory of discipline. Of the two following assertions, the first refers to theoretical issues, and the second to the empirical focus.

My first assertion is that a social psychology which is local in character is more likely to be theoretically appropriate or more accurate, in the sense of matching the understanding to the social reality. I have previously likened social psychology as a science to a blueprint, and the social system to a complex machine (Berry, 1974a, p. 138), and asked the question:

> "If our blueprint was printed elsewhere, how can we hope to make sense of the complex machinery we see here? One way to resolve the inconsistency between the machine and the blueprint is to make the machine match the blueprint; this we are in danger of doing. The other is to discard the present blueprint, and make a new one based upon the machine as it is; this is what I hope we will be able to do."

A more balanced way to view this issue is through the schema set up by Campbell (1961). He has argued that ethnocentrism may bias any observation of social phenomena. Thus it is necessary to conduct every comparative study four times: twice by observer A (looking at the phenomenon in Culture A and in Culture B) and twice by observer B (again looking at the phenomenon in both cultures). In this way observer biases may be disentangled, and acutal differences between cultures (if they exist) may be established. Applying this schema to the present assertion (within a single culture) we note that ethnocentric observations may be made by either observer (the "insider" or the "outsider"; Merton, 1972). Thus we should not be content with either one. But without the local or insider's view, the very question of an alternative to the outsider's view (that of an assumed universal social psychology) would never arise. This argument establishes the necessity, but it cannot claim the sufficiency, of the insider's view. It is for this reason that those advocating a local perspective in social psychology must logically also pursue their work within a comparative framework. Without it, the choice is merely between two ethnocentrisms; with it, the relative accuracy of the views may be discerned.

A second assertion is that a social psychology which is local in character is likely to be more useful, in the sense of making some (positive) difference in the lives of individuals and of the group. It is probable that a local focus will lead to the inclusion of issues and problems of concern, whereas those attuned only to the general may overlook questions which are vital to the community. The Symons Commission, indeed, has asserted that such ignorance characterizes much scientific research in Canada. Of course applying a social psychology based on general principles to the solution of international problems is also important (cf. Deutsch and Hornstein, 1975), but such a perspective should not blind us to the local questions, nor delude us into thinking that current social psychology is sufficiently general to be of use in all local and international situations.

Over the years we have witnessed hundreds of internationally-mounted, centrally-directed, theoretically-guided and technically-researched projects fall flat on their faces. Something is wrong, and my hunch is that local issues were not grasped, that the insider's view was not articulated. In both these assertions, I claim that an understanding of the local societal bases of phenomena is a necessary condition for an accurate and useful discipline.

We have argued above that if we wish to avoid ethnocentric observations, the advocacy of a local view logically requires also the advocacy of an outsider's view (and of course *vice versa*). Further, if *one* other view is necessary, then many other views may be desirable. Two further assertions may be made: that the collection and comparison of numerous local exemplars is necessary for testing the limits of current theory; and that only with such collection and comparison can general (perhaps universal) statements be made about human behaviour.

The development of theory, of course, requires both empirical observation and creative reflection. And the purpose of theory development is the production of general statements, abstract in nature, which are applicable to as wide a set of phenomena as possible. Since all theories are based upon a limited set of observations and upon the reflections of minds enculturated in a limited set of cultures, then it follows that all theories could be made more general if based upon wider empirical and analytic foundations. The building of these broader foundations will, in the first instance, indicate the limits of current theory, and in the long run, permit the development of more general, perhaps even universal, theories of human behaviour. Thus the very goal of theory building requires, in social psychology at least, a cross-cultural, comparative endeavour.

These four assertions should demonstrate the desirability of developing many local understandings of behaviour which reflect their own societal bases, and of comparative analysis of these variations which may permit the emergence of pan-cultural regularities. These assertions may, of course, be rejected on the grounds that we already have such universal theory, or that such universal theory itself is undesirable. However, I am assuming that neither position is likely to be advocated.

How Possible?

The basic argument in this section is that the search for the general or universal is only possible after wide ranges of local, specific phenomena and relationships have been observed; that is, the integration follows the differentiation of knowledge. And the way to differentiate and integrate is by the use of the comparative method. As documented in the recent special issue of *The International Journal of Psychology* (1976, 11, no. 3) there are many dimensions of comparison in addition to the cross-cultural (e.g. the historic, the phylogenetic, and the ontogenetic), and they all share some common advantages and problems. However, for our present purposes we will focus only on the cross-cultural form.[3]

In their text *Comparative Perspectives on Social Psychology* Lambert and Weisbrod (1971, p. 3) assert that "the comparative perspective in social psychology requires a movement toward more general models of social processes — models involving more abstract and less culturally specific variables, whose hypotheses have been confirmed in widely varied settings . . .". The first part of our proposition, and most of the previous section, constitutes a plea not to step quickly over (or even ignore) the often difficult groundwork in these "varied settings". But how is this work to be accomplished? And once it has been done, how is it possible to proceed toward the general?

One approach which has been adopted in cross-cultural psychology is through the use of the terms *emic* and *etic*. These two terms were initially proposed by Pike (1966) and derive from the two special approaches in linguistics of phonemics and phonetics. In phonemics, the focus is upon sounds which are employed within a single linguistic system, while in phonetics, the emphasis is upon more general, or even universal, aspects of language. By dropping the root, the two suffixes become terms which are applicable to this local versus universal distinction in any discipline. By analogy, emics apply in only a particular society, while etics are culture-free or universal aspects of the world (or if not entirely universal, operate in more than one society).

The emic approach involves the discovery of native principles of classification and conceptualization and avoids the use of *a priori* definitions and conceptual models (Sturtevant, 1964). Stated in other terms "the final goal . . . is, briefly, to grasp the native's point of view . . . to realize his vision of his world" (Malinowski, 1922, p. 25).

(3) For a comprehensive review of cross-cultural methods, see Triandis and Berry (1979).

In contrast, the *etic* approach is characterized by the presence of universals in a system. Often these universals are assumed to exist; in such cases they have been termed an *imposed etic* (Berry, 1969, p. 124) or a *pseudo etic* (Triandis, Malpass and Davidson, 1972, p. 6). In such cases, these etics are usually only Euro-American emics, imposed blindly and even ethnocentrically on a set of phenomena which occur in other cultural systems (for example, "intelligence" or "personality" tests). On the other hand a true etic is one which emerges from the phenomena; it is empirically and theoretically derived from the common features of the phenomena. Such an etic has been termed a *derived etic* by Berry (1969, p. 124).

Our major problem is how to describe behaviour in terms which are meaningful to members of a particular culture (an emic approach) while at the same time to compare validly behaviour in that culture with behaviour in another or all other cultures (the etic aim). The proposed solution (Berry, 1969, p. 124) involves the initial application of extant hypotheses concerning behaviour. We must tackle a research problem from some point of view, and the conventional one is to try out what we already have; this has been termed an imposed etic approach. In doing so, however, we must recognize the culturally specific (perhaps even ethnocentric) origins of our approach, and deliberately remain open to new and even contrary kinds of data variation. If we enter into the behaviour system of another culture, knowing that our point of entry (imposed etic) is probably only a poor approximation to an understanding of behaviour in that system, then the first major hurdle is passed. Modification of our external categories must be made in the direction of the behavioural system under study, until we eventually achieve a truly emic description of behaviour within that culture. That is, an emic description can be made by progressively altering the imposed etic until it matches a purely emic point of view; if this can be done without entirely destroying or losing all of the etic character of the entry categories, then we can proceed to the next step. If some of the etic is left, we can now note the categories or concepts which are shared by the behaviour system we knew previously and the one we have just come to understand emically. We can now set up a derived   etic which is valid for making comparisons between two behaviour settings, and we have essentially resolved the problem of obtaining a descriptive framework which is valid for comparing behaviour across behaviour settings. This new derived etic can then be transported to another behaviour setting (again as an imposed etic), be modified emically, and thence form the basis of a new derived etic which is valid in three behaviour settings. When all systems which may be compared (limited by the initial functional equivalence requirement) have been included, then we will have achieved a universal for that particular behaviour.

A further concept has been proposed by Naroll (1971), that of *theorics*. For Naroll, "theoric concepts are those used by social scientists to *explain* variations in human behaviour" (1971, p. 7). They represent an even higher level of abstraction than etics, and these etics in turn are more abstract than emics. Thus emics are local concepts employed by a people to classify their environment; etics are pan-cultural concepts employed by social scientists to analyse the emic phenomena; and theorics are theoretical concepts employed by social scientists to interpret and account for emic variation and etic constancies.

In order to compare and integrate the wide range of local or emic observations there must be *comparability*. For comparability to be established, one important criterion must be met: there must be some common baseline upon which the local variation takes place. In other words, "comparison requires dimensional identity" (Duijker and Frijda, 1960, p. 138; Frijda and Jahoda, 1966, p. 115). In a similar vein, Campbell (1964, p. 325) has argued that only when a common underlying process exists can there be the possibility of interpreting differences in behaviour. When such dimensional identity of a common underlying process is demonstrated, then *comparability* is established.

There are two routes to the demonstration of dimensional identity in psychology: one is by adoption of *universals* from biology, linguistics, anthropology or sociology; the other is by the empirical demonstration of *equivalence* in the data collected from two or more samples cross-culturally. The question of universals has been considered in detail by Lonner 1979. Suffice it to say that from these sister disciplines, it is possible to adopt universals which may be in the form "all human beings . . ." or "all human groups . . .". For example, from biology, behavioural researchers may adopt a list of primary needs; from anthropology, we take over a list of common cultural components (language, tool use, myth, etc.); and from sociology there is provided a set of functional prerequisites for social life (Aberle *et al.*, 1950) such as role differentiation, normative regulation of behaviour, and socialization. No known cultural group or individual lacks such common features; thus they may be termed cultural universals, and as a result, they may be employed as common dimensions along which groups and individuals may vary, and may be compared.

With respect to the notion of *equivalence,* the demonstration is not so simple. An earlier outline (Berry and Dasen 1974) suggested that three kinds of equivalence could be demonstrated, each providing some evidence for dimensional identity: *functional, conceptual* and *metric equivalence.*

Firstly, *functional equivalence* exists when two or more behaviours (in two or more cultural systems) are related to functionally similar problems. This term has been coined simultaneously by Frijda and Jahoda (1966) and Goldschmidt (1966) to refer to the same notion and in pursuit of the same argument: "obviously if similar activities have different functions in different societies, their parameters cannot be used for comparative purposes" (Frijda and Jahoda, 1966, p. 116).

Turning to *conceptual equivalence,* Sears (1961) has argued that the *meaning* of research materials (stimuli, concepts, etc) or of behaviour must be equivalent before comparison is possible. Within anthropology, Tatje (1970) has considered this problem in some detail, and within psychology, Price-Williams (1974) has examined the issue with some special emphasis upon categories. Essentially, both argue that the researcher must search for and discover the local meaning of concepts within the cognitive systems of the people and groups being compared. Only if common meaning is discovered can comparison legitimately take place. Note that, as in the case of functional equivalence, conceptual equivalence is a precondition of comparison.

, A number of attempts have been made to operationalize this requirement. One is through the use of forward and back translations of words, sentences and test items to demonstrate *translation equivalence* (Brislin, 1970; Werner and Campbell, 1970). This technique usually involves an initial translation to a target language by one bilingual person, and a back translation to the original language by another; discrepancies will often indicate the presence of conceptual non-equivalence. Variations on this basic technique have been elaborated by Brislin, Lonner and Thorndike (1973, Chapter 2).

A second approach to conceptual equivalence has been by way of semantic differential analyses (Osgood, 1965). For example, the meaning of a concept can be explored by having a respondent judge its position on a set of bipolar adjective scales. Excellent use of this technique has been made by Wober (1974) who explored the Kiganda concept of "intelligence" *(obugezi)*, and its differences from the Western notion represented both in psychological tests and common usage.

A final type of equivalence has come to the fore in recent years: *metric equivalence* exists when the psychometric properties of two (or more) sets of data from two (or more) cultural groups exhibit essentially the same coherence or structure. Within this general approach, two lines of argument have developed. One, termed *subsystem validation* (Roberts and Sutton-Smith, 1962), requires that statistical relationships remain fairly constant among independent and dependent variables, whether one employs the variance available intra-culturally or cross-culturally. In this version the basic argument is that covariation among variables should be stable, regardless of the source of the variation. A second requirement is that statistical relationships among dependent variables should be patterned similarly in two or more cultural groups before comparisons are allowable. Essentially the various forms of this argument are attempts to demonstrate *scalar equivalence* (Poortinga, 1975a, b). It may be demonstrated by similarity in correlation matrices (Poortinga, 1975) or by common factor structures (Irvine and Carroll, 1969; Buss and Royce, 1975). In both cases, the requirement is that behavioural measurements (observations, test data, etc.) should be structured in similar ways *within* groups before comparisons *across* groups are allowable. Note that unlike functional and conceptual equivalence, metric equivalence can usually be established only after the data have been collected and analysed.

Once the three forms of equivalence are established and comparability is asserted, it may be possible to demonstrate *construct validation* across the cultural groups in the comparisons. Such demonstration, however, also requires theoretical argument and abstraction, and these too require a further process of transcultural adaptation. Comparisons may be appropriate with only the demonstration of comparability; but interpretation demands construct validation as well.

In summary, we have argued that comparability is a prerequisite for valid comparison, and that comparability may be attained either by adopting *universals* from other disciplines or by demonstrating the equivalence of psychological concepts and data across groups. A theme which has run through this argument is that it is necessary to keep track of two levels, of both local (single cultural) meaning, function and structure, while at the same time seeking the broader trans-cultural dimension or framework on which basis comparisons might be made.

Some Universals

As noted both in the last section (on the method of comparative integration) and by Kluckhohn (1953, p. 517), the existence of universals in other disciplines can provide the necessary dimensional identities upon which social psychological work can proceed. Particularly important for social psychology are the writings of Malinowski (1944), Murdock (1945) and Aberle *et al.* (1950), where universal features of social and cultural life are proposed.

In the work of Malinowski a list is presented of seven "basic needs" (metabolism, reproduction, bodily comforts, safety, movement, growth and health) which are thought to stimulate a set of universal cultural responses such as economic activity, social control, education and political organization. In a similar functional vein, Aberle and his co-workers have presented a list of nine prerequisites to social life. These include *inter alia* the presence of role differentiation, a shared symbolic communication system, a shared articulated set of goals, the normative regulation of behaviour and the socialization of newcomers to the group.

The most comprehensive proposal has come from Murdock. His list of 73 cultural universals has been classified by Lonner (1979) into five categories: individual behaviour (e.g., hair styles), social behaviour (e.g., courtship), social control and education (e.g., etiquette and penal sanctions), technology (e.g., obstetrics) and collective beliefs (e.g., magic and ritual).

These proposals remind us of the early attempts in social psychology to provide a list of human instincts (e.g., McDougall, 1908) upon which a psychological understanding could rest. They are easily criticized as "vague tautologies and forceless banalities" (Geertz, 1965, p. 103) or as being overly general. However, they are the product of a century of anthropological reflection on the common properties of human social and cultural life, and they do receive some empirical support in factor analytic studies of empirical observations of cultural variation (e.g., Sawyer and Levine, 1966). And given that they are often based upon prior ecological, biological and linguistic considerations, these suggestions of cultural universals surely provide the social psychologist with an excellent basis for comparative enquiry.

Thus far in this paper, I have argued that social psychology needs to include both local or societal and pan cultural or universal phenomena if it is ever to generate an understanding of behaviour as it is exhibited in all mankind. I have argued, further, that it is possible to pursue both when emic and etic levels are employed, and when comparisons are made either on the basis of universals provided by other disciplines, or on the basis of derived etic equivalence which has been generated by comparative integration of data within psychology.

Some Examples

We may examine the recent literature in social psychology to see whether such grandiose goals and methods are anywhere in evidence. Two candidates are easy to spot: the work of Foa and Foa (1974) and of Triandis and his colleagues (1972, 1975, 1976a, b, c). In both, there are attempts to construct universal theories of aspects of social behaviour, mainly the individual's understanding of his social environment and his interpersonal relationships within it. And in both, the comparative method is employed to evaluate ideas and data deriving from a variety of cultures.

In the work of Foa and Foa, analyses of universal features of social interaction (such as the distinctions between self and other, and between acceptance and rejection) lead to the distinction between *"who* is doing the action and towards *whom* it is directed" (p. 36) and between *giving* and *taking away*. The obvious question of *what* is the subject of the inter-action is answered by Foa and Foa in terms of six classes of resources: love, status, information, money, goods and services. These analytical concepts are then structured to yield typologies of possible universal modes of interpersonal interaction which are then evaluated in the light of some cross-cultural data.

Work by Triandis has also yielded typologies of social be-haviour which are thought to be universal. His basic distinctions are between what might be called the "valence" of the inter-action (Associative or Dissociative), the relative status of the interaction (Superordinate, Coordinate or Subordinate), the formality of the interaction (intimate, informal, formal) and the overtness of the interaction (action *vs.* feeling). These are integrated by way of a model formula which may be universal, but whose weights may vary from culture to culture.

At a more modest level, I have been exploring one particular aspect of social behaviour in a wide variety of cultural settings, and the nature of one particular phenomenon within the Canadian multicultural setting. The first involves tracking the relationship between an individual and his group (see Berry 1976b, and in press), while the second involves the structure of ethnocentrism in a culturally plural society (see Berry, Kalin and Taylor, 1977). The first has passed through the imposed etic-emic-derived etic stages, while the second is still in an emic wallow.

In capsule, I have been interested in the degree of independence which characterizes an individual's relationship to his group's norms (Berry, 1967, 1974b). Starting with the social and cultural universals of socialization (enculturation) and the normative regulation of individual behaviour, and with the imposed etic concept of independence (and an Asch type test of it), I was able to consider in each society the local or emic nature of the individual-group relationship. Then with the help of an etic concept of "cultural complexity" (see for example Murdock and Provost, 1973) and an ecological model of cultural variation (see Berry, 1976b), I was able to account for about 65% of variation across seventeen subsistence-level societies, and about 45% of the variation across the 780 respondents in these samples. Those societies which had a hunting and gathering ecological base, which were "loose" (Pelto, 1968) in social and political structure, and which emphasized "assertion" (Barry, Child and Bacon, 1959) during socialization tended to exhibit more independence during test performance. In contrast, those societies which had an agricultural base, a "tight" social structure, and emphasized "compliance" exhibited less independence. Of course there were individual differences within each cultural sample, but it was still possible to account for a major portion of the variance at this individual level of analyses. Details of the model, and its theoretical base, are available in Berry (1976b), while some comments on this approach to studying social psychology cross-culturally can be found in Faucheux (1976, pp. 295-307).

The second study has attempted to explore emically the concept of ethnocentrism within a society which is culturally plural and which promotes a multicultural, rather than an assimilationist, ideology. It seemed reasonable to start with the concept of ethnocentrism since it has been developed as a research concept largely within the American tradition (Sumner, 1906; Levine and Campbell, 1972), but has recently been the subject of emic analyses in a variety of cultures (e.g., Brewer and Campbell, 1976).

It is fairly clear by now that most (and perhaps all) cultural groups tend to positively evaluate their own (in) group and negatively evaluate other (out) groups; that is, an inverse ethnocentric structure to cultural group attitudes is generally thought to be universal. However, the cultural context of such an inverse relationship is usually where one cultural group is dominant in a particular national setting, and where clear in- and out-group distinctions are fostered. In Canada there is a culturally plural situation, and the question may be reasonably asked: does the ethnocentric theory hold in a multi-cultural context?

This question is particularly important at the present time because the Federal Government is promoting a policy of multi-culturalism which is based upon the assumption that the development of one's ethnic identity will lead to an increased acceptance of the ethnicity of other groups. That is, a direct covariation of own (in) group and other (out) group attitudes is expected. Our results (Berry, Kalin and Taylor, 1977) suggest that the structure of attitudes varies depending upon which group's attitudes are being examined. Ethnocentrism theory does not hold in a simple and straightforward way, nor does the multi-culturalism assumption receive support entirely. Clearly the overall multi-cultural context causes problems for one imposed etic (ethnocentrism theory), and theoretical variations are required within that context, depending upon which specific groups are being examined.

These two examples are presented (albeit briefly) to illustrate that it is not psychologically dissonant to carry the two notes of my original proposition simultaneously. A focused interest in emic analyses *and* a comparative integration in the pursuit of potential universals are joint goals, both desirable and possible. It is my hope that these illustrations will serve to show that an interest in societal bases and more universal goals are entirely compatible, and that the earlier arguments will persuade that, indeed, they are both necessary to the development of social psychology.

References

Aberle, D.F., Cohen, A.K., Davis, A.K., Levy, M.J. and Sutton, F.X., The functional prerequisites of a society, *Ethics,* 1950, *60,* 100-11.

Barry, H., Child, I. and Bacon, M., Relation of child training to subsistence economy, *Amer. Anth.,* 1959, *61,* 51-63.

Berry, J.W., Independence and conformity in subsistence-level societies, *J. Pers. Soc. Psychol.,* 1967, *7,* 415-18.

Berry, J.W., On cross-cultural comparability, *Int. J. Psychol.,* 1969, *4,* 119-28.

Berry, J.W., Canadian Psychology: Some social and applied emphases, *Canadian Psychologist,* 1974a, *15,* 132-9.

Berry, J.W., Differentiation across cultures: Cognitive style and affective style. In J.L.M. Dawson and W.J. Lonner (Eds.), *Readings in Cross-Cultural Psychology,* Hong Kong: University of Hong Kong Press, 1974b.

Berry, J.W., Critique of Triandis' Social psychology and cultural analysis. In L. Strickland, F. Aboud & K. Gergen (Eds.), *Social Psychology in Transition,* New York: Plenum, 1976a.

Berry, J.W., *Human Ecology and Cognitive Style: Comparative Studies in Cultural and Psychological Adaptation,* New York: Sage-Halsted, 1976b.

Berry, J.W., Social psychology: comparative, societal and universal, *Canadian Psychological Review,* 1978a.

Berry, J.W., Implications of the cross-cultural method for research in multicultural societies. Paper presented to American Educational Research Association, Toronto, 1978b.

Berry, J.W., A cultural ecology of social behaviour. In L. Berkowitz (Ed.), *Advances in Experimental Social Psychology,* New York: Academic Press, in press.

Berry, J.W. & Dasen, P. (Eds.), Introduction to *Culture and Cognition,* London: Methuen, 1974.

Berry, J.W., Kalin, R. and Taylor, D., *Multiculturalism and Ethnic Attitudes in Canada,* Ottawa: Government of Canada, 1977.

Berry, J.W., Kalin, R. and Wilde, G.J.S., *Brief to Commission on Canadian Studies* (Symons Commission), Subcommittee of CPA, 1973.

Berry, J.W. & Lonner, W.J. (Eds.), *Applied Cross-Cultural Psychology,* 1975, Amsterdam: Swets & Zeitlinger.

Berry, J.W. and Wilde, G.J.S., *Social Psychology of Canada: and Annotated Bibliography*, Kingston: Queen's University, 1971.

Berry, J.W. & Wilde, G.J.S. (Eds.), *Social Psychology: The Canadian Context,* Toronto: McClelland & Stewart, 1972.

Bhatnagar, J., Alternative approaches to the study of experience and behaviour. In J.W. Berry & W.J. Lonner (Eds.), 1975.

Brewer, M. and Campbell, D.T., *Ethnocentrism and Intergroup Attitudes: East African Evidence*, New York: Sage-Halsted, 1976.

Brislin, R., Back translation for cross-cultural research, *J. Cross-Cultural Psychology*, 1970, *1*, 185-216.

Brislin, R., Lonner, W.J. and Thorndike, R. *Cross-Cultural Research Methods,* New York: Wiley, 1973.

Buss, A. and Royce, J.B., Detecting cross-cultural commonalities and differences: Intergroup Factor Analyses, *Psychol. Bull.*, 1975, *82*, 128-36.

Cairns, A.C., Political science in Canada and the Americanization issue, *Can. J. Pol. Sci.*, 1975, *8*, 191-234.

Campbell, D.T., The mutual methodological relevance of Anthropology and Psychology. In F.L.K. Hsu (Ed.), *Psychological Anthropology*, Homewood: Dorsey, 1961.

Campbell, D.T., Distinguishing differences of perception from failures of communication in cross-cultural studies. In F.S.C. Northrop & H.H. Livingston (Eds.), *Cross-Cultural Understanding*, New York: Harper & Row, 1964, 308-36.

Canadian Psychological Association, *The Future of Canadian Psychology*, 1971.

Clark, S.D., The American takeover of Canadian sociology: Myth or reality? *The Dalhousie Review*, 1973, *53*.

Deutsch, M. & Hornstein, H.A. (Eds.), *Applying Social Psychology*, Hillsdale: LEA, 1975.

Duijker, H.C.J. and Frijda, N.H., *National Character and National Stereotypes,* Amsterdam: Noord-Hollandse, 1960.0.

Faucheux, C., Cross-cultural research in experimental social psychology, *Europ. J. Soc. Psychol.*, 1976, *6*, 269-322.

Felt, L.F., Nationalism and the possibility of a relevant Anglo-Canadian Sociology, *Can. J. Soc.*, 1975, *1*, 377-85.

Foa, U.G. and Foa, E.G., *Societal Structures of the Mind*, Springfield: Thomas, 1974.

Frijda, N.H. and Jahoda, G., On the scope and methods of cross-cultural research, *Int. J. Psychol.*, 1966, *1*, 110-27.

Geertz, C., The impact of the concept of culture on the concept of man. In J.R. Platt (Ed.), *New Views on the Nature of Man*, Chicago: University of Chicago Press, 1965.

Gibson, D., Enculturation stress in Canadian Psychology, *Canadian Psychologist,* 1974, *15*, 145-51.

Goldschmidt, W., *Comparative Functionalism,* Berkeley: University of California Press, 1966.

Gurstein, M., Towards the nationalization of Canadian sociology, *J. Can. Studies,* 1972, 7.

Ho, D., Traditional Chinese approaches to socialization. In J.W. Berry & W.J. Lonner (Eds.), 1975.

Ingleby, D., The job psychologists do. In N. Armistead (Ed.), *Reconstructing Social Psychology*, Harmondsworth: Penguin, 1974, 314-28.

International Journal of Psychology, 1976, *11,* no 3. Special Issue on Methodological Problems of Comparative Research.

Irvine, S.H. and Carroll, W.K., Testing and assessment across cultures: Issues in methodology and theory. In H.C. Triandis and J.W. Berry (Eds.), *Handbook of Cross-Cultural Psychology,* (Vol. 2) *Methodology,* Boston: Allyn & Bacon, 1979.

Jarvie, I.C., Nationalism and the social sciences, *Can. J. Soc.,* 1976, *1,* 515-28.

Kluckhohn, C., Universal categories of culture. In A.L. Kroeber (Ed.), *Anthropology Today,* Chicago: University of Chicago Press, 1953.

Kornberg, A. and Tharp, A., The American impact on Canadian political science and sociology. In R.A. Preston (Ed.), *The Influence of the United States on Canadian Development,* Durham: Duke University Press, 1972.

Lambert, W.W. & Weisbrod, R. (Eds.), *Comparative Perspectives on Social Psychology,* Boston: Little Brown, 1971.

Levine, R.A. and Campbell, D.J., *Ethnocentrism: Theories of Conflict, Ethnic Attitudes and Group Behaviour,* New York: Wiley, 1972.

Lonner, W.J., The search for psychological universals. In H.C. Triandis & W.W. Lambert (Eds.), *Handbook of Cross-Cultural Psychology,* (Vol. 1) *History,* Boston: Allyn & Bacon, 1979.

Lyons, G.M., Globalizing the social sciences, *PS,* 1973, *1.*

Malinowski, B., *Argonauts of the Western Pacific,* London: Routledge, 1922.

Malinowski, B., *A Scientific Theory of Culture,* Chapel Hill: University of North Carolina Press, 1944.

McDougall, W., *Introduction to Social Psychology,* London: Methuen, 1908.

Merton, R.K., Insiders and outsiders: a chapter in the sociology of knowledge, *Am. J. Soc.,* 1972, *78.*

Moscovici, S., Society and Theory in Social Psychology. In J. Israel & H. Tajfel (Eds.), *The Context of Social Psychology,* London: Academic Press, 1972, 17-68.

Murdock, G.P., The common denominator of cultures. In R. Linton (Ed.), *The Science of Man in the World Crisis,* New York: Columbia University Press, 1945.

Murdock, G.P. and Provost, C., Measurement of cultural complexity, *Ethnology,* 1973, *12,* 379-92.

Myers, R., Whatever happened to Canadian Psychology? *Canadian Psychologist,* 1970, *11,* 128-32.

Naroll, R., Conceptualizing the problem, as seen by an anthropologist. Paper presented at Amer. Pol. Sci. Assoc. Annual Meeting, Chicago, 1971.

Nisbet, R., Ethnocentrism and the comparative method. In A.R. Desai (Ed.), *Essays on Modernization of Underdeveloped Societies,* Bombay: Thacker, 1971, Vol. 1, 95-114.

Okonji, M., African approaches to the study of behaviour. In J.W. Berry & W.J. Lonner (Eds.), 1975.

Osgood, C., Cross-cultural comparability in attitude measurement via multilingual semantic differentials. In I. Steiner & M. Fishbein (Eds.), *Current Studies in Social Psychology,* Chicago: Holt, Rinehart & Winston, 1965.

Patel, A.S., An approach to behaviour as expounded in the Indian scriptures. In J.W. Berry & W.J. Lonner (Eds.), 1975.

Pelto, P., The difference between "tight" and "loose" societies, *Transaction,* 1968, (April), 37-40.

Pike, R., *Language in Relation to a Unified Theory of the Structure of Human Behavior,* Glendale: Summer Institute of Linguistics, 1954 and Den Haag: Mouton, 1966.

Poortinga, Y., Limitations on intercultural comparison of psychological data, *Nederlands Tijdschrift voor de Psychologie*, 1975a, *30*, 23-39.

Poortinga, Y., Some implications of three different approaches to intercultural comparison. In J.W. Berry & W.J. Lonner (Eds.), *Applied Cross-Cultural Psychology*, Amsterdam: Swets & Zeitlinger, 1975b, 329-32.

Price-Williams, D., Psychological experiment and anthropology: the problem of categories, *Ethos*, 1974, *2*, 95-114.

Roberts, J. and Sutton-Smith, B., Child training and game involvement, *Ethnology*, 1962, *1*, 166-85.

Sawyer, J. and Levine, R.A., Cultural dimensions: a factor analysis of the world ethnographic sample, *Amer. Anth.*, 1966, *68*, 708-31.

Sears, R.R., Transcultural variables and conceptual equivalence. In B. Kaplan (Ed.), *Studying Personality Cross-Culturally*, New York: Row, Peterson, 1961, 445-55.

Smiley, D., Must Canadian political science be a miniature replica? *J. Can. Studies*, 1974, *9*, 31-42.

Smith, D.E., What it might mean to do a Canadian sociology: the everyday world as problematic, *Can. J. Soc.*, 1975, *1*, 363-76.

Stoltzman, J. and Gamberg, H., The national question and Canadian Sociology, *Can. J. Soc.*, 1975, *1*, 91-106.

Sturtevant, W.C., Studies in ethnoscience. In A.K. Romney & R. D'Andrade (Eds.); *Transcultural Studies in Cognition*, *Amer. Anth.*, 1964, *66*, 99-131.

Sumner, W.G., *Folkways*, Boston: 1906.

Sweet, L.E., What is Canadian anthropology? *Amer. Anth.*, 1976, *78*, 844-50.

Symons, T.H.B., *To Know Ourselves*, Vols. 1 & 2, Ottawa: AUCC, 1975.

Taft, R., Cross-cultural psychology as a social science: comments on Faucheux's paper, *Europ. J. Soc. Psychol.*, 1976, *6*, 323-30.

Tatje, T.A., Problems of concept definition for comparative studies. In R. Naroll & R. Cohen (Eds.), *Handbook of Method in Cultural Anthropology*, New York: Natural History Press, 1970, 689-706.

Triandis, H.C., Culture training, cognitive complexity and interpersonal attitudes. In R. Brislin, S. Bochner & W. Lonner (Eds.), *Cross-Cultural Perspectives on Learning*, New York: Sage-Halsted, 1975.

Triandis, H.C., *Interpersonal Behaviour*, Monterey: Brooks Cole, 1976a.

Triandis, H.C., Social psychology and cultural analysis. In L. Strickland, F. Aboud & K. Gergen (Eds.), *Social Psychology in Transition*, New York: Plenum Press, 1976b.

Triandis, H.C., On the value of cross-cultural research in social psychology: reactions to Faucheux's paper, *European J. Soc. Psychol.*, 1976c, *6*, 331-41.

Triandis, H.C. *et al.*, *The Analysis of Subjective Culture*, New York: Wiley, 1972.

Triandis, H.C. and Berry, J.W., *Handbook of Cross-Cultural Psychology*, (Vol. 2) *Methodology*, Boston: Allyn & Bacon, 1979.

Triandis, H.C., Malpass, R.S. and Davidson, A., Cross-cultural psychology, *Biennial Review of Anthropology*, 1972.

Trimple, J., The intrusion of Western psychological thought on native American ethos. In J.W. Berry & W.J. Lonner (Eds.), Amsterdam: Swets & Zeitlinger, 1975.

Werner, O. and Campbell, D.T., Translating, working through interpreters, and the problem of decentering. In R. Naroll & R. Cohen (Eds.), *Handbook of Method in Cultural Anthropology*, New York: Natural History Press, 1970.

Weyant, R.G., A typically Canadian Psychology: Fact or myth? *Canadian Psychologist*, 1974, *15*, 152-6.

Wober, M., Towards an understanding of the Kiganda concept of intelligence. In
J.W. Berry & P.R. Dasen (Eds.), *Culture and Cognition,* 261-80, London: Methuen,
1974.

Wright, M., Should we rediscover Blatz? *Canadian Psychologist,* 1974, *15,* 140-4.

Discussion

HOLMES: John, in your comments you pointed out that if we're to move from a
local psychology to a general or universal one, then we need a set of methods where
we can have convergence — where we can have observers from different cultures
observing the same thing. What are the implications then for integration of the
scientific community? Surely this implies changes in our journal structure, in the
relationships between communities, and so on, that you really haven't gone into?

BERRY: There are two terms which I have used previously in discussing this issue:
"restrain" and "resist". The dominant scientific communities (those which usually
contribute the *imposed etics)* should restrain themselves from further imposing their
views; the non-dominant ones (those which are struggling to develop their own
emics) should "resist" such influence for the time being. Eventually, when local
emic views are well-developed, more balanced scientific discourse will be possible.
However, at the present time, those societies without a social psychological tradition
of their own must examine their own assumptions and phenomena without pressure
from outside.

KIESLER: It might be of interest to our guests, John, to say a few words about the
discussion in Canada about dominance in the social sciences.

BERRY: Well, if you look at the papers I've cited on that debate, you will notice
that the titles frequently have question marks after them: "Must Canadian Political
Science be a Miniature Replica?", or "What is Canadian Anthropology?, or "The
American Takeover of Canadian Sociology: Myth or Reality?" The titles, at least, are
open-minded. But the comments that are made in them are often highly divisive and
dogmatic, with people arguing that it is old-fashioned to consider that the culture
or national background of a social scientist could or should interfere with the way he
does his work. This assertion seems to me almost impossible to accept, because as
social scientists we look at the relationship between social/cultural/political structure
and the development of our behaviours. And yet many of the papers published in
the last three or four years have made dogmatic statements: that advocating a Canadian
social science is simply witch-hunting, it's anti-American, it's an attempt to get back
at the history of dominance of social science in this country. I take heart from the
very straightforward statement of the assumption of the alternative position by the
Soviet delegation. Speakers have said, "our social science flows from our cultural/
ideological/philosophical basis, and this is obvious to us". So it's up to us now to
specify what these bases are in Canada — and in Nigeria and Zambia and Timbuktoo.

BAREFOOT: This may be impossible to answer, but how local is local? If one thinks
of trying to take on this task within a multi-cultural society like Canada, where
regional differences are so great, at what level is it practical, at what level do you
start working?

BERRY: Well, there's no clearcut rule, but I would say to begin with functioning socio-cultural units, which are self-aware, which are able to generate a perspective on themselves, and are able to be a focus of study by outsiders. You might look at my recent attempt to solve this problem in Berry, 1978b.

KIESLER: So it could be a province?

BERRY: Well no — I was going to give some examples. French Canada obviously has a different social science tradition from us. And from our work in the North, I see a broad pattern of understanding social behaviour common to Inuit, Cree, Ojibwa, and Athabascan peoples. So it's arbitrary to an extent — but if our interest is culturally-based views of man, then the answer reasonably can be in terms of cultural units.

KIESLER: I think that's why you can't expect this kind of approach to push strongly on a universal theory. If you take this approach, then you must draw arbitrary lines to determine between what the groups are, what the decisions are, and what is studiable. In one sense you're asking that psychology support research in smaller groups (actually, they turn out being larger than the usual groups that we study), cultural groups, without reference to hard-core theory, or overlays of behavioural models as we may think we understand them. It's a plea for intellectual freedom — to investigate existing subgroups without such fine definitions.

SEGALOWITZ: A rhetorical question: when *you* work in a French Canadian setting, are you providing the outsider's view or are you doing local psychology?

BERRY: As a different example, my work with Cree people at James Bay has proceeded with Cree school-teachers who were released from their teaching jobs, and who were trained by me in the techniques of interviewing, testing, data gathering — but not in the theoretical aspects of the study. Later we combine efforts and try to put it all together. Both insiders and outsiders are required.

SEGALEWITZ: I wonder if that's very different in principle from an American social psychologist training us how to do social psychology in Canada.

BERRY: But if there's no "us" as part of the team, there's no insider. There's no self-aware point of view. There's no alternative.

ANDREEVA: I have no quarrel with the basic premise that cultural conditions form a base for the study of social psychology. And I will not touch on the Canadian-American example because it is a matter of sovereignty. I will discuss another point from the presented paper, general theory of psychology. I want to propose two meanings of "general theory", and show them in this figure:

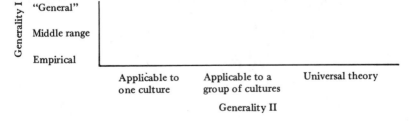

The vertical axis represents level of theory, and here I indicate three levels of generalization. The first is empirical, the second is "middle range", and finally we have the general, so-called "all embracing theory" (such as Parsons', for example). I feel that there is another dimension which can be presented diagrammatically on the horizontal. One can speak about theories applicable to a single culture; then there are theories applicable to a group of cultures; the third level could be called either "general" or "universal" theory. I am interested in the relationship between what is represented on the horizontal and the vertical, and because of this, there is one point in the paper where I have some doubts. You say, "My first assertion is that the social psychology which is local in character is more likely to be theoretically appropriate, or more accurate, in the sense of matching the understanding to social reality". If you carry this transitivity notice to the vertical axis, then there is a danger of making an error. One might think that the middle range theory, which is closer to the empirical level than a general theory, would be a more exact method of describing reality than the general level. But that would not be fair to say. The explanatory functions of a general theory and middle range theory are essentially different. One cannot say that the middle range is better because it is more exact. They each should be looked at separately as having different functions. The functions of general theory are very important, too: it gives the philosophical comprehension of the subject matter of social psychology. This aspect has not been discussed in your paper.

BERRY: You asked me to consider relationships amongst levels of theory, and what I did was essentially to equate these two dimensions on the assumption that it is the relationship between them that is important — both can be swung into the same dimension. The reason for doing this is that I would not want to progress very far up the vertical axis from unicultural observations. On the other hand, I'd be happy to progress up to general theory, on the basis of multi-cultural observations.

ANDREEVA: How or where do you introduce "social context" at the various levels in constructing theory?

BERRY: Can I ask a question in return? Is the word "social" being used deliberately in distinction from "cultural"?

ANDREEVA: Social or cultural, it could be either.

BERRY: Social context is introduced at the level of data collection, at the level of what anthropologists do during field work; the parameters are not set in advance, but are to be discovered.

The Level of Social Psychological Analysis
A Plea for a More Social Psychology

WOLFGANG STROEBE

Introduction

Since changes in social psychological theorizing are typically due to satiation rather than refutation, it seems only fitting that the so-called "crisis of social psychology" was never resolved but repressed. Everybody got sick and tired hearing about it and the prophets of doom, having lost their audience, turned to new and more fashionable issues. However, unlike people, problems are rarely made to go away by disregard. It is therefore even more timely today to search for solutions to those unresolved issues than it was ten years ago, when the discontent with social psychology broke to the surface in April 1967 with Ring's "sober questions" about the frivolous values apparently guiding most of the experimental research in social psychology.

It is the argument of this paper that the cause of our discontent has typically not been seen very clearly and that, with a few exceptions (e.g. Gergen, 1973; Harre and Secord, 1972 – who furthermore could be accused of going to the opposite extreme), prescriptions have been directed at minor symptoms rather than attacking the real problem. We have wasted a decade blaming our methods while the real problem lies with our theories. It is my conviction that what has been hailed as the "emerging new paradigm" (McGuire, 1967, 1973) or the "new look" (Smith, 1972) was nothing but a methodological fashion, and the new paradigm, if and when it emerges will be a new theory, and not a new method.

The first section of this paper analyzes the reasons for the discontent with social psychology. The second section discusses some of the suggested solutions and demonstrates that a purely methodological solution is bound to fail, and that a reorientation of theory rather than research method is called for. In the third section some suggestions will be made as to the nature of this theoretical reorientation.

I. The Cause of Discontent

Ring's (1967) paper has often been represented as being concerned with the lack of applicability of social psychological findings. For example, "The crux of the controversy", as McGuire (1967) summarized Ring's position, "seems to be whether one should choose his next step in research in order to clarify a theoretical issue or to guide action in the natural environment" (p. 126). Although McGuire merely rephrased similar statements by Ring, his summary does not present the true flavour of the Ring article. There is more to the conflict than the old argument over the relative virtue of applied versus basic research. Phrased in a general way, the accusation that social psychological research cannot be applied is wrong anyway and could be refuted quite easily. One only has to read Varela's (1971) book to get quite worried about the immense applicability of social psychological theories and findings. Any text on consumer psychology or advertising relies heavily on social psychological knowledge. Although the clinical applications of social psychological findings are only just being explored, one feels that the possibilities in this area are also immense.

However, it is obvious to the reader of Ring's article that influencing the *attitudes of individuals* was not the kind of application he had in mind. As one of his major examples of the anti-applied attitude predominant among experimental social psychologists he quotes McGuire (1965), who attacks some misguided colleagues for being "too preoccupied with the Berlin wall, the urban plight, the population bomb, and the plight of the Negro in the South" (p. 115). Thus, the crux of the controversy is not merely whether social psychologists should do applied or basic research: the real cause of the problem: is that Ring, like a lot of other people, felt that social psychologists should do research which would help to understand and solve social problems, such as ethnic and racial tensions, prejudice, and other sources of social conflict, that is *structural* conflicts, which, unlike interpersonal conflicts, cannot be explained in terms of individual motives but derive from the structure of the social units involved.

It is not surprising that these concerns became prevalent in the sixties when social and political conflicts were fought again more openly, and when students became politically involved in North America as well as in Europe. It is also not surprising that people looked to social psychologists for advice and guidance. After all, to the naive layman, the name "social psychology" suggests that this should be the study of social relations and that therefore social psychology should offer guidelines for the understanding and handling of large scale social conflicts. *Unfortunately it does not, and this, I believe, is the real cause of the present discontent with social psychology.*

The reason for our ignorance is common knowledge. For the past twenty years we have been so busy doing the work of personality psychologists, that we have had little time for social psychology. Admittedly, we have been doing such a great job that we have caused an identity crisis among personality psychologists. In a recent (annual) review of the field of personality psychology, Sechrest (1976) admits this fact frankly:

> "It is very difficult to distinguish between social and personality psychology today, but clearly a large part of what might be, and probably even should be, personality is, by passive consensus, within and/or dominated by social psychology. ... *The Journal of Personality and Social Psychology* is heavily oriented toward social psychology. The study of emotions and other internal states is widely seen as "social" psychology because a social psychologist, Schachter, started the area. Edward Jones, another social psychologist, nabbed off attribution theory for social psychology, even though much of that theory is as relevant to personality as to social psychology. Leonard Berkowitz, social psychologist, has been the central figure in research on aggression and catharsis for the past 15 years or so. Sex-role research has been a topic of interest for social psychologists for the past 2 or 3 years. The list could go on, but just to give final substance to the notion that the study of personality really lies in large part in social psychology, along the way Schachter and his students added obesity and smoking to social psychology's domain" (p. 5).

But however well we have been doing our job in the eyes of the personality psychologists, the fact remains that this individualistic brand of social psychology is of little use as soon as it has to be extended beyond the interpersonal level. As sociologists have stressed since Durkheim, one cannot fully account for social organizations (e.g. family, small group) in terms of the motives of the individuals forming that organization. Consequently one cannot *fully* understand interactions between members of such organizations in terms of their individual motives. Or as Tajfel (e.g. 1974) has emphasized over and over again, individuals on opposing sides of race riots or other intergroup conflicts do not interact in terms of their individual characteristics, but in terms of their group memberships and their behavior cannot be *fully* accounted for by studying individual motivation. Thus, by focusing on the study of the individual as an individual, social psychologists have neglected the study of the individual as part of social systems, which should be their proper subject matter.

II. The Methodological Solutions and Their Failure

All crises have their moments of irrationality. During the industrial revolution bands of workers stormed factories to destroy the machines to which they attributed all their troubles. A similar movement developed during the height of the crisis of our discipline. What had started out as a discussion of the applicability of social psychological research to social problems turned into a campaign against laboratory experimentation. Professional bodies which only ten years earlier had proudly garnished their names with the qualifier "experimental" suddenly considered dropping it as if to rid themselves of incriminating evidence. Even reasonable people like McGuire were carried away into hailing field research as the cure for all our problems. He forecast "that the ingenuity now exercised in creating laboratory surrogates for the real world will be steadily replaced by equal ingenuity in utilizing the natural environment as a field in which to test these deductions."

"The solace", he perceived, "in this prospect offering for those who are concerned with the social uses of science is that a theory tested in the real world is almost certain to prove relevant to the problems existing in the natural environment" (1967, p. 126). One only has to look into accounts of the research on altruism or other areas dominated by field research to realize, which on epistemological grounds could have been known all along, that "irrelevant" theories do not become any more relevant when tested in the field rather than the laboratory.

The attack on the laboratory experiment and the frantic search for new methods seems partly to be guided by an outdated epistemology, by the Baconian myth that theories are *logically derived from* observations. As we have known since Kant, this has never been true in the history of science and cannot be true for good reasons. Kant's position is accepted nowadays by most philosophers of science. As Popper rephrased it — "our intellect does not draw its laws from nature, but tries — with varying degrees of success — to impose upon nature laws which he freely invents" (1963, p. 191). Popper elaborates this point even further when he states that "theories are . . . free creations of our minds, the results of almost poetic intuition, of an attempt to understand intuitively the laws of nature" (1963, p. 192). It should thus be obvious, that since we do not derive our theories from our data, but merely use the data to check the validity of our theories, the content or relevance of our hypotheses cannot increase miraculously depending on the methodology used.

However, while the explanatory power of a theory remains unaffected by the methodology used to test it, poor methodology can be misleading in other ways. It can lead to the apparent corroboration of a hypothesis which should have been refuted had the test been conducted properly, or to the erroneous refutation of hypotheses which should have been corroborated in a proper test. It is in this sense that the investigation of the experimental method is perfectly legitimate.

The work on demand characteristics (Orne, 1969) and on experimenter bias (Rosenthal, 1966) appears to be guided by concerns of the first kind, that a great deal of the evidence which is apparently corroborating our social psychological theories is *de facto* due to artifacts of the experimental situation. It is suggested that subjects frequently support hypotheses either intentionally, because they guessed them and wanted to be nice, or unintentionally, because they were subtly influenced by experimenter expectations. It does not have to concern us here whether these fears are well founded. If they were it would merely mean that there should be even fewer theories around than there are at present.

Similar objections, though for different reasons, are raised against the laboratory experiment by the adherents of the "ethogenic approach". Ethogeny, which takes its model from ethology, "is the study of human lives as they are really lived, not in the strange and impoverished world of the laboratories, but out in the streets, at home, in shops, cafes and lecture rooms where people really interact" (Harré, 1974, p. 250). The observation of behavior in the natural setting is necessary, because the meaning of social action can be understood only in its social context. We understand the behavior of a given individual in a given social situation only if we know the "rules" governing that situation and the specific application of these rules to the actor (his role-prescriptions for that situation). Since the behavior of subjects in experiments is determined by their perception of their role and of the rules prescribing actions in that particular situation, it does not tell us anything about their behavior outside the laboratory situation. The object of social psychology, according to the ethogenic approach, "is to obtain so detailed a knowledge of the rules, conventions, situational meanings and so on, by which skilled and intelligent actors manage their social lives, that any particular fragment of social reality can be reconstructed" (Harré, 1974, p. 258).

Although only the methodological implications of the ethogenic approach are discussed here, a few remarks should be made about its potential as a general theory of social behavior. While one can agree with Harré on the importance of concepts like rule and role, knowing the norms and role-prescriptions governing the behavior of individuals in all kinds of situations does not seem sufficient for an understanding of social behavior. In addition, social psychologists should be able to explain how these roles and norms developed and what function they serve for the individual as well as for the larger social unit involved. The ethogenic approach does not offer any guidance as to how such an understanding could be achieved.

The second kind of criticism, that hypotheses were erroneously refuted because the experimental method did not provide a proper test, is typically not raised in this actual form. Rather, a more hypothetical version is used in suggesting that certain types of theories were never developed because they *could* not have been properly tested. Smith (1972), for example, remarked that in "building an experimental social psychology, we do well to recognize a certain incongruity between the experimental method and the interactive phenomena with which social psychology is supposedly concerned. When pressed, most of us will agree that social behavior involves interactive systems in which feedback loops are more characteristic than linear causation. . . . With its independent and dependent variables, experimental design inherently produces a unidirectional snapshot. Experimentation in social psychology is most powerful when it is used for the analytical dissection of the interactive process" (p. 94). In the same vein Swingle (1976) has recently warned that in "its extreme form, the causal fixation gives rise to complete myopia with respect to the reciprocal and circular nature which, as one moment's reflection must indicate, characterizes all social processes" (pp. 103-4).

In his thoughtful and perceptive analysis of the reasons for the decline of the "groupy" social psychology of the forties and fifties, Steiner (1974) argued too that the experimental methodology with its quest for ever stricter controls was partly to blame. But he also mentions the total lack of theory as another important reason for the loss of interest in small group research.

In the light of all the evidence, it cannot be denied that the independent-dependent variable format of the experimental method, in conjunction with analysis of variance procedures, has encouraged a fixation on simple linear models (although one could argue whether this is really an *inherent* characteristic of the experiment). However, I firmly believe that the best antidote against this bias are theories which take account of the alleged circular nature of social processes. Methods are tools. As long as we work to the same old blueprints, we will continue to turn out the same old line of products, even if provided with a new fancy set of gadgets.

III. Towards a Theoretical Reorientation

Time has not been too kind to previous prophecies of "emerging new paradigms" and prophets have recently become distinctly more careful in their forecasts (e.g., compare McGuire, 1967 and 1973). It is thus with great apprehension that I take my turn at the crystal ball.

However, equipped with the analysis presented earlier, I feel that I am on slightly firmer ground than my predecessors. The discontent with social psychology, I argued in Section I, developed when social psychologists proved to be either unable or unwilling to apply their knowledge to large scale social conflicts. This inability, I argued in Section II, was due to the individualistic nature of social psychological theorizing during the last twenty years and could not be explained in terms of the restrictions placed on research by our experimental methodology. The solution to our crisis or the emerging new paradigm can therefore not consist merely of a new methodology, but has to come from a reorientation of social psychological theorizing.

Descriptions of what is hoped to become the "new paradigm", and I am using the term here in the sense Kuhn (1962) used it, as "accepted examples of actual scientific practice — examples which include law, theory, application, and instrumentation together" (p. 10), have already been given by Steiner (1974) and Tajfel (1974). The paradigm is not completely new either, but is partly a return to the "groupy" social psychology of our founding fathers. It is suggested that social psychology, which during the last 20 years has undergone a Copernican revolution in reverse, should stop treating man as the center of the universe and foster again the development of theories which look at man merely as a subsystem in a larger system, e.g. the group, the organization, or even society.

The individualistic orientation, which social psychologists have increasingly adopted during the last two decades, studies the individual as a system in his own right. Although lip-service is paid to the fact that the individual system functions in a social context, the social context is typically perceived as consisting of *unstructured homogeneous collections* of other individual systems. Individual behavior is explained by relating it to other elements of the individual system, typically unobservable constructs such as attitudes, motives, and needs.

As a consequence of this individualistic orientation, interactions between individuals or between groups must be explained in terms of individual motives. The position taken by Berkowitz in his book on aggression is typical for this general point of view. Berkowitz (1962) writes:

"Granting all this, the present writer is still inclined to emphasize the importance of individualistic considerations in the field of group relations. Dealings between groups ultimately become problems of the psychology of the individual. Individuals decide to go to war; battles are fought by individuals; and peace is established by individuals" (p. 167).

The socio-psychological or "groupy" (Steiner, 1974) approach shares with the individualistic orientation the emphasis on the study of individual behavior. This makes it a psychological rather than a sociological discipline. However, it shares with sociology the belief that individual behavior ought to be explained in terms of events outside the individual. The individual is studied as part of a larger system, e.g. a group or an organization, and his behavior is assumed to reflect the state of the larger system and the events that occur in it. The basic assumptions, which this approach shares with sociology, are made quite explicit by the sociologist Chinoy (1967) when he writes:

"The close dependence of the individual upon his social milieu makes it possible to account for some aspects of human behavior without direct reference to psychological characteristics. Since people tend to follow the norms of the groups to which they belong, knowledge of an individual's group affiliations and of the attributes of those groups is likely to be sufficient to predict and account for his actions" (pp. 73-4).

Such a socio-psychological approach trespasses on the demarcation line between sociology and psychology. The dividing line between the two disciplines is the concept of social role. While for the sociologist, the social role is the smallest unit of analysis which cannot be broken down any further, the psychologist looks at the role from the inside, from the side turned towards the individual, and thus reduces it further (Dahrendorf, 1965). However, social psychology was intended to trespass on this border line by the founding fathers. It was supposed to occupy a mediating position between the sociological and the psychological points of view. *De facto,* however, social psychology has become very law abiding and stays precisely within the limits of a psychological analysis. The individualistic social psychologist is thus in a position similar to that of the experimental psychologist studying rats in a Skinner box. He has excellent theories to account for the lever pressing in relation to the food pellets dropped into the box. But it is *he* who drops the food pellets and he has no idea about the dropping rate or dropping contingencies of pellets in a natural environment.

The individualistic social psychologist has constructed a Skinner box of his own making. He is busily simulating counter-attitudinal role pressures, normative pressures, group interactions and so on. He can explain what happens to an individual's attitude if pressure is exerted on him to behave counterattitudinally, but he has no theories about how those pressures come about in the natural social context. He knows a great deal about conformity and the motives of the conforming individual. But beyond the individual need for cognitive clarity, he has little interest in the reasons why norms develop, what function they serve for the group, and why they develop for certain areas of group behavior rather than others.[1] Similarly, he cannot explain how roles develop, what kind of roles develop in different social contexts or how role conflicts come about.

Instead of merely paying lip-service to the fact that there

(1) One notable exception to this is the functional analysis of norms by Thibaut and Kelley (1959).

is a social context and that it affects individual behavior as, in turn, individual behavior affects the context, social psychologists should study individuals as parts of that context. If we admit that an individual's behavior is affected by such structural elements as status, position, role, and norms, we must also concede that a social psychology is incomplete without a theory of the development, maintenance and dissolution of such social structures.

It is actually quite intriguing, that two disciplines based on such different assumptions as sociology and (individualistic) social psychology could, both in their own way, be quite successful in predicting individual social behavior. If behavior is influenced by our private motives, needs and attitudes, as social psychologists assure us, how come sociologists do quite well in predicting it from a knowledge of the individual's sociological characteristics? If, on the other hand, people always followed the norms of the groups to which they belonged and knowledge of their sociological characteristics was sufficient to predict and account for their actions, as sociologists assure us, how come social psychologists do quite well in predicting, for example, interpersonal attraction from partner attitudes and personality traits?

Internalization of norms and values through socialization is certainly part of the explanation, but it cannot be the whole story, or sociologists would not have missed much in using role as the smallest unit of their analysis. A second reason is probably that the two disciplines account for somewhat different parts of the total variance. However, I believe that there is a third reason. It may be that there are some situations in which individual behavior is mainly influenced by individual motives, while in other situations it is mainly directed by group memberships and other sociological characteristics. While social psychologists have been doing quite well in predicting social behavior in the first type of situations, sociologists have been better in the second type. I would even argue that the discontent with social psychology is due to the failure of social psychologists to account for individual behavior in situations of the second type. This analysis is taking up and expanding a point made earlier by Tajfel (1974) in developing his theory of intergroup conflict. Tajfel hypothesized that social interactions can be placed on a continuum ranging from *interindividual* to *intergroup* behavior. At one extreme, which cannot be found in its "pure" form in "real life", is the interaction between two or more individuals which is *fully* determined by their interpersonal relationships and not at all affected by the various social groups or social categories to which they respectively belong. The other extreme, for which "real life" examples can be found, consists of interactions between two or more individuals (or groups of individuals) which are fully determined by their respective memberships of various social groups or categories and not at all affected by the interindividual personal relationships between the people involved. Examples of behaviors near the interpersonal extreme would be the interaction between husband and wife or between old friends. Examples of situations near the other extreme would be the behavior of soldiers from opposing armies during a battle or of participants involved at different sides of a race riot.

Since individual motives have little impact on behavior in such intergroup situations, it is not surprising that individualistic social psychology has typically had problems in accounting for this type of behavior. *It is therefore an important task for social psychological theory to identify the conditions which determine the adoption of forms of social behavior nearing one or the other extreme of this continuum.*

One such condition has been identified by Tajfel, who argued that intergroup conflict forces members of opposing groups to behave towards each other in terms of their respective group memberships rather than in terms of their individual relationships. To elaborate this statement, I will briefly outline Tajfel's theory of intergroup conflict. Intergroup conflict is the result of a competition between groups for some scarce resource. This resource may be material, as in the case of a "conflict of interest", or social, as in the case of competition for relative status. The reason for "social competition", Tajfel argues, is that individuals define and evaluate themselves in terms of the social groups to which they belong, by comparing the status of their membership groups to that of other groups. Since Tajfel assumes that people find a negative social identity unsatisfactory, he suggests that unless an individual accepts his social inferiority as God-given (e.g. serfs in a feudal system or women before women's lib), he will be motivated to change his social identity. His way of attempting this change will depend on his position on a continuum of beliefs which ranges from a belief in *social mobility* to a belief in *social change*. If the individual perceives the society he lives in as flexible and permeable, permitting free social mobility, he will attempt to leave his group as an individual and to move into groups which are higher up on the status hierarchy. On the other hand, if he perceives the society as inflexible and impermeable, he will feel enclosed within the walls of the social groups to which he belongs. He cannot leave his group. His fate is firmly linked to the fate of his group. The only way open to him to improve his condition is to improve the condition of his *group as a whole.*

There is thus a close relationship between the position of members of a group on the belief continuum of social mobility or social change and their behavior towards members of relevant outgroups. While a shared belief in social mobility should lead to a decrease in the cohesiveness of a low status group, a shared belief in social change should increase cohesiveness and cause strong negative feelings towards relevant outgroups. Thus, the nearer group members are to the social change extreme on the belief continuum, the more uniformity they will display towards members of relevant outgroups and the less they will take into account the individual differences between members of that group. They will react *en masse,* treating them as undifferentiated items in a unified category. Empirical support for these assumptions comes from Tajfel's (e.g. Tajfel *et al.,* 1971) own work with "minimal groups" and from Sherif's (e.g. Sherif, 1966) field studies. In both situations, it could be demonstrated that assignment to "opposing" groups overruled previously existing relationships.

However, to anybody familiar with military or naval hierarchy, similar examples will come to mind of personal relationships being overcome by powerful role-prescriptions. While the relationships between fellow captains can mainly be determined by their personal characteristics, role-prescriptions take over when they find themselves on the same ship as captain and rear admiral. The difference between these two examples might seem that conflict destroys the previous personal relationship while role requirements only suspend it. Off duty the two officers could still be good friends. However, one could as easily imagine the generals of opposing armies having been good friends before the war and taking up their personal relationship some time afterwards. This probably depends on the intensity of conflict, how personally involved one gets and on the implications of the concept of opponent or enemy at that particular time.

Conceptually inter-role and intergroup behavior are actually not that different. After all, role-prescriptions originate from groups and the interaction between captain and admiral could be conceived of as an interaction between members of two different groups. Nevertheless, such instances of inter-role behavior cannot be explained in terms of intergroup or interpersonal conflict and other determinants of such "intercategory" behavior have to be identified. It may be that any factor which increases group cohesiveness or otherwise makes salient the membership to a certain social category moves interactions towards the "intercategory" extreme of the behavior dimension and that intergroup conflict is only one of these factors. However, as Tajfel clarified the close dependence of intergroup behavior on intergroup conflict when he developed a theory of intergroup relations, the general conditions determining interactions in terms of roles rather than personal characteristics as well as the interactions between personal motives and role-prescriptions will certainly be clarified when social psychologists join the sociologists in the development of a socio-psychological theory of social organizations.

References

Berkowitz, L., *Agression: A Social Psychological Analysis*, New York: McGraw-Hill, 1962.

Chinoy, E., *Society: An Introduction to Sociology*, New York: Random House, 1967.

Dahrendorf, R., *Homo Sociologicus*, Köln: Westdeutscher Verlag, 1965.

Gergen, K.J., Social Psychology as history, *Journal of Personality and Social Psychology*, 1973, *26*, 309-20.

Harré, R., Blueprint for a new science. In N. Armistead (Ed.), *Reconstructing Social Psychology*, Harmondsworth: Penguin, 1974.

Harré, R. and Secord, P., *The Explanation of Social Behaviour*, Oxford: Blackwell, 1972.

Kuhn, T.S., *The Structure of Scientific Revolutions*, Chicago: The University of Chicago Press, 1962.

McGuire, W.J., Discussion of William N. Schoenfeld's paper. In O. Klineberg & R. Christie (Eds.), *Perspectives in Social Psychology*, New York: Holt, Rinehart & Winston, 1965.

McGuire, W.J., Some impending reorientations in social psychology: Some thoughts provoked by Kenneth Ring, *Journal of Experimental Social Psychology*, 1967, *3*, 124-39.

McGuire, W.J., The Yin and Yang of progress in social psychology, *Journal of Personality and Social Psychology*, 1973, *26*, 446-56.

Orne, M.T., Demand characteristics and the concept of quasi-controls. In R. Rosenthal & R.L. Rosnow (Eds.), *Artifact in Behavioral Research*, New York: Academic Press, 1969.

Popper, K.R., *Conjectures and Refutations*, London: Routledge & Kegan Paul, 1963.

King, K. Experimental Social Psychology: Some sober questions about some frivolous values, *Journal of Experimental Social Psychology*, 1967, *3*, 113-23.

Rosenthal, R., *Experimenter Effects in Behavioral Research*, New York: Appleton-Century-Crofts, 1966.

Sechrest, L., Personality. In M.R. Rosenzweig & L.W. Porter (Eds.), *Annual Review of Psychology*, 1976, Palo Alto: Annual Reviews Inc.

Sherif, M., *Group Conflict and Cooperation: Their Social Psychology*, London: Routledge & Kegan Paul, 1966.

Smith, B., Is experimental social psychology advancing? *Journal of Experimental Social Psychology*, 1972, *8*, 86-96.

Steiner, I.D., Whatever happened to the group in social psychology? *Journal of Experimental Social Psychology*, 1974, *10*, 94-108.

Swingle, P.G., Critique: On "Resolution versus Revolution?" In L.H. Strickland, F.E. Aboud & K.J. Gergen (Eds.), *Social Psychology in Transition*, New York: Plenum Press, 1976.

Tajfel, H., Intergroup behaviour, social comparison and social change, Katz-Newcomb Lectures, University of Michigan, 1974.

Tajfel, H., Flament, C., Billig, M. and Blundy, R.P., Social categorization and inter-group behaviour, *European Journal of Social Psychology*, 1971, *1*, 149-78.

Thibaut, J. and Kelley, H., *The Social Psychology of Groups*, New York: Wiley, 1959.

Varela, J.A., *Psychological Solutions to Social Problems*, New York: Academic Press, 1971.

108   *Wolfgang Stroebe*

Discussion

KIESLER: I'd like to comment on a couple of things. First, I think we all agree that social psychology has over-emphasized individual psychology to the exclusion of the social context in which social behavior occurs. Further, probably psychology in general over-emphasizes the psychology of the individual; but I disagree that sociologists have had much success in predicting or understanding behavior when ignoring individual psychology. Psychology should be more balanced, but I hope that you're not advocating that we be equally imbalanced in the opposite direction. Sometimes when I talk to people who are interested in structural variables, which is what this approach advocates — structural variables, not simply group variables — I get the impression that they not only want to work on structural variables themselves, but they want me to stop working on individual variables; the former I would agree with and the latter I would disagree with.

STROEBE: I would fully agree with that statement. If sociology had really done such a great job, it wouldn't need us to work on those problems. Sociologists have gone to the opposite extreme, and have completely neglected individual motives. That becomes particularly obvious if one reads books on organizational sociology. But I feel it is necessary for one area to overlap the psychological aspects on the one hand, and sociology on the other. We cannot say "Let's leave the sociology to the sociologists, and we'll stay on our side of the fence". And I think that social psychology was specifically designed to be an area which *should* overlap, and that we have neglected that task by moving more and more into an individualistic orientation.

LOMOV: How to connect the individual and the sociological — that's a big problem.

STROEBE: If you talk about social psychology moving too much toward one extreme, to clarify things, one has to present the two extremes. This does not mean I perceive the psychological and sociological as absolutely different approaches which can in every instance be clearly differentiated. I am simply trying to clarify the issue by showing both extremes. Furthermore, my main concern is really for the generation of theories about the development of groups, not theories which just take the individual as one part of a system where you related one part to the other. I could think only of two such developmental theories in social psychology: the one was Bales' approach involving leadership, and the other is Tajfel's theory.

THORNGATE: When you argue that social psychologists should become more interested in sociological variables, and when you argue that sociologists should become more interested in individual variables, it seems to me that what you're arguing is that we should have theories with more variables in them. If so, how do you propose to test these theories?

STROEBE: I would not necessarily advocate more variables, but I would stress different variables. As a good example of what I say has happened, consider functional theories of attitudes. We've not been interested what functions these attitudes would serve for a group; but immediately we have asked what function they serve for the individual and we have based predictions on functions of attitudes for individuals.

KIESLER: But that's been the least productive approach to attitudes in the history of attitude change. Probably less than six experiments exist on the whole issue.

STROEBE: Yes.

ANDREEVA: I agree with you that further development of methodology will not lead out of the content of the current crisis, and that there is a need for reorganization of theories in the field. But I would like to come to the defense of McGuire, whom you have discussed. McGuire, in speaking about the crisis in social psychology, spoke to two paradigms. He criticized the paradigm where a social psychologist accepts theory-oriented hypotheses and uses a laboratory experiment to test them, and he prescribes another one. I think that McGuire also criticized the paradigm where a social psychologist accepts, not theory-oriented, but socially oriented hypotheses and uses the field of experiment to test them. I agree with his point of view. If we accept field experiments as the basic form of analysis, and if we do not change anything in the *strategy* of the research, it means that we simply repeat laboratory methods in a natural setting; then we will not be achieving anything new. This is what McGuire is saying. And he then proposes a completely new, third paradigm. He seems to be close to your own point of view, and I am surprised that you seem to criticize him as a man who believes in field experiments as the be-all and end-all. As to me, I think that this third paradigm proposed by McGuire does not solve all the problems, but it is another question.

STROEBE: I feel a little guilty about sounding so critical — McGuire simply provided me with such lovely quotes that his position was very clear. I would admit that he moved away from his 1967 position in his 1973 paper. However, even in 1973, on the new paradigm, he still sees the solution in new methods, and I would still criticize him in that respect, because I do not think that by using new methods we will achieve anything unless we have different theories.

LOMOV: Every science has its own way of looking at phenomena and its own method of abstraction. Human life is sufficiently complex, considering just social, biological or psychological factors. If we are speaking of the inter-relationship between psychology and sociology, it is very important to define the characteristics of each of the disciplines. If we do not do that, we shall create something eclectic. In order for the sciences to find mutual dependence and their inter-relationships, each must define its own aspect. And in this connection, I would like to hear from you, what are the very specific characteristics of social psychology? In your opinion? What do you think are the special social psychological aspects in the analysis of human life? It's a difficult problem.

STROEBE: Miller, in his new text book, has refused to define social psychology, because he argued that one could not really satisfactorily define such a field of study. But even if one were to loosely define it as the study of individual social behavior as influenced by the social context, although it doesn't really tell us a very great deal, then I think I would again make my argument that social psychology should be the one area that should overlap between psychology and sociology. Because, if both stay on their respective fences, there will not be any interaction between the two areas.

BERRY: I'm a bit concerned about the tendency to think in either/or terms, or mixing both psychology and sociology as if they were discrete. In one study of ethnic attitudes in Canada, we included the conventional, individualistic personality measures, such as ethnocentrism, authoritarianism, value systems, religious beliefs on the one hand; and we included the conventional sociological elements on the other, like ethnicity, social class, education, etc. We got reasonable and acceptable prediction from the sociological categories to attitudes, and from the psychological categories to attitudes. But we improved prediction a lot by taking a set of variables, conceptually in-between the sociological and psychological. In this particular case, to give an example, it was based on one's ethnicity, and based on one's position in the socio-economic hierarchy. But it involved the individual's *conceptualization* of his position — which we termed "cultural threat" and "economic threat", two new variables generated out of the sociological and psychological original variables. This was a new level of analysis, that we hadn't used before.

ZAJONC: I don't really see that there is a disagreement here. I think that the issue that we're talking about is not whether to import sociology into social psychology lock, stock and barrel. If I understand Wolfgang correctly, he simply meant that we must consider certain collective phenomena. The problem here is, and in the past has been, that we have tried to do it without translation of their variables into terms that are commensurate with the concepts in individual psychology. We can't just take SES and bring it in, and try to explicate certain psychological phenomena, without translating the psychological processes that are involved where people of different socio-economic levels behave differently in some particular situation. It is this translation that will cause our problems, and it's very difficult to achieve. But once achieved I think there's no particular difficulty in proceeding. Now I think we considered earlier an attempt where both individual and collective aspects were involved, and there were problems. What is the meaning of the statement that one group perceives another group? Is it the average? Is it the distribution of the individual perceptions? Is it some parameter of the distribution? Is it a typical perception, or is it some other transformation of this distribution? We have to decide on this, and I think it's a matter of trying to find a solution to this problem and not accepting point-blank a sociological concept. Whatever there is in this collective aspect must be translated into terms that we can use, that we know, at other levels of abstraction.

The Unity of Activity and Social Relations in the Construction of General Theory in Social Psychology

LYUDMILLA P. BUEVA

The phenomena which are studied in any science are subject to its general principles and laws, and these principles are independent of the particular social context in which scientific knowledge is developing. But this does not mean that the unique features of the given context do not influence the condition and development of that science. In fact, the characteristics of the social structure of society influence the development of social psychology in several different ways:

(1) The object of research (man's social behaviour) is itself changing in the process of historical development. Social psychological processes are taking place in different ways in communities of different types;

(2) Certain aspects of the society under consideration are reflected in the scientific problems it chooses to address;

(3) The social and social psychological contexts of a science influence its development, its direction, and the application of its results to social practice.

It is obvious that social psychology would have a closer connection with the social system than would such sciences as physics, mathematics, etc., because the object of social psychological research is man's social behaviour. But acknowledging this does not mean the abrogation of the general princi-

111

ples of the development of science for social psychology.

Social psychology faces both general and unique problems in its development as a science. Among them is the fact that socially determined individual behaviour takes different forms in the different groups which constitute society. For example, current data illustrate how communication processes vary among large and small communities, nation-ethnic, and social demographic groups. Also, differences in group dynamics, particularly those processes of consolidation and unification, will depend on the type of social relations within and among the groups, on the system of values in the groups, and on the social trend of group activity.

But does this mean that a general theory for social psychology must disintegrate into different kinds of separate, "local" theories, reflecting the specificity of the social structures and regions where they are developing? Is it possible to have *any* general principles of social psychological science? And if there are such principles, how must they relate to the peculiarities of scientific development in different socio-cultural systems?

The idea of a general theory of social psychology presupposes the existence of initial, general principles of theory construction, but since social structures in relation to which social psychology has been developing differ (sometimes they even conflict with one another), one may doubt the possibility of ever finding such principles. There have been different proposals for solution of this problem.[1] One of them is that these principles must be formulated at the mathematical level, and that only in this way can they gain recognition by everyone. But this approach prompts certain objections:

(1) Such formalization does not *reveal* anything about the quality of the objects being studied, and it may mask many substantial differences between them;

(1) The necessity of dealing with both generalities and specifics in the development of social psychological theory does not itself provoke disagreements. Usually, the polemics begin on the questions of which phenomena to attribute to general principles, and which phenomena to consider to be specific peculiarities of different groups of social systems of different types.

(2) Extreme formalization leads, as a rule, to a result which is not useful for solution of real, practical problems.

In the USSR we feel that formalization is reasonable only in combination with judgements of quality. By itself, it has limited use.

Another approach offers pluralism as a principle, on the basis of which problems of theory will be worked out in a future, "universal" social psychology. This principle hardly seems acceptable, because by its nature it can generate only a collection of heterogeneous conceptual schema; it is apparent that nobody has succeeded as yet in attempting to develop a universal theory with a pluralistic approach.

In Soviet psychology, the Marxist *principle of activity* is the most important initial methodological principle for explaining mental phenomena and the determination of consciousness. The principle of *the unity*[2] *of activity and social relations* has a special significance for social psychology, because social and social psychological processes occur in terms of the *activity* of people *united* in groups and communities of different kinds.

The social structure of a society is defined in terms of relations among individuals and groups. These groups differ in their "ways of life", i.e., in terms of the type and direction of their activity, according to their own systems of values and norms. If we undertake to analyse different forms of activity of social organizations (classes, groups, communities) and of individual subjects (personalities) several things become possible:

(1) The study of social psychological phenomena not only in laboratories but also in real social contexts;

(2) The discovery of social (not only small group) determinants of personality, consciousness, and behaviour;

(3) The analysis of both small and large groups on the basis of principles and combining them into a social unity.

Use of the principle of *unity of activity and social relations* offers explanatory and heuristic advantages:

---

(2) "Unity" is perhaps best construed here as meaning "interdependence".

(1) It exposes the essence of objects under investigation in their actual development, and explains the origin and functioning of mental phenomena in intentional activity, both individual and social;

(2) It permits one to combine theoretical research with empirical research;

(3) It makes possible the integration of different sciences by restricting their specific approaches to the appropriate areas of research.

This last point requires some elaboration. Social psychology was born of a "crossing" of sociology with general psychology. This parentage was naturally reflected in social psychology's conceptual systems and in its methods of research. The development of integrative connections among sciences studying society and man makes necessary the correlation of different "scientific languages". The fact that one concept, when used by different authors, often yields wide variations in content has hampered the progress of research. However, the concept of *activity* is common for the whole complex of sciences, including general psychology and sociology. This means we must examine the different levels of this notion, so as to construct, scientifically, the entire "model" of the activity of persons in social systems of different levels. For example, the study of one aspect of human activity, such as action at the level of the biological sciences, may be limited to physical actions with the help of which the organism establishes balance with the environment. At another level, general psychology studies goal-directed or intentional actions, those based in the experienced needs and interests of individual subjects. At yet another level, sociology studies actions which make up social processes and changing social conditions in general.

What level of *activity* falls within the sphere of social psychology? There are grounds to believe that traditional social psychology has narrowed its research area, because on the one hand it construes *activity* as individual behaviour in small groups or lab situations, and on the other hand, because it treats *social relations* as interpersonal interactions. The narrowness of this approach locks social psychological phenomena into the framework of the small group, isolating them from the laws of the whole society. We believe that the possibilities for social psychology are significantly broader than the study of processes in small groups. The explanatory force and practical significance of social psychology will depend on whether it can pass from a focus on small groups and interaction within them to the study of activity of social systems in general. This is not to deny that it is, of course, most important that the general laws of social activity and social relations determine social psychological processes in small groups. However, there exists a certain danger in reduction to the small group level; transfer of the peculiarities of one level of study of social activity to another level may distort the entire "model". It is impossible, for example, to explain personal behaviour in social systems in terms of (say) the relations between organism and environment, or according to the laws of animal communities. Each higher form of activity subsumes previous forms, but it cannot itself be reduced to them.

Social psychological study of the subjective side of social activity supposes another kind of correlation that is between individual and social activity. The analysis of different systems of societal and personal objectives shows that correlation and coordination of these systems is a contradictory and complex process. The same may be said about systems of values, necessities, interests, etc.

In the solution of these problems, there are three questions that must be asked:

(1) How are social and group aims and tasks adopted into, and revealed in, individual consciousness and behaviour?

(2) How are personal plans and aims realized in the activity of different groups?

(3) How is the essential coordination between person and group actions achieved?

Empirical research on group activity has exposed essential differences among social psychological processes dependent on group character and those dependent on group aims, or on values. *Collective* unity and *collective* relations differ in their content, and dynamics from those processes in group activity which are irrelevant for persons, i.e., processes determinating behaviour of persons in collectives are different from those in groups of little significance. Much depends on the "group character" and on how it is included in the system of social relations. It is felt that the principle of *the unity of activity and social relations* will enable us to deal with such complexities and questions.

Discussion

ABOUD: I still haven't really got an idea of how you operationalize activity or how you study activity as you have defined it.

BUEVA: Social activity cannot be studied through the description of external activities. It can be studied operationally through its subjective aspect — the system of goals, values, orientations — all that concerns the motivation of activities and which depends on the person's belonging to small or large groups of various types.

ABOUD: Do you study each individual's values, or do you look mostly at the group values?

BUEVA: We study both. And we also study the relationship between the individual's values and the group values. The individual may accept the values of his group, but he may accept them to different degrees, and when he does accept them, then he carries them out through his activity — he implements them. And here problems arise at the point where various social, group and individual values meet.

KIESLER: This question of what is activity — activity as defined by the word *dyeyatelnost* — earlier it was said that this might be seen as goal-directed activity. Was that it?

ANDREEVA: It's always a problem of terminology or translation of this very difficult notion — activity — as we use it in Russian. We can turn to German again, because activity in our sense corresponds to the German *Tatigkeit,* and not *Activitate.*

STROEBE: Is *Tatigkeit* really the best German word? Isn't it *Handlung*? I think the English expression for it would be "social action", which implies goal direction.

ANDREEVA: "Activity" is for us a special kind of general activity, because activity is not a quality unique to human beings. Activity is a general quality of all organisms. If we speak about "activity" in our present sense, we include in this notion one major aspect of *human* activity: that it has some goal, and that it has intentional character. Without this emphasis on intention or direction, human activity can't be understood very well. Putting it briefly, I can say activity means the unique human kind of activity, in comparison with other kinds of activity — it is activity as a goal-directed process, as a process in which some intentional capacity of human beings is realized. It's not very clear, but unfortunately I can't explain it better.

KIESLER: Let me ask two questions. When someone is learning with rewards, is that *dyeyatelnost*?

ANDREEVA: No, because "learning" has a certain specific connotation of the behaviouristic model of behaviour.

KIESLER: When wolves are running in packs, is that *dyeyatelnost*?

ANDREEVA: No.

KIESLER: The reason I use these examples is because there's no explicit social perspective in either.

ANDREEVA: Right, there is no social perspective, no process of goal construction, which is an inevitable element of activity in our sense. First I construct my goal, and after that I realize my activity. You know, maybe goal-directed behaviour *is* the word.

KIESLER: But *social* goals, not just goal-directed behaviour itself — but social.

ANDREEVA: Of course, goals that are a part, an element of social activity, perhaps as with activity of big social units.

KIESLER: So the wolfpack would not be *dyeyatelnost*, because it's not goal directed.

ANDREEVA: If we're speaking of the system of activity (i.e. *dyeyatelnost*) in general psychology in the Soviet Union, such a system of activity involves activity as a whole. The units of this activity are *actions,* and then as a unit of each action, *operation* — more or less mechanical action. And *dyeyatelnost* as a whole activity is the summary of all social actions, and so is directed by the highest motives. I can perform an operation: for example, I can move my eye glasses from this point to that point, and I have no special goal for this, it's more or less mechanical. At another level, I can make some action, social action — for example, I can just stand up and go away. This is more or less of a social action, but it is not social activity as a whole. What I can interpret as social activity is the fact that I am with my colleagues and friends here. That is influenced not only by my immediate motives, but by more high-level motives. These include my image about the importance of scientific exchange between countries, or my image about the inevitability of the development of social psychology within socialist society or other types of society and so on. This last is social activity and is more or less what I mean by it.

KIESLER: This discussion is an interesting example of how the perspective of the fields in the two countries — identical fields in one sense — vary so much and depend so much on specific terms.

SEGALOWITZ: Would it help if perhaps you gave an example of the kind of research one might do, under the heading of studying activity? Could you give an example of what kind of question you might study in an experiment, or in any project? Maybe that would help us understand.

ANDREEVA: It seems to me that there are two possible approaches to research from the point of view of the principle of activity. First I might study different things,

118 *Lyudmilla P. Bueva*

but always having in my mind activity as a principle of the explanation of different phenomena. But the second thing I might do is study the given activity itself. Your question concerns this second approach, but what is typical is not the second but the first approach. I don't mean to imply that each of us each day conducts empirical research on the study of activity. We study *different* phenomena — group cohesiveness, or maybe leadership within groups, or maybe processes of interaction or attraction within the group; but we do this having in our mind that all these phenomena are elements of human activity. So my answer is that all of our researches are researches *from the point of view of activity*, but not in the way you mean in your question. Perhaps we could select some research on activity in your way, but it's not very typical, and in my opinion this type of research is not the most important. What is most important is research in different fields, on different phenomena, but only with the principle of activity as "equipment". When we interpret the results of these different researches, we must include the concept of activity in our interpretation.

KIESLER: I think of it as "goal oriented, intentional social behaviour".

ANDREEVA: Yes, but with reservations concerning "behaviour". We must exclude behaviouristic connotations — behaviour not only as learning, not only as conditional responses, you know?

ZAJONC: It is my impression to some extent, that it is not really a matter of identifying aspects of behaviour which will allow us to distinguish between activity and other forms of social psychological phenomena; it is rather the way that we conceptualize behaviour, or the object of scientific study, and the commitment to what aspects of these phenomena must be included in the analysis. As I see it, activity includes not only intentions, goals, and the social context, but it includes a requirement that these intentions and goals be interpreted in the language of social value which surround the individual. Is that correct?

ANDREEVA: Not only is this correct, but I can accept your addition to "goal directed". It is not only the "goal directedness" of the activity but activity with the interpretations like yours.

KIESLER: This relates to previous discussions, when you said that in your approach to research, epistemology played much more of a role in the context of research than is typical of the West. That is, this motivated behaviour is also seen not only in the context of values in which the individual sees it, but in the concept of values in which the observer sees it, as well.

ANDREEVA: It seems to me that if we had tried to find some operational definitions and had in this way interpreted "activity", actually we would have dealt in empirical studies. I can agree with your use of "behaviour", but with only one addition. Each act of behaviour is to be a unit of "social activity". If this is done, I accept "behaviour".

KIESLER: There is one difference. When we speak of behaviour, we often mean it to be a "pure event", which any observer could see. Whereas from your perspective, you try to avoid the term, because you maintain that you cannot avoid the meaning of the behaviour. That's one reason why a second term might be useful.

B. THEORY AND CONTENT AREA

The Role of Nonhuman Behaviour in
North American Social Psychology*

JOHN C. BAREFOOT

If we judge from the literature, North American social psychology has not been very concerned with social behaviour in any species except humans. Only one of the prominent introductory texts (Brown, 1965) considers nonhuman social behaviour in a separate systematic fashion. A very small percentage of the articles in our major journals have been based on data obtained from other species and those studies which have tested nonhumans have often used them as simple substitutes for human subjects. Perhaps the most telling sign of our disinterest in other species is the fact that our neglect of them is so infrequently lamented.

Social psychologists do not appear to be hostile to the study of other species, for few argue against it and some studies of nonhumans have played prominent roles in our thinking. We just don't seem to be convinced that serious systematic attention to other species would be worthwhile. In this paper I would like to offer some hypotheses about why we feel that way and suggest a strategy which might help make the study of other species more useful for us. In the last half of the paper, I will attempt to apply this strategy to a particular problem area:

*This research was supported by a Canada Council Leave Fellowship. The author wishes to thank Irwin Altman for his comments and encouragement during the early stages of the project.

119

the effects of crowding.

Potential Roles for Nonhuman Behaviour in
Social Psychology

A number of works based on nonhuman behaviour have been influential in our field. Hebb's work on emotions (Hebb, 1946; Hebb and Thompson, 1968), Harlow's studies of love and social isolation (Harlow, 1958), and Calhoun's studies on the effect of population density (Calhoun, 1962) are three obvious examples. Of course, studies of learning in other species have been prominent in our thinking, especially when their results have been imaginatively applied to human problems, as in Seligman's work on learned helplessness (Seligman, 1975). These and other important studies of nonhumans have had their impact by serving a number of functions, illustrating the potential of nonhuman behaviour to serve a variety of roles in the research process. Nonhuman subjects are not simply substitutes for humans and we underestimate their usefulness if we limit them to this role.

THE PROBLEM OF CROSS-SPECIES GENERALIZATION

The most frequent and controversial way to treat nonhuman behaviour is as an indicator of possible human tendencies. It is often argued that this procedure is necessary when ethical or practical considerations prevent experimentation on human subjects, but in practice it is used at other times as well. While this strategy has served us well and many fruitful contributions to the field have been based on it, undisciplined generalizations across species have led to some of the most heavily criticized works on human social behaviour (e.g., Ardrey, 1966; Lorenz, 1966).

Cross-species generalization is a risky game and there are no clear agreed-upon rules to guide the researcher. Harlow, Gluck, and Suomi (1972) have summarized the dilemma well:

> . . . it is commonly believed that some animal data generalize to man and some data do not. The only problem then is that of selecting between or among the

data that generalize and those that do not. This is never an easy task since there is no completely logical or absolutely objective way to make the separation (p.175).

It should be pointed out that these difficulties are not unique to cross-species generalization. Hebb and Thompson (1968) have pointed out that many of the objections to the cross-species generalization are based on a misunderstanding of the nature of generalization. Strictly speaking, there are equivalent difficulties in generalizing across cultures, time, and individuals; yet we proceed to do so. It is done flexibly, however, always subject to disconfirmation and the rules of plausibility. The same should be true of our approach to cross-species generalization. Nevertheless, the dangers are serious enough to warrant our taking a conservative strategy. If we err in this matter, let us err on the side of caution.

PROBLEM CLARIFICATION

Even if one rejects the possibility of cross-species generalization, the study of nonhumans can be justified on the grounds that the process of studying a problem in another species results in a kind of problem clarification which can later be applied to the study of similar problems at the human level.

For example, data from nonhumans can suggest new variables or reconceptualizations of problems. Latane's work on affiliation in rats (Latane and Hothersall, 1972) suggested the importance of responsiveness during interaction as a variable leading to attraction. This was later confirmed for humans as well (Insko and Wilson, 1977; Werner and Latane, 1976).

This kind of cross-fertilization can also take place on the methodological level. Miller's (1967) studies of nonverbal communication in monkeys served as a stimulus for those interested in the accuracy of human nonverbal communication, leading to the adaptation of the Miller paradigm to human subjects (Buck, Savin, Miller, and Caul, 1972; Lanzetta and Kleck, 1970). This particular example also illustrates that this kind of stimulation can go both ways, for the Lanzetta and Kleck study produced a pattern of individual differences which Miller, Levine and Mirsky (1973) later sought and found in a study of monkeys.

In addition, Zajonc (1969) has argued that the study of animals improves our theories and designs by forcing us to abandon our own experience as a guide, serving as a kind of discipline for the researcher by removing the temptation of introspection. The fact that we share subjective experiences with our human subjects is in many ways an advantage, but if we rely too heavily on introspection, we may fail to consider alternatives which are not suggested by subjective experience. The act of studying a phenomenon in another species prevents us from limiting ourselves in this way.

THE EVOLUTIONARY PERSPECTIVE

The most obvious reason for studying animal behaviour is its intrinsic importance and interest. If this were our motivation, we would study the naturally occurring behaviour of a wide range of species. Psychologists have not done that. Our over-whelming concern with our own species has led us to concentrate our attention on those aspects of animal behaviour which appear to have some immediate relevance for human problems. Beach (1960) has argued that this anthropocentrism has, ironically, robbed us of the most important lesson about humans that comparative psychology has to teach: an under-standing of our place among the species.

While the goal of cross-species generalization compels us to search for cross-species similarities, the evolutionary approach suggests that differences between species are just as informative as similarities. When the social behaviour of another species differs from our own, it may be because it faces different problems or because it has made different adaptations to cope with problems also faced by humans. In either case, it serves to illuminate our own condition by delineating the alternative forms and functions of social behaviour.

Animal Behaviour and Social Psychology

I doubt that many social psychologists would object to the

goals that have been expressed thus far. Few would argue against the study of animal social behaviour. Why, then, have we failed to incorporate the area into our field? I suspect that most of us take the attitude that "animal behaviour is interesting, but it just isn't relevant to my goals". There are several bases of this attitude.

First of all, many of us are in the field because we wish to help find solutions to relatively immediate social problems and the relevance of animal behaviour for this goal is dubious at best. Zajonc (1969) cites the historical roots of social psychology in "action research" as the main reason for our past neglect of nonhuman behaviour. Problems such as job discrimination, gun control, and organization effectiveness have no parallel in other species. For those of us interested in solutions to such immediate problems, animal behaviour must remain an interesting, but marginally relevant topic.

Secondly, some (e.g., Young, 1973) fear that theories based on a comparative approach might be used to justify the *status quo* as biologically "natural" and therefore "good". In the same vein, there are fears that these theories will be used to justify racism and sexism. Others feel that the view of humans as animals will result in a kind of fatalism which will prevent us from striving to achieve our uniquely human potential. These dangers are real and the potential for misuse is great, but the same is true for other approaches to social behaviour as well. Let me also point out that these objections are based on a view of animals and nature which is static and, therefore, limiting. There are alternative images which I believe to be preferable to this traditional view.

The existence of this static, limiting view of nature leads to the final and most important basic of our attitude: animal behaviour appears to be so different from our own, both in form and principle, that we don't believe that it can tell us much about the human condition. The most popular recent attempts to comment on human behaviour from the perspective of animal behaviour (Lorenz, 1966; Ardrey, 1966) have been so fraught with difficulties and widely criticized (e.g., Montagu, 1968) that further attempts hardly seem worthwhile. This point of view is based on the assumption that generalization is the goal of comparative research and, therefore, cross-species similarities are necessary. As we have seen, however, cross-species generalization is only one of several ways to use nonhuman research.

This traditional image of animal behaviour plays an important role in our neglect of other species. There are alternative images and I wish to argue that they are preferable to the traditional view, which fails to account for the existing empirical evidence and unnecessarily limits our perspective of nonhuman behaviour.

The Traditional Image of Nonhuman Behaviour in Social Psychology

Most of us have formed our ideas about nonhuman behaviour from reading the most influential theorists in the field: Lorenz and Tinbergen.[1] Their model of innate behaviour has been the basis of a vast amount of work and has been so successful that it has become the basis of our image of nonhuman behaviour.

In this model, behaviour is "driven" by instinctual energy which accumulates until the animal senses the stimulus which will trigger its release. Once this releaser stimulus is sensed, the energy "flows" into the performance of the behaviour, which is done in a rigid, unvarying fashion. This model, so blatantly hydraulic in its concepts that it has been called the "flush toilet" model of behaviour (Johnson, 1972), implies that: (a) the organism is impelled to behave in certain ways by the pressure of accumulating instinctual energy; (b) there is little variability in behaviour between individual conspecifics; and (c) there is little or no variation between repeated performances within an individual. These aspects of the ethological model have crept into our image of animal behaviour as assumptions, and have profoundly influenced our thinking about animal social behaviour.

---

(1) I do not wish to place the credit and/or blame for the traditional view on the shoulders of these men alone, for the ideas have a long history (Beach, 1955). The ethologists were the immediate source of our knowledge, however.

While the ethological model has been successful within its original domain, it has problems which make it inadequate for general application. The ethologist's simplistic division between innate and learned behaviour is no longer useful. The idea of an instinctual energy which "drives" behaviour is an unsatisfactory model of motivation on both theoretical and empirical grounds (Berkowitz, 1975; Hinde, 1960; Johnson, 1972).

While I believe that these objections to the traditional model are important, I would like to emphasize another issue: the traditional model fails to convey the degree of plasticity present in animal behaviour. Current studies are revealing this plasticity, resulting in a decline of the use of instinctual explanations for behaviour. As Beach (1955) has noted, we appear to be less and less likely to employ the concept of instinct as we learn more and more about the behaviours we are studying. Even sociobiologists, who emphasize the role of genetics in behaviour, seem to reject the rigidity of the traditional model. Barash (1977) refers to genetically based influences on behaviour as "a flexible, modifiable, and perhaps rather fragile set of inclinations . . ." (p. 286).

I believe that this past emphasis on the rigidity and simplicity of animal behaviour has been unfortunate and unnecessary. We can choose to seek interpretations of nonhuman behaviour within frameworks that are closer to those which we employ for the explanation of human social behaviour. The potential rewards may be significant, for I believe that such a strategy would make the study of nonhuman behaviour more interesting and relevant for our goals. As an illustration of the need for this new perspective and the advantages of this reconstrual, let us review the literature on the effects of crowding on nonhumans.

The Effects of Crowding on Nonhumans: Two Perspectives

THE TRADITIONAL VIEW

Most social psychology texts and articles on crowding cite

two works which deal with nonhumans: Calhoun's (1962) demonstration of the "behavioural sink" and Christian's (1950) theory on the physiological effects of high population density.

Calhoun studied the behaviour of rats in a confined, but freely growing colony. As the population size increased, Calhoun witnessed the emergence of a number of "abnormal" behaviours, such as hypersexuality, pansexuality, cannibalism, inadequate maternal care, fighting, and withdrawal.

Christian's theory is based on Selye's concept of the General Adaptation Syndrome, which states that the presence of stress will be reflected in the action of the pituitary-adrenal system. While this stress reaction is beneficial in the short run, the chronic application of a stressor can have a number of detrimental effects, including retarded growth, poor reproductive functioning, and decreased resistance to disease. Christian extended Selye's line of thought by suggesting that high population density might result in enough stress to activate the GAS. Since one by-product of the stress reaction is a lowered reproductive rate, the system might provide a means by which the birth rate could be lowered in times of overpopulation. While most of Christian's work has been done on rodents in laboratory settings, social psychologists frequently cite a study of deer who were living on an island in the Chesapeake Bay (Christian, Flyger and Davis, 1960). This herd of deer suffered a severe and sudden increase in the mortality rate during the winter of 1958. Working from data obtained from autopsies, the authors concluded that the die-off was probably due to a stress reaction resulting from the high population density at the time.

Studies such as these have led most social psychologists to the conclusion that crowding has automatic, massive, and deleterious effects on nonhumans. Since this conclusion does not appear to hold for human responses to crowding, it is often cited as a case of the assertion that, "proving something to be true for animals does not prove it to be true for man". This conclusion and the assumptions of the traditional model have been explicitly stated by Kutner (1973):

> . . . the relevance of these (animal) results for human behavior is questionable. Although even temporary increases in population density can overload a lower

species' system of mechanistic, instinctual behavior, this may not be true for man. Humans can survive the extreme crowding of subways and elevators for short periods of time without apparent adverse effects. This is not to say that humans do not experience agitation when encroached upon by others, but only that the origin of this agitation is probably far more complicated than in animals. Human experience appears to be mediated by more adaptive, conscious cognitive processes as well as patterns of sociocultural learning (p. 31).

Similar, if less extreme, conclusions are found in many social psychological discussions of crowding in animals.

SOME PROBLEMS WITH THE TRADITIONAL MODEL

While I must admit that this popular conclusion appears to be quite reasonable if it is based on the usually cited data, a further examination of the literature reveals some gaping holes, both from the omission of important studies and problems in the interpretation of the studies which are cited. While there is not time to survey this literature in detail, let me discuss a few outstanding examples.

Replication and Interpretation

The interpretations of several key studies underlying the traditional model of crowding are open to question. For example, the famous study of deer by Christian, Flyger and Davis (1960) certainly deserves more careful scrutiny. While it is certainly possible that population density could have been a contributing factor in the deaths, there are other equally plausible alternatives. Illness cannot be ruled out as a factor, although the authors claim that the mild cases of kidney problems and hepatitis uncovered in the autopsies were the effect of the stress syndrome. A more likely culprit is the unusually severe winter weather which occurred at the start of the die-off. Weather could not only serve as a stressor, but it might have had significant effects on the food supply. In this regard, it is important to note that Klein (1970) and Flyger (1960) attributed the deaths of these animals to malnutrition. At the very least, the data of this study are ambiguous.

Calhoun's studies of the behavioural sink are more straightforward, except for the fact that the findings are not always replicable. While some researchers (e.g., Brown, 1953; Crowcroft and Rowe, 1963; Southwick, 1955b) have observed similar phenomena, there are other instances in which the behavioural sink phenomena did not appear (e.g., Brown, 1953; Lloyd, 1975; Southwick, 1955b). The critical conditions for the appearance of the phenomenon are not known. Calhoun (1971) suggested that a centralized feeding area was necessary for the effects to occur, but Southwick manipulated this variable without success. The behavioural sink phenomenon is undoubtedly real, but incompletely understood.

Individual Differences

The traditional model of animal behaviour has little place for individual differences; yet they are of great importance. Large individual differences are probably the cause of some of the failures to replicate studies in this area. For example, Southwick (1955b) has noted that it is much easier to obtain differences from within-subject designs than with between-subject designs because the between-subject variability is so great. This is especially important in studies of aggression, for one aggressive individual can inflate the amount of aggression in an entire colony of animals by starting fights which lead to other fights. In one of Southwick's mice colonies, the mean number of aggressive acts per hour fell from 20 to 4.4 with the death of one animal. A similar phenomenon was cited by Smith and Porter (1976) as the reason for their failure to find a monotonic relationship between population density and aggression in deermice.

Another example of the importance of individual differences pertains to Christian's hypothesis of a physiological stress reaction to the experience of crowding. Only some animals in the colony show evidence of the response. It turns out that these animals tend to be low in the dominance hierarchy (Thiessen and Rogers, 1961). This is actually support for Christian's theory, for he proposes that population density serves to produce social stress and aggression which, in turn, produce the stress reaction. The animals lowest in the dominance hierarchy are likely to bear the brunt of this aggression and disorder. In other words, the stress response is produced not by crowding, but by intraspecific aggression. The relation between crowding and aggression is the phenomenon for social psychologists to explain.

Severity of the Effects

There is great danger in attempting to assess the degree of severity of crowding effects, a point which I will pursue in the next section. Nevertheless, the traditional image that crowding has a devastating impact on animals must be tempered by studies which show that the effects are much milder than usually portrayed.

Aggression is a dependent variable which appears to be reliably related to crowding manipulations. It may also be the key to the understanding of the area, for aggression appears to be related to many other of the behaviours alleged to be the result of crowding. For example, the stress response discussed by Christian (Bronson, 1963), poor maternal care (Southwick, 1955a), cannibalism (Boice, 1972), have all been shown to be the results of aggression. Therefore, it may be that crowding simply produces heightened levels of aggression which, in turn, produces the other effects. The centrality of aggression in the problem of crowding makes it a logical target for well-controlled assessments of crowding effects. Fortunately, two excellent studies of monkeys appear to speak to the problem.

Southwick (1967) enclosed 25 rhesus monkeys in a 1000 square foot cage, allowing them 15 weeks to adapt to their environment and each other before introducing the manipulations. After a stable base rate of aggression had been obtained, he introduced a number of manipulations, including crowding. When the animals were restricted to half of their former cage, a 70% increase in the aggression index was observed. This increase is highly significant and may seem to be an enormous change, but it is actually rather small when compared to the effects produced by disruptions in the social organization. For example, the introduction of two unfamiliar males into the uncrowded colony produced a 540% increase in the aggression index.

The Southwick study not only demonstrates the effect of crowding on aggression, but it argues for the importance of familiarity in intraspecific aggression. Some studies have crowded unfamiliar animals together, perhaps leading to an inflated estimate of the amount of strife in high density situations.

Alexander and Roth (1971) nicely controlled for the problems of conspecific familiarity by experimenting on an intact troop of Japanese macaques with a pre-existing social structure. They manipulated crowding by alternatively placing the animals in a large corral (8058 meters) or a small pen (186.7 meters). There were three crowding and three control periods, each lasting 4-6 days. Alexander and Roth divided their observations of aggressive acts into two classes: severe physical attacks (mobbing) and milder threats (squabbling). The first time the animals were placed in the crowding pen, there was an increase in both mobbing and squabbling. In the second crowding period, heightened squabbling was still apparent, but the mobbing effect had disappeared. The authors suggest that the initial increase in mobbing was due not to crowding but in the change from a familiar to an unfamiliar environment, noting that another troop of monkeys had shown a similar increase in mobbing when moved from a small to a larger pen.

Finally, another note should be added about the severity of the stress response hypothesized by Christian to be the result of aggression and social disruption. Despite the problems with his study of deer, many well-controlled laboratory studies have supported the basic theory. While the crowding-stress effect clearly can occur, there is some question about its severity, for Krebs and Myers (1975) have argued that the supporting data for the theory have been obtained at artificially high densities and that the hypothesized stress response is too weak at natural densities for the process to operate as a population control mechanism.

Anthropocentric Comparisons

In discussing the severity of crowding effects, I have tried to compare crowding effects to other phenomena which occur in the same species. Making comparisons of relative severity across species is associated with a number of conceptual problems; problems which are especially apparent in our literature on crowding.

One example stems from the fact that we have tended to label crowding effects as "pathologies", a trend which has led to the temptation to find their equivalent in human abnormal behaviour. The very term "pathology" implies a value judgment based on human (and usually Western) standards. For example, the labelling of cannibalism as a pathology overlooks the fact that it is fairly common in other species and even in some human societies which we consider to be healthy in their functioning (Dickeman, 1975; Fox, 1975). It also overlooks the fact that cannibalism can be adaptive for the species (Day and Gallef, 1977). A far more pathological behaviour pattern in high population density might be the continuation of "normal" behaviour and rates of reproduction until the population size outstripped the resources available in the environment.

The second argument against cross-species comparisons of severity is based on the simple principle that such comparisons should be based on the responses to manipulations of equivalent magnitude. Since nonhumans are subjected to densities which would not be tolerated in human research, this biases any cross-species comparison in the direction of finding greater effects in nonhumans. Many laboratory studies of rodents provide the animals with less floor space than the average body size of the species, meaning that the subjects must be living stacked on top of one another. One is tempted to suggest that these studies should be compared to those effects found when humans were subjected to similar densities, such as in the slave ships or the Black Hole of Calcutta. Even this approach would be invalid, however, for there are wide species differences in the capacity for mutual toleration. An environment where animals are stacked on top of each other may be more comfortable for a rat than an elevator is for humans.

Attempts to label humans as more or less affected by crowding than other species not only involve these conceptual problems, they distract researchers from the more critical questions, such as the form of the mechanism mediating the effects.

AN ALTERNATIVE APPROACH

The inadequacies of the traditional model in dealing with crowding phenomena demonstrate the need for an alternative. One simple attempt at a solution may be borrowed from research on human crowding: assume that organisms are active participants in their interaction with the environment rather than passive recipients of stimulation. This means that the organism is capable of initiating coping responses to alleviate the stress associated with stimuli such as crowding. The animal may not always be successful, but we can specify the conditions under which negative crowding effects can be expected.

The first condition is the most obvious: negative effects will appear if the organism is prevented from performing its coping responses. Stress reactions and their by-products would be unavoidable.

The second source of effects is the chronic use of a particular coping strategy which itself has undesirable ramifications. This might be illustrated by reference to the literature on human reactions to urban stress. Urban dwellers may cope with the excess social stimulation by reducing their involvement with others, producing the apparent unfriendliness of cities (Milgram, 1970). Children living in noisy environments may become inattentive to sounds, eventually impairing their ability to discriminate speech sounds (Cohen, Glass and Singer, 1973). The form of the effect will be mediated by the type of coping strategy employed by the organism.

The third source of effects is related to Christian's hypothesis in that it is based on the idea that the effort of continual coping carries with it a degree of psychic and/or physiological cost.

This will eventually be reflected in the organism's reduced resistance to physical or psychological insult.

This model assumes a more complex organism than does the traditional model, but it is capable of explaining a wider variety of findings as a result. Negative consequences of crowding may or may not occur depending upon the presence or absence of the above-mentioned conditions.

COPING STRATEGIES IN NONHUMANS

How could animals cope with the problems of a crowded environment? The simplest response is to leave, an option taken by most nonhumans as well as humans. As a result, most studies of crowding in animals take place in confinement with the animals' dominant response blocked. It is difficult to find naturally occurring high density situations.

Aside from such obvious responses, we can talk about possible coping strategies on both the group and individual levels.

Group strategies are usually subsumed under the term "social organization", and include concepts such as territoriality and dominance hierarchies. Both would reduce stress by providing means for the settlement of dispute over resources with minimum conflict.[2]

As the population density increases, so does the potential for conflict. Space may be considered a resource which can become the object of competition. In addition, inhibitions against fighting over other resources may be harder to maintain in crowded settings, since many animals ordinarily maintain these inhibitions through spacing practices (e.g., Kummer, 1971). As a result of this heightened conflict potential, the necessity for a coping response such as social organization increases in crowded settings.

Note that this way of treating social organization as a strategy differs significantly from the traditional view that a species-

(2) While it is commonly assumed that social organization serves a stress-reducing function, Rowell (1974) has noted that much of this evidence is correlational and that organization might occur as a response to stress without being functional in its reduction. See Deag (1977) for a discussion of this issue.

John C. Barefoot

specific pattern of social organization is inborn and rigid. There are a number of observations in the literature which support the idea of flexibility in social organization. For example, Davis (1958) has suggested that dominance and territorial systems define poles on a continuum and that animals (in his studies, mice) will adopt an organization which is appropriate for the population density in the colony at the time. While low densities produce territorial systems, the same mice will adopt a dominance hierarchy if the population is increased to a point where territoriality is impractical. In addition, Kummer (1971) and Leyhausen (1971) have described a number of subtle ways that dominance and territorial organizations can coexist in the same animals in complementary ways.

Coping responses which occur at the individual level are more difficult to discuss, partially because little attention is paid to the individual when studying other species. However, the withdrawal of animals in the behavioural sink would certainly qualify (Calhoun, 1962). This withdrawal has been seen as a pathology in the past literature, but it may be as effective in reducing stress in animals as it is in humans (Milgram, 1970). A second possibility comes from Kummer (1971), who suggests that "cut-off" behaviours (Chance, 1962) such as eye aversion may serve the same tension-reducing functions in nonhumans that they do in humans (Argyle and Dean, 1965). Kummer has also noticed a number of behaviours in baboons which he classifies as "privacy-seeking".

While I realize that no real catalogue of coping strategies is now possible, I do feel that there are enough supportive hints in the literature to justify a search for them.

COPING AND CROWDING EFFECTS

As far as I can tell from my reading of the literature, every study which demonstrated negative crowding effects has also disrupted social organization. I admit that I cannot be confident in this conclusion, for extreme crowding can itself disrupt social organization, confounding the variables. There is the additional problem that few studies have looked at social organization independently of crowding, Southwick (1967) being a notable exception. Nevertheless, I feel that it is worthwhile to pursue the hypothesis that negative crowding effects will be alleviated as long as social organization can be maintained. Notice that there will be two interpretations of the data if the hypothesis is confirmed. Crowding may produce negative effects which can be prevented by social organization or crowding is simply a way of producing social disorganization which is the real culprit in the matter. Let's save that debate for another time.

THE GENERALIZATION PROBLEM REVISITED

If this approach were to prove fruitful, the resulting picture of nonhuman social behaviour would be much more like that of human social behaviour. The temptation to generalize across species to human problems might be greater. Let me reiterate that I do not see this generalization as an important goal of the approach. The stimuli which produce crowding and the form of the response to crowding may differ widely across species; yet these differences may clarify underlying processes. I hope that we might learn something about processes of crowding and coping by observing them in a variety of forms.

Conclusions

Crowding is but one problem area in which social psychology might gain from the study of nonhumans. We will not utilize this resource, however, if our theories portray other species as simple automatons bound by instincts. If comparative social psychology is to fulfill its potential and be intrinsically interesting as well, a more realistic protrayal is necessary.

References

Alexander, B.K. and Roth, E.M., The effects of acute crowding on aggressive behaviour of Japanese monkeys, *Behaviour,* 1971, *39,* 73-90.

136   *John C. Barefoot*

Ardrey, R., *The Territorial Imperative*, New York: Atheneum, 1966.
Argyle, M. and Dean, J., Eye-contact, distance and affiliation, *Sociometry*, 1965, *28*, 289-304.
Barash, D.P., *Sociobiology and Behavior*, New York: Elsevier, 1977.
Beach, F.A., The descent of instinct, *Psychological Review*, 1955, *62*, 401-10.
Beach, F.A., Experimental investigations of species-specific behavior, *American Psychologist*, 1960, *15*, 1-18.
Berkowitz, L., *A Survey of Social Psychology*, Hinsdale, Illinois: Dryden Press, 1975.
Boice, R., Some behavioral tests of domestication in Norway rats, *Behaviour*, 1972, *42*, 198-231.
Bronson, F.H., Density, subordination, and social timidity in *Peromyscus* and C57bL/10J mice, *Animal Behaviour*, 1963, *11*, 475-9.
Brown, R., *Social Psychology*, New York: Free Press, 1965.
Brown, R.Z., Social behavior, reproduction, and population changes in the house mouse *(Mus musculus* L.), *Ecological Monographs*, 1953, *23*, 217-40.
Buck, R., Savin, V., Miller, R. and Caul, W., Nonverbal communication of affect in humans, *Journal of Personality and Social Psychology*, 1972, *23*, 362-71.
Calhoun, J., Population density and social pathology, *Scientific American*, 1962, *206*, 139-48.
Calhoun, J., Space and the strategy of life. In A. Esser (Ed.), *Environment and Behavior: The Use of Space by Animals and Men*, New York: Plenum, 1971, 329-87.
Chance, M.R.A., An interpretation of some agonistic postures: the role of "cut-off" acts and postures, *Symposium of the London Zoological Society*, 1962, *8*, 71-89.
Christian, J., The adreno-pituitary system and population cycles in mammals, *Journal of Mammalogy*, 1950, *31*, 247-59.
Christian, J., Flyger, V. and Davis, D., Factors in the mass mortality of a herd of sika deer, *Cervus Nippon, Chesapeake Science*, 1960, *1*, 79-95.
Cohen, S., Glass, D.C. and Singer, J., Apartment noise, auditory discrimination, and reading ability in children, *Journal of Experimental Social Psychology*, 1973, *9*, 407-22.
Crowcroft, P. and Rowe, F.P., Social organization and territorial behavior in the wild house mouse *(Mus musculus* L.), *Proceedings of the Zoological Society of London*, 1963, *140*, 517-31.
Davis, D.E., The role of density in aggressive behaviour of house mice, *Animal Behaviour*, 1958, *6*, 207-10.
Day, C.S.D. and Gallef, B.G., Pup cannibalism: One aspect of maternal behavior in golden hamsters, *Journal of Comparative and Physiological Psychology*, 1977, *91*, 1179-89.
Deag, J.M., Aggression and submission in monkey societies, *Animal Behaviour*, 1977, *25*, 465-74.
Dickeman, M., Demographic consequences of infanticide in man, *Annual Review of Ecology and Systematics*, 1975, *6*, 107-37.
Flyger, V., Sika deer on islands in Maryland and Virginia, *Journal of Mammalogy*, 1960, *41*, 140.
Fox, L.R., Cannibalism in natural populations, *Annual Review of Ecology and Systematics*, 1975, *6*, 87-106.
Harlow, H.F., The nature of love, *American Psychologist*, 1958, *13*, 673-85.
Harlow, H.F., Gluck, J.P. and Suomi, S.J., Generalization of behavioral data between nonhuman and human animals, *American Psychologist*, 1972, *27*, 709-16.

Hebb, D.O., On the nature of fear, *Psychological Review*, 1946, *53*, 259-76.
Hebb, D.O. and Thompson, W.R., The social significance of animal studies. In G. Lindzey & E. Aronson (Eds.), *Handbook of Social Psychology*, Vol. II, Reading, Mass.: Addison-Wesley, 1968, 729-74.
Hinde, R.A., Energy models of motivation, *Symposium of the Society for Experimental Biology*, No. XIV, 1960, 119-213.
Insko, C.A. and Wilson, M., Interpersonal attraction as a function of social interaction, *Journal of Personality and Social Psychology*, 1977, *35*, 903-11.
Johnson, R.N., *Aggression in Man and Animals*, Philadelphia: W.B. Saunders, 1972.
Klein, D.R., Food selection by North American deer and their response to over-utilization of preferred plant species. In A. Watson (Ed.), *Animal Populations in Relation to their Food Resources*, British Ecological Society, Symposium X, Oxford: Blackwell, 1970, 25-44.
Krebs, J. and Myers, M., Population cycles in small mammals. In A. MacFadyen (Ed.), *Advances in Ecological Research*, Vol. 8, New York: Academic Press, 1975.
Kummer, H., Spacing mechanisms in social behavior. In J.F. Eisenberg & W.S. Dillon (Eds.), *Man and Beast: Comparative Social Behavior*, Washington: Smithsonian Press, 1971, 219-35.
Kutner, D.H., Overcrowding: Human responses to density and visual exposure, *Human Relations*, 1973, *26*, 31-50.
Lanzetta, J.T. and Kleck, R.E., Encoding and decoding of nonverbal affect in humans, *Journal of Personality and Social Psychology*, 1970, *16*, 12-19.
Latane, B. and Hothersall, D., Social attraction in animals. In P.C. Dodwell (Ed.), *New Horizons in Psychology II*, Harmondsworth, England: Penguin, 1972.
Leyhausen, P., Dominance and territoriality as complemented in mammalian social structure. In A. Esser (Ed.), *Environment and Behavior: The Use of Space by Animals and Men*, New York: Plenum, 1971, 21-33.
Lloyd, J.A., Social structure and reproduction in two freely-growing populations of house mice *(Mus musculus L.)*, *Animal Behaviour*, 1975, *23*, 413-24.
Lorenz, K., *On Aggression*, New York: Harcourt, Brace & World, 1966.
Milgram, S., The experience of living in cities, *Science*, 1970, *167*, 1461-8.
Miller, R.E., Experimental approaches to the physiological and behavioral concomitants of affective communication in rhesus monkeys. In S.A. Altmann (Ed.), *Social Communication Among Primates*, Chicago: University of Chicago Press, 1967, 125-34.
Miller, R.E., Levine, J.M. and Mirsky, I.A., Effects of psychoactive drugs on nonverbal communication and group social behavior of monkeys, *Journal of Personality and Social Psychology*, 1973, *28*, 396-405.
Montagu, M.F.A., *Man and Aggression*, Oxford: Oxford University Press, 1968.
Rowell, T.E., The concept of social dominance, *Behavioral Biology*, 1974, *11*, 131-54.
Seligman, M., *Helplessness*, San Francisco: Freeman, 1975.
Smith, H. and Porter, H., Personal Communication, 1976.
Southwick, C.H., Regulatory mechanisms of house mouse populations: Social behavior affecting litter survival, *Ecology*, 1955, *36*, 627-34 (a).
Southwick, C.H., The population dynamics of confined house mice supplied with unlimited food, *Ecology*, 1955, *36*, 212-25 (b).
Southwick, C.H., An experimental study of intragroup agonistic behavior in rhesus monkeys, *Behaviour*, 1967, *28*, 182-209.
Thiessen, D.D. and Rogers, D.A., Population density and endocrine function, *Psychological Bulletin*, 1961, *58*, 441-51.

Werner, C. and Latane, B., Responsiveness and communication medium in dyadic interactions, *Bulletin of the Psychonomic Society,* 1976, *8,* 569-71.
Young, R.M., The human limits of nature. In J. Benthall (Ed.), *The Limits of Human Nature,* London: Allen Lane, 1973, 235-74.
Zajonc, R.B., *Animal Social Psychology,* New York: John Wiley, 1969.

Discussion

STROEBE: I feel that the paper is extremely interesting, but it has, in a way, made me feel good about *not* studying animal behaviour. Your argument was not really that we should learn from the animals and then know a bit more about human behaviour, but rather that we should start explaining animal social behaviour with the knowledge we have gained from human social behaviour. Now if I'm not interested in explaining animal behaviour then I can feel free to ignore it.

BAREFOOT: No — I feel that my point is more that if we take a view of animals as being more complex than we used to, then we will find that their behaviours are actually more relevant to ours. The particular example I gave was one where we try to apply to humans a model from animal behaviour, but I don't see that as the main message.

ZAJONC: I think it's a little bit unfair to bring in such old views as Lorenz and Tinbergen, or Calhoun and Christian as examples of the study of animal behaviour. They are two views, but they are no longer followed in any systematic or serious research in the study of animal behaviour, except perhaps by some old students of either Lorenz or Tinbergen. I also think that the views of Christian and Calhoun are no longer very much regarded as bases for the study of crowding, *especially* when it applies to humans, for a number of reasons. First, it seems to me that the selection of the example of crowding is a bit unfortunate, if we want to draw parallels between animal and human behaviour, or animal and human social organization. One of the big problems here is that we forget that one of the most important aspects of reaction to crowding in animals involves a scarcity of resources to which the animal responds; in humans, there are adaptive mechanisms which can restore scarcity of resources by a number of means, such as transportation, or building innovation, or other adaptive processes. Another thing that differentiates reaction to crowding in animals as opposed to humans is the repeated demonstration that many effects we attribute to crowding occur *before* the crowding conditions. That is, you see animals withdrawing mating privileges to young adults, there is a decrease in gonadal weights in many animals, and delay of micturition of the females before the actual crowding condition. A condition which will result in crowding, such as, for example, the scarcity of certain seeds in the area, will affect the birds in terms of eggs laid, the number of individuals allowed into the territory, and so on. Now — the regulation of numbers among animals is a completely different story from regulation of numbers among humans. I think there are many areas of behaviour in animal social psychology which can be profitably studied at some level, but I think maybe crowding is not one of them, and perhaps you will learn little by drawing parallels between crowding in animals and crowding in humans.

LOMOV: I don't hesitate to agree that it is very important and useful to study human behaviour to understand animal's behaviour, and *vice versa*. But I think there are *qualitative* differences between human society and human social behaviour, and animal society (so-called society) and so-called animal social behaviour. If you agree, what are the differences? What are the *real* differences? Principles? Qualitative differences between them?

BAREFOOT: I do not doubt there are significant qualitative differences, based primarily on the importance of our language and on our ability to change and manipulate the environment.

LOMOV: But don't animals do this?

BAREFOOT: No — not much.

LOMOV: A little bit?

BAREFOOT: A little bit, yes. But to find out about human behaviour is not the most important reason for studying animals. I think maybe that by studying animals, it might give us some ideas; it might help us clarify problems, and we then can go back and test these ideas out on humans to see if humans are different. It's good for the theoreticians, I think.

LOMOV: Maybe it would be better to use another term for animal behaviour. I don't think that "society" is a good term to analyse animal behaviour. Maybe "groups", or something like that, would be better. There are in my opinion very interesting researches concerned with animal behaviour in our country, which show that animal group behaviour is very flexible, and so on. But with respect to "society", I don't think that you realize that when we try to generalize something, we must keep in mind problems of qualitative difference. That's why it's important to understand what is society, and what type of qualities it has.

ABOUD: Well, what do you think are the major qualitative differences?

LOMOV: There are many analogies in the behaviour of animals and humans. When we talk about goal-directed behaviour, we find similarities in the behaviour of humans and animals. When we say that man uses weapons for his actions, we can find an analogy in the animal world. When we say that people inter-react in the process of their activities, we can find that in the animal world as well. But the main difference would appear to be that the human individual, as a basis of his qualities, has the feeling of belonging to a social system. We have a special term — we talk about "system qualities". These are qualities which belong to any object that belongs to a certain system: they are determined by the object's belonging to a particular system. When we talk about man, about man's qualities, about the society from which he comes, then we discover these analogies that I have been mentioning are somewhat superficial. When we talk about goal-oriented behaviour, then we have to remember that man's goal orientation is determined by the society in which he lives: it is not something which is inborn. When we talk about weapons, then the weapons that man uses are different from the weapons used by the animal, because man's weapons have been produced by the society in which he lives. When we talk about human interaction in society, this is determined by the structure of society — primarily by its economic structure. Therefore, when we talk about analogies and comparisons, we must bear in mind those particular qualities of men that are determined by society. In the human, activity is determined by and directed toward productivity. And productivity is society oriented and society determined. Animals do not produce anything. They have no economic relationships. Therefore they have no ideological, or any other, inter-relationships. And this determines the cardinal differences between animals and humans — including differences in the way they react to crowding.

When German Fascists occupied our country, large groups of our population were taken prisoner, in order to be used as labourers. These people were crowded during their transportation in large numbers into railway cars and then into the camps. For long periods of time they had to exist in highly crowded conditions. However, they still behaved as humans. Therefore, we see the qualitative differences.

ZAJONC: I want very much to agree with you, and I do agree about the danger of drawing analogies between some superficially similar behaviour pattern or activity pattern in animal and human groups. Let's not call them societies, because "society" may have a special meaning. I think there is a real danger of making a mistake in drawing analogies between phenotypes rather than genotypes, that is, in relying on superficial similarities, superficial occurrences of behaviour and organization which seem to have similar form. The causal antecedents of those similarities may be completely different. This is where we can make a very serious mistake. There is, however, another point of view, which would advocate the study of animal behaviour in a social context, and which may benefit social psychologists as well; here I am in agreement with John Barefoot. When we study microbiology, we make no distinctions between the cells of animals and the cells of humans. Many of the processes are the same — we ignore these differences. When we study certain physiological processes, we make no distinction again between certain *genera*, human and animals or between different species of mammals. We are perfectly comfortable drawing upon animal behaviour or animal processes to make generalizations to humans, and these generalizations are valid. I think we do this fairly well and fairly successfully, perhaps because we are dealing with something terribly basic. We don't have any fear of making errors here, because time and time again these generalizations have not been disconfirmed; they have been fairly stable, and fruitful. When we come to social behaviour, immediately there is a reluctance and fear that maybe we are dealing with something that is qualitatively different, and I really feel that on many levels there is an important qualitative difference. But surely, if we are able to point to some basic similarities between animal and human phenomena, in microbiology, and physiology, and anatomy, *perhaps* there are basic phenomena in social psychology which apply equally to animals and to humans. For example, there may be some reactions to novelty, or there may be some forms of early attachment, which have certain basic components that are common to humans and to animals. There may be certain forms of reaction to social control, social punishment, or socialization at a very basic level, which are common both to animals other than humans and to humans as well. And I think that while there is a qualitative difference, perhaps we should not forget the possibility, by not doing research, to see if there *are* these genotypical commonalities that govern the behaviour — social behaviour — underlying both animal and human aggregations. It seems to me that starting with a premise that they aren't there, we'll end up with a conclusion that they aren't; starting with a premise "Let's find out", we might be able to discover if there exists such a common basis of behaviour or not. And I think that the great advantage of looking at animal behaviour this way is that it will force us to look at the very fundamental basis of social behaviour, rather than concentrating on sorts of phenotypical, overt, easily detectable, outward manifestations of what is essentially human.

LOMOV: Well, I don't object to the study and comparison of human behaviour and animal behaviour; I don't object. But I think we must keep in mind the qualitative differences between them in our investigations. You mention physiology — there is some research in our country which shows that physiological or psychophysiological characteristics of animals and humans are *different,* in some situations, at any rate. It has been shown that electroencephalograms, for example, are different when man is leading or when he is following, for example. But I think that in all qualities — perhaps not all, but in the most important qualities — man, the human being, differs from the animal because he is a *social* animal, as Aristotle told us. Aristotle told us that man is a political animal; we have corrected him a little and we usually say that he is a *social* animal. And these social characteristics have the primary influence on his behaviour.

KIESLER: I think though, that one has to say that these issues you mention are largely empirical questions. One can say that, as in humans, there are forms of social organization in animals — and ants or bees and the like — very complex social organizations.

LOMOV: Yes, of course.

KIESLER: And so one cannot necessarily say that the distinguishing characteristic between animals and humans is one of society. One might as easily say, and it's a matter of belief rather than a matter of fact or theory, that man distinguishes himself because he can *choose* his form of society, rather than have one *per se.* But those are not issues of empirical fact.

LOMOV: I described before an instance where people found themselves under conditions of extreme crowding. And I said that they behaved in a completely different fashion from animals under similar conditions. And the explanation is that they remained social creatures. Certain principles determine their behaviour. One could cite many other empirical facts. We are coming back again to the problem of *activity* that we have discussed earlier, and the social/historic characteristics of its nature. We're still coming back to the same problem.

KIESLER: It's less a problem than a different approach. I would agree that indeed the animals and humans acted differently, and I'm pleased to see that you describe that as an empirical fact. I would agree with that. But as with all empirical facts, it's quite another question as to what they mean, and what their implications are, what the theory is underlying them, and how they may be generalized. It's on those issues that we may legitimately disagree. Perhaps by disagreeing we will be motivated to establish other empirical facts. And I think that's what Professor Zajonc was referring to.

LOMOV: No objection to that.

BUEVA: Science is one way to knowledge.

LOMOV: But I think that we must be very, very careful when we try to generalize. You know — *very* careful.

ZAJONC: Absolutely.

On the Study of Some Cognitive Processes in Soviet Social Psychology

A. A. BODALEV

A substantial increase in interest in both theoretical and applied problems of the psychology of communication may be observed in recent Soviet psychology. It is quite clearly evinced by the increasing number of publications in which various aspects of this complex process are considered, in such areas as general psychology, psychophysiology, social and differential psychology.

Without discussing the reasons for such a considerable increase in this interest, it is necessary to emphasize that among the monographs and articles written by the Soviet psychologists during the last decade, a conspicuous place is occupied by the works which demonstrate the cognitive characteristics invariably present in that multicomponent process of social interaction, communication. Some of these studies are devoted to the analysis of the regularities and mechanisms of the formation of different kinds of awareness of the situation which results from verbal contacts which participants have to establish with each other, for whatever reason. (The above problems are studied by Evrastov N.P., Leontiev A.A. . Ruzskaya A.G., Ryzhkin Y.E. Rybalko E.F. and others.)[1]

Another group of work focuses on details of the development of interpersonal perception in the communicating individuals, as well as on their understanding of those personality charac-

---

(1) An attempt to obtain the addresses of these and other investigators was not successful (Ed.).

144   *A. A. Bodalev*

teristics which are found to be related to their bodily characteristics: their appearance, the expressiveness of their behavior as participants of the communication process, etc. (The studies in this field are those by Valciner Ya., Golovey L.A., Zinin A.M., Labunskaya V.A., Lestsepp H., Meigas M., Mikkin G., Podberezin J.M. . Snetkov V.A., Tommings E. and others.)

The monographs and articles of a third group are focused primarily on discovering the effects of the psychological characteristics of the participants in the communication process (considering each as a "cognizer" of other people, not an object of that process) on their cognition of one another, as well as changes in the communication process itself which may result from this cognition. In this connection, the works of the following group reveal the significance of the most essential characteristics of various psychological processes on man, such as his perceptions (Bodalev A.A., Galunov V.J., Zolotnyakova A.S., Lasko M.A., Manerov V.H., Panferov V.V., Petrovskaya V.A., Smirnova E.E. and others), his memory (Zinin A.M., Ivanskaya L.I., Lisina M.I., Semyenova L.F. and others), his imagination (Gavrilova G.P., Drankov V.A., Karandyshev Yu. N., Kashtanova T.R. and others), his speech (Bazhin E.F., Eremyev B.A., Galagudze S.S., Labunskaya V.A., Manerov V.H., Nitchenko A.K., Persianova N.A. and others), his thinking (Dvoryshina M.D., Magun V.S., Kondratyeva S.V., Razdobudko V.A., Rytchik and others), and his desire for more or less accurate cognition of the people with whom he is to interact (Dzhos, V.V.).

There have also been an increasing number of publications in which attempts are undertaken to pursue the dependence of the results of cognizing of one individual by another in the communication process on the emotional states of the participants (Mazmanyan M.A., Kulikov V.N., Ruzskaya A.G., Safin V.F., Talyan L.Sh., Shafranskaya K.D. and others).

Of similar scientific import are recent studies demonstrating the effect of certain personality characteristics of the cognizing subject on the cognition of another person in the communication process (Berman M.Ya., Esareva Z.F., Kondratyeva S.V.,

Labunskaya V.A., Obozov N.N., Okoneshnikova A.P., Repina T.A., Sekun V.I., Fedotova N.F. and others).

While enumerating these trends in the studies which aim at analyzing different aspects of the cognitive component of communication, it should also be mentioned that there have appeared a great number of recent works in which the effects of integral characteristics of psychological processes, states and personality traits on the formation of concrete-imaginal and abstract-conceptual knowing of other people are studied; these include the age of the individual (Bodalev A.A., Valciner Ya., Zaporozhets A.V., Lisina M.I., Maksimova R.A., Mescheryakova S.Yu., Repina T.A., Sosnovnikova Yu. E. and others), his sex (Eremyev B.A., Ivashkin V.S., Kondratyeva S.V., Kunitzina V.N., Panferov V.N., Fedotova N.T. and others) and his profession (Bodalev A.A., Kondratyeva S.V., Kuzmina N.V., Kukosyan O.G., Tyshlukov V.A., Ungal V.V., Shultz S.P. and others).

An independent line among the studies of the cognitive components of the communication process is followed by works in which the formation of the knowledge about another person during interpersonal contacts is considered in relation to the effect of various socio-psychological factors (for example, the opinion of the perceiver's reference group about his person, his position in the informal structure of the collective, "the emotional climate" in the collective and so on) (Kolominsky Ya. I., Krichevsky R.L., Umansky L.I., Fedotova N.F., Khanin Yu.L. and others).

And finally, to complete this survey of the principal trends in the study of cognitive components of the communication process, it should be noted that a number of works have been published recently which were primarily devoted to the revelation of the role played by different spatio-temporal characteristics involved in each of the communication situations, in the formation and actualization of the knowledge about the other person (Eremyev B.A., Zinin A.M., Ivanskaya L.N., Karandyshev Yu.N., Kondratyeva S.V., Krutova E.M., Maryanenko A.P., Snetkov V.A. and others).

While speaking about all these research trends in the studies performed by Soviet psychologists, which are of great importance for understanding the principal phenomena, regularities, and mechanisms involved in the cognition by people of each other, it should be specially mentioned that recently there have appeared works in Soviet social psychology which aim at revelation of the specificity of relations between cognitive and "praxic" characteristics of communication (Andreeva G.M., Bodalev A.A., Kondratyeva S.V.). These studies, some of which have already been published, show how different kinds of concrete-imaginal and verbal-conceptual knowledge possessed by man about other people mediate various individual acts, both in the communication area and beyond it, how they interact with the knowledge of the individual about the other aspects of reality, and how they may jointly control his behavior in the most important situations he faces in his life in the sphere of labour (in all its diversity), his everyday affairs, and in the sphere of his leisure.

But the study of only one cognitive component of the communication process, as well as its emotional characteristics, or the description and the analysis of its praxis component, although being of interest for science, has on the whole only a specific significance, both theoretically and practically. One should not fail to see that in everyday life, in the case of most people, their object-praxic activity is intricately interwoven with their communication. This interrelation with communication invariably exists with respect to the goals of these activities, the motives which influence the performance of these activities, and the operational structures of these activities. That is why the study of a "psychological inside" of the communication process should not be reduced solely to the revelation of principal phenomena, and regularities and mechanisms of social perception. The solution of a more complex task is obligatory. First, we must determine the essence of the combination of various types of psychological processes and the manifestation of different personality characteristics; there are, so to speak, possible "syndromes" of both at different stages of all the known kinds of human activity carried out together with other people. Second, it is necessary to pursue the nature of the correlation between the changes in such "syndromes", the causes of such changes, and the actual behavior of the individual.

Discussion

KIESLER: Could you describe a typical experiment, so we can develop some feeling for your experimental approach?

BODALEV: During the period 1962 to 1967, work in the field of cognition of interpersonal relationships was done with experiments modeled on a methodology built up by Soviet psychologists who had studied in England, in the Soviet Union, and in Canada; but starting in 1967, essential modifications were introduced into the methodology, and I shall try to explain why.

It is interesting to study the cognition of one person by another, but it is more important to discover the *significance* of the way people imagine other people to be. What are the consequences of the impressions that we gain from other people for the regulation of our behaviour towards that person? What we are studying is, essentially, the interdependence of our reflection of other people, our emotional response to them, and the type of behaviour we choose on that basis. Accordingly, a number of works have been carried out in our country, where the people to be studied are physicians and patients, or teachers and schoolchildren, managers and subordinate personnel, sport trainers and athletes, and many other groups which represent the same relationship of manager and worker, or actors and spectators. The object of the study is to comprehend the interdependence of the reflective, emotional and behavioural components of the communication process. As an example, we could consider a teacher and a student. An observer will study over a long period of time what method the teacher employs — both his behaviour and his attitude toward the student. What qualities he attributes to his students are recorded with questionnaires and scales. And even using this extremely simple method, we can find profound differences between master teachers and novice teachers.

From memory, I will describe a recently completed work on wrestlers who had not met each other previously in a wrestling bout. First one determines the way they picture their opponent and how they assess their own potential. After that they start the wrestling bout, and following the actual fight they are again questioned, and we determine how their opinion of themselves and of their opponent has changed. The important thing is the wrestler's initial self-concept and his evaluation of his opponent; we ask him what strategy he is going to employ in this wrestling bout based on his self-concept and his evaluation of the opponent. We find that there is a most striking difference in the accuracy of evaluation of the opponent between a beginning wrestler and an experienced one, each one meeting a new opponent that he has not wrestled with before.

We also carry out this type of study with personnel managers, and we compare the evaluation of a job applicant by experienced and inexperienced personnel managers. And we are trying to determine what personality characteristics determine the ease and depth of understanding of the other person. Recently in the laboratory of

Dr. Andreeva, they have attempted to develop a special system of exercises which would raise the level of social perceptive skills of people whose job consists of influencing other people.

SEGALOWITZ: Is there much research on the impressions people form about others from the way they speak?

BODALEV: At the Bekterev Institute researchers are studying the impressions gained by one person from the voice and manner of speaking of the other person. The researchers of this particular institute studied a group of mentally ill patients diagnosed as manic-depressive psychotics. These particular patients were selected because there is an established correlation among various metabolic, physiological, biochemical parameters with either the manic or depressive stage of their illness. They were all filmed. Each one was studied separately; a film was made for each particular patient, and his voice was recorded during the various stages. In some experimental sessions, the picture and the sound would be presented together. In another session, the film would be played without sound, or the sound would be played without the film. Observers were asked to differentiate, from both the visual image and from the sound, the stages of change from the manic to the depressive. They would not be given cues from the extreme of the elation or the extreme of the depression; they would be presented with some intermediary stage, on the way down or on the way up, and they were asked to study both pictures and sound. It was found that there were profound differences among observers in their ability to differentiate; some people are able to differentiate only between extremes and others are very sensitive, and can make the diagnosis during a subtle change. Women prove to be more sensitive in this respect than men, and the most sensitive of all were women psychiatrists. One interesting and rather funny fact came to light. If the people who were tested for this differentiating ability were given a lot of time to reflect, their errors rose by a factor of three. Their immediate response was usually correct — if they reflected on it, it became wrong. We think that the explanation may lie in the fact that this waiting period lets our stereotypic images interfere with our spontaneous judgement.

ABOUD: Most of the dyadic situations you have mentioned were complementary — there were two wrestlers in conflict, a teacher and a student, and so on. But if we want to study some things, social learning for example, it is clear that we learn a lot from people who are similar to us, and with whom we are not in conflict. Do you ever study social perception in the family group? Does the same theory and same methodology apply to that?

BODALEV: Some studies are now being carried out on the perception and understanding by small children in a family unit of each other, looking at the sibling hierarchy and the differences in social perception of the first, second and third child. They are looking at the significance of sibling self-perception and evaluation as related to their acceptance by the parents, and especially by the head of the family unit — whether father or mother.

HOLMES: I was wondering if there is a set of research studies on social conflict, on conflict situations.

BODALEV: I am not a specialist in this area, but a colleague from Leningrad

University, Professor Kuzmin, together with his students, is working in a number of industrial installations of Leningrad. Along with a number of other problems, he is studying the nature of the conflict which can arise among the members of a particular labour team, or which may arise between manager and subordinate. And he studies the relationship between the components of the conflict itself and the way people in this conflict perceive themselves and perceive one another. They are attempting to form a system of classification of conflict, a causal classification. They see a very sharp distinction between conflicts that are useful to the cause and conflicts that are harmful to the cause, that is, those that provide a hygienic or sanitary influence on the collective, as opposed to the type of conflict that produces a negative influence on the collective. There are other social psychologists in the Soviet Union who devote their time to the study of psychological conflict.

STRICKLAND: You mentioned some of the studies on collectives, and I wondered if these tended to be experimental or observational, or what?

ANDREEVA: Our programme of studies in this particular field involves a very complex analysis of the problems of social perception. We try to determine all the possibilities of social perception. For example, consider the following possibilities: the most frequently described model is one where two people belonging to the same group are perceiving each other; there is the type of study where the person inside the group perceives not only the other person but the group as a whole; there is the context where a person belonging to one group perceives the other person as a member of another group; there is the instance where a person identified as a member of a particular group identifies with the different group — as an example, a hospitalized patient identifies with the hospital staff; another model is of the case where a group perceives one of its members (the traditional way of putting this one used to be the way a group accords status to the individual, but we feel we can also take it as a model of social perception). Another model is where a whole group assesses a member of a different group, for example, when a class of students accepts a new teacher. This has not been studied very well, experimentally, although in real life it presents a factual situation and an important one, because when a new teacher is assigned to a classroom of students, their learning performance will depend on how they accept that teacher. Finally we have a model where one group perceives the other group — one group is the perceiving subject and the other is the perceived object, for instance former students — how they accept former teachers. For me the social psychological aspect of the problem of intergroup relations is the process of perception of one group by another group.

After developing all the possible variations of this type of perceptual relationship, a number of experiments were designed on some of the models. All the experiments are essentially guided by one general idea: they are carried out in a natural setting, not laboratory experiments, and the point of each study is how mutual social activity affects the social perception processes. In other words, it means that these groups become collectives (according to Petrovsky's idea) and we try to study in which way this new group quality modifies the perception process. One colleague has been carrying out observations over a long period of time in a setting of a children's summer camp. The summer camp is a particularly useful model because there are time limits for the formation of the group. The children usually spend one month in that camp, so as they arrive the group is formed, then it exists and behaves as a group and within a month it is terminated. He then can study during that month how one group of these campers accepts another group of the campers, and how their attitudes change from their first encounter to later on. These two groups might then be asked to engage in activities which are dependent on their ages; if they are very young, the activity will be play — if they are older it might be some type of work. A month later a study is done on how the members of this one group perceive the members of the other group, after they have had this mutual activity. The same idea is carried through with respect to other kinds of groups.

Ethnocentric Reactions to Social Threat

JOHN G. HOLMES and PETER GRANT

The notion that intergroup conflict increases internal cohesion is treated almost as a truism in the social science literature. Sumner in 1906 proposed that "outer hostility is associated with inner cohesion" and that this ethnocentric syndrome characterizes both primitive societies and modern intergroup relations. The proposition has now achieved a stature consistent with its old and venerable place in the sciences. Authors like Boulding (1962) do not bother to offer any citations when referring to it. Levine and Campbell (1972) in their recent book on "Ethnocentrism" have called it the "ubiquitous principle". Few authors deem it necessary to mention any qualifications or caveats.

In our view this state of affairs is unfortunate. The empirical evidence for the hypothesis is rather weak and points to a set of restricting conditions that will require further theoretical elaboration. In this paper, we will first present a short overview of research on conflict and cohesion in the small-group context. We hope to demonstrate that the principles that emerge have clear parallels with those in another research domain, that of group reactions to stress and social threat. Our goal in drawing this comparison is to develop a theory that will help to explain some of the apparent contradictions in the research literature, and second, to suggest that certain psychological principles are common to both areas. Let us first examine some of the research on the ingroup/outgroup hypothesis.

151

Conflict and Cohesion

The general notion is that conflict with outgroups is associated with cohesion and solidarity in the ingroup. The relationship is assumed to be negative: hostility to outsiders implies the opposite tendency, or mirror-image in the ingroup. There are two distinct hypotheses merged within this theme, depending on the causal direction that is assumed. First, a unified, cohesive group may be more likely to instigate conflict with other groups and depreciate their members. Second, involvement in an external conflict with outsiders may serve a unifying function for the ingroup, creating a more positive social climate and solidarity.

Research studies have focused almost exclusively on this latter principle in their choice of experimental manipulations. The paradigm usually involves confronting small groups of individuals with a situation of intergroup competition, and comparing it to one that is either cooperative or non-competitive in nature. For instance, in a series of field studies, Fiedler and his associates report that competition has a quasi-therapeutic effect on internal relations in military and industrial settings (Fiedler, 1967; Julian, Bishop and Fiedler, 1966). Task efficiency increased, as did personal adjustment and attraction to the group. In laboratory experiments, seven or eight studies have found increased cohesion as an aftereffect of competition, though usually with limiting conditions. The indicators of ingroup attraction range from overevaluation of its products, increased sociometric ratings of members, equitable allocation of rewards, and a positive bias in judging the motives and intentions of one's fellow group members (see Dion, in press). Four or five studies have failed to find such differences.

There are several problems with these studies. First, most of them predicted an ethnocentric reaction to competition, with a positive shift in ingroup feeling, and a negative bias towards the outgroup. This hypothesis is normally based on cognitive balance or frustation explanations. This result is usually claimed by the authors, since they subtract the ingroup evaluations from the outgroup ratings. But in most cases, only ingroup attraction has changed. Second, the external conflict dimension is invariably manipulated in an all-or-none fashion, with competition being compared to a control. The degree of conflict, the chances for success or achieving a solution, and the characteristics of the outgroup are seldom considered. Thus, Kahn and Ryen (1972) and Rabbie *et al.* (1974) do in fact report increased hostility to outsiders, but only when the group expects to be successful. Therefore, at the present stage of development of the hypothesis, it seems critical to identify the particular set of conditions that will elicit both aspects of the ethnocentric reaction.

The omnibus, broad manipulations discussed above also make it difficult to distinguish among the various theoretical perspectives. For example, "realistic group conflict theory" (Campbell, 1965) emphasizes the functional relations between groups, and contends that direct competition for scarce resources produces outgroup antagonism and associated changes in ingroup solidarity (Deutsch, 1973; Sherif, 1966). Other perspectives rely more heavily on the perceptual dynamics that are responsible for separating social units into the value-laden categories of "ingroup and outgroup" (Dion, 1973; Tajfel and Billig, 1974; Billig, 1976). Most experimental studies arrange a direct confrontation between groups, selecting procedures that do not allow clear tests of these differing explanations. However, several studies find evidence for intergroup discrimination in the absence of direct interaction or objective competition (e.g., Kahn and Ryen, 1972; Rabbie and Horwitz, 1969; Tajfel and Billig, 1974). These trends highlight the importance of designing studies that are capable of distinguishing between theoretical explanations or discovering the conditions under which each of these various perspectives becomes more critical.

Given the present state of affairs, it therefore seems reasonable to conclude that a group will react to a competitive relationship with outsiders by becoming more internally cohesive and integrated, given a special set of limiting conditions.

However, the *psychological processes* that catalyze this reaction are not clear at this point in time. Second, there is little evidence to support the idea that this increased attachment to one's own group is a *sufficient* condition to precipitate hostile attitudes toward the outgroup, eliciting the spectre of the more insidious ethnocentric reaction. In fact, several experiments have directly manipulated the level of internal cohesion. These studies failed to find an associated shift in outgroup evaluations. If anything, Wilson (1971) notes that members who hold their own group in high esteem tend to be more positively disposed toward outsiders.

Group Reactions to Shared Threat

There is a marked parallel between these results and those concerned with group reactions to stressful experiences. In their review of the cohesiveness literature, Lott and Lott (1965) note that groups appear to cope with external pressure or stress by increasing their internal coherence. There is empirical support for this conclusion across a rather diverse set of definitions for the external stress and a wide variety of methodologies. For example, the stress or threat can result from natural disasters (see Stein, 1976), economic uncertainty (Mulder and Stemerding, 1963; Sales, 1973), potential frustration or evaluation (Wright, 1943; Burnstein and McRae, 1962; Lanzetta, 1955), a decision crisis (Hamblin, 1958), expected electrical shock (Schachter, 1959; Rabbie, 1963), and so on. In other words, people tend to depend on and feel closer to other members in their group when they experience a shared threat which has important psychological consequences for their well-being and equilibrium.

This research perspective has generally remained theoretically and empirically isolated from the study of intergroup conflict. However, a rather elaborate set of propositions can be derived from this evidence (Holmes, 1974). In our opinion there are convergent themes and processes in the two areas, and these propositions can help to clarify the theory of ethnocentrism in intergroup relations.

The general hypothesis is that groups will react to threat by increasing their internal cohesion. Cohesion includes a syndrome of attraction to fellow members, increased conformity to group norms, perceptions of similarity among group members, solidarity and efficacy. This reaction will depend on certain conditions at the onset of the perception of threat:

(1) The threat must be a salient motivational force with important psychological consequences attached to it for the group as a whole. That is, important group values and goals must be perceived to be in danger by the majority of group members;

(2) The cause of the threat must be perceived as external to the group, rather than resulting from stress that is caused by failures or incapacity on the part of its members;

(3) The members must believe that their concerted actions can have instrumental value. They must be capable of constructing cognitive alternatives to their present state, and believe that they have a reasonable chance of achieving some degree of success in coping with the threatening situation;

(4) Propositions (1) and (3) imply that group members identify with their group. Group identity has two aspects in this context. The social unit must be sufficiently cohesive to support the internal dynamics of social evaluation and consensus (Schachter, 1959). And, second, the rewards that members draw from ingroup identification must be sufficient to motivate them to work to preserve group values and goals, rather than allowing the unit to disintegrate.

An Integration

These propositions can be rather directly applied to an analysis of intergroup conflict by considering the outgroup as a source of threat, in this case, one with social origins. But this approach is not very satisfying, given the atheoretical nature of the enterprise. We will therefore present a model of intergroup conflict derived from both the empirical results and several theoretical assumptions. Our goal is to integrate the findings in a way that takes our understanding of the ethnocentric process one step further, but by no means will this formulation unravel all of the contradictions that abound in this complex literature.

The model involves a systems-theory approach to intergroup conflict (see Miller and Rice, 1967). It is proposed that an ethnocentric reaction involving distortions in evaluations of both the ingroup and outgroup will depend to a critical degree on two characteristics of the intergroup system. The first variable consists of the degree of polarization between groups from the egocentric point of view of one particular ingroup — that is, the extent to which this group feels that it is cognitively differentiated from a particular outgroup and has an integrated identity of its own. The second variable consists of the degree of social threat experienced by ingroup members that can be subjectively associated with the outgroup. These two factors are postulated to work together in a multiplicative fashion to produce an ethnocentric reaction. If either factor is not present, then the relation is not expected to result.

This formulation implies that under threatening conditions a group's identity becomes increasingly reliant on social comparison with the outgroup, which stresses ingroup superiority and outgroup inferiority. Thus high status, powerful groups who are not easily threatened will be unlikely to have strong ethnocentric reactions toward other groups. Further, differentiation refers not only to a perceptual contrasting of group differences but also to a *functional* process that leads to the group coping more effectively with the threat. For example, a steel-producing country faced by a slump in the world market for steel (an amorphous external threat) will select another steel-producing country as the "cause" of this threat because of certain threat-relevant attributes (low labor costs) and will differentiate itself from the country using these attributes. Thus the ethnocentric reaction will be in the form "They exploit their steel workers", i.e., a negative evaluation stressing ingroup superiority and outgroup inferiority, using these threat-relevant differentiated attributes. In the following sections, the two critical theoretical variables will be discussed in more detail to clarify why the model is presented in this particular form.

Dion's (1973) cognitive differentiation hypothesis was chosen as a point of departure. Dion contends that intergroup biases can be understood from the point of view of balance theory. He first adopts Gestalt principles of perceptual organization. Bias will occur if the ingroup and outgroup form cognitively distinct or differentiated entities-unit-formation in Heider's (1958) terms. This categorization into separate social units is furthered by perceptions of "homogeneity" in the ingroup, of a type that distinguishes it from the outgroup. Homogeneity is increased by assumed similarity of the members on critical issues, heightened cohesiveness, status equity, and a common fate.

But how do these perceptual distinctions get converted into positive and negative affect, into attraction and hostility? According to Dion, the perceptual unit relationships and the sentiment or emotional relationships will tend toward consistency over time. Balance theory suggests that the tension between these cognitive and emotional systems is the mechanism that produces the change.

This theory appears to be a step forward. It suggests ways of dealing with the more subjective processes of social perception and group structure that are given little prominence in the realistic conflict theories (Campbell, 1965). It also integrates many of the features of previous findings without undue strain. For instance, intergroup competition is thought to cause internal cohesion and bias because of the common fate shared by insiders and the opposed fate experienced by outsiders. It also manages to incorporate the finding that cohesion is often reduced if a group expects to fail. Supposedly, the spectre of failure would reduce the perceived unity of the group.

Our main point of contention with this theory relates to the meagre place in the scheme of things that it accords to the motivational components that convert perceptual principles into emotional ones. The "strain toward symmetry" from cognitive inconsistency (Newcomb, 1956) seems to be but a pale, static force when compared to the profound allegiances and hatred that often result from group confrontations. It is essentially a cognitive theory, without a strong drive component to energize the system. The strength of consistency motivation has recently been questioned by authors in other fields, particularly when it is pitted against other drives, such as esteem maintenance (see Jones, 1973).

Other recent studies contribute in important ways to our understanding of perceptual differentiation between groups. Brewer and Campbell (1976) in their discussion of extensive survey data from East African tribes apply the notion of "accentuation" (Eiser and Stroebe, 1972) to this process. To illustrate this phenomenon, consider two sets of people who have a number of differences between them. These differences could be on continuous dimensions such as *outgoing-withdrawn,* or on discrete dimensions such as *black-white.* If these two sets of people are now labelled group A and group B, then this theory predicts that the existing differences between the groups will be accentuated (a contrast effect). The application of the binary social category tends to polarize other associated continuous attributes into more discrete classes. However, usually people belong to several overlapping groups and there is a lack of convergence of group differences with group boundaries. Only when the convergence takes place do Brewer and Campbell agree that an ethnocentric reaction will occur. That is, "the ethnocentric syndrome will be characteristic only for those social groups in which multiple criteria for intergroup differentiation converge" (p. 137).

Billig (1976) agrees that the application of social categories enhances perceived dissimilarities between groups on other traits. But in his discussion of the research program with Tajfel in the minimal group context, he stresses that the formation of social categories does *not* imply an inductive model where group membership is decided by similarity or dissimilarity of traits. He suggests that social labelling by the person and by outsiders is the critical process. The social and linguistic categories may have little objective basis, but if they are accepted, they then become the social reality for differentiation.

Finally, Hamilton (1977) has demonstrated how an "illusory correlation" can develop between minority member status and anti-normative behavior. Both events are distinctive, since they are less frequently encountered, and are therefore more vividly recalled.

These various theories describe the process by which intergroup differentiation *could* occur at the cognitive level. But the questions remain as to why certain outgroups would be selected as targets for this polarization process. And, given the innumerable differences among groups, why do certain critical dimensions of comparison emerge? Finally, as we argued before, what is the motivation to convert perceptual "differences" between social categories into value — laden evaluations involving feelings of hostility and superiority?

Our hypothesis is that intergroup differentiation represents much more than the exaggeration of group differences. It reflects the *functional distortion of group differences in service of group goals and values.* Broadly speaking, the social threat elicited both by the relative position, actions, and cultural identity of an outgroup, and the particular fears and problems the ingroup is experiencing, motivates a coping process in the group. The success of this coping process and the particular pattern of adjustment depend on the degree of differentiation between these groups.

A particular outgroup is chosen because it appears from the ingroup's members' point of view to interfere with the achievement of important group goals (e.g., through competitive relations) and/or calls into question their status and social identity as members of the ingroup. The definition of threat is therefore tied both to the actual character of the outgroup and the threat it poses (the kernel of truth), as well as the egocentric, identity and status concerns of the ingroup.

Thus, social threat often motivates concern about dimensions of identity. In a differentiated, cohesive group, each person experiences acceptance and a sense of identification that help to create and define a sense of self-esteem, a "social self".

A group that has culturally distinct qualities is better able to fulfill the need for group identification. However, when the group or ethnic bloc confronts outsiders, certain aspects of their value system are implicitly placed in comparison to another, and in a sense, put into question. This conflict of values will be more pronounced if the groups are differentiated along a number of convergent dimensions.

Thus, the threat value of an outgroup will increase to the extent that the social comparison process becomes *invidious* — that is, if the contrasts imply superiority and inferiority in a more Darwinian sense, rather than simply "differences" between the cultural units (Holmes and Miller, 1976; Lerner, Miller and Holmes, 1976). Intergroup competition often induces this perspective, so that winning or losing takes on far more value than the objective issues would suggest. In the absence of such comparisons, a group may develop cohesion and a "separate identity", without the associated negative feelings for outgroups. However, if the social threat of invidious comparison increases in intergroup relations, then group identity will become more *"comparative"* in nature. The particular pattern and lines of intergroup differentiation that then develop will reflect these salient dimensions of comparison. The ethnocentric pattern of attitudes that emerges will therefore not constitute formless, undifferentiated positive affect for the ingroup and negative affect for the outgroup, but rather, a distinct pattern of beliefs that reflect the nature of the social threat that energized the process. (These ideas may help to explain why the correlation between ingroup and outgroup evaluations has been so variable in the literature. The present theory predicts a positive association under low degrees of threat, but a more negative one as threat increases.)

The perceptual process suggested by these ideas is consistent with Campbell's (1967) general model of intergroup stereotypes. Campbell applies the Spence (1956) model from learning theory and postulates that four factors interact multiplicitively to determine whether a particular attribute will be attended to by the ingroup. The first is the actual prevalence of the attribute in the outgroup *compared to* its prevalence in the ingroup. However, three other factors, including drive, incentive and familiarity, also play a role, and serve to enhance the perception of particular attributes. Although Campbell doesn't really develop this theme or directly apply it to his later empirical studies, it does seem consistent with our assumption about the critical role of motivational forces in intergroup differentiation and our emphasis on the idea that attributes that are "drive" (threat) relevant will be highlighted in the process.

The particular form of intergroup differentiation is therefore important in defining the emergent dimensions of a perceived social threat and the lines of adjustment. However, differentiation also controls the ability of the ingroup to cope effectively with the threat, both in terms of goal achievement and social evaluation processes. This coping process leads to further affective separation between the group in the following way.

First, goal locomotion is served best in the confines of a cohesive, coherent ingroup structure (Lott and Lott, 1965). The group is also more capable of instrumental action to reduce the threat if the outgroup is clearly differentiated from it, and represents a symbolic, integrated social unit. That is, the ingroup members need a clear, "frozen" *target* that they can direct their actions and emotions *"against"*. Note in particular that Korten (1962) and others have argued that the need for distinct, uniform targets or goals increases dramatically under conditions of stress. or threat. A contrient relationship with the outgroup where realistic group competition exists (Deutsch, 1973) serves to highlight these perceptions. At the same time, it more directly emphasizes the promotive aspects of relationships in the ingroup.

Intergroup differentiation also furthers an ethnocentric reaction by facilitating the social evaluation process among group members. This involves dynamics described by Schachter (1959; 1964) and others, where people turn to others both for socio-emotional support and evaluation of their feelings and emotions in stressful circumstances. There is evidence from this line of research that the group climate will serve this purpose best if the members are attracted to each other, perceive themselves as similar on dimensions critical to the issues in question, and believe that they are subject to a common source of stress. On the other hand, a distinct, dissimilar outgroup with an opposing fate will enhance the psychological or emotional distance between the groups. In addition, a differentiated outgroup provides a context where the emotions and possible plight of the ingroup can be *externalized,* and the outsiders blamed for the distress being experienced. This involves a labelling or attribution process mediated by the group. It serves to divert blame, preserve ingroup cohesion, and select a target for group action to counteract the threat they feel.

Group polarization dynamics (see Lamm and Myers, in press) are likely to play a critical role in this process, and in the sharpening of group attitudes along the critical attitude dimensions made salient by the social comparison dynamics that we discussed earlier. It is important to emphasize in this analysis of the coping process that direct *social influence* is viewed as an integral part of the development of ethnocentric attitudes. The recent applications of perceptual and cognitive models give little weight to this process.

In conclusion, we have tried to illustrate that three sources of group-mediated motivation can be set in motion by external threat. In intergroup relations, the outgroup represents a powerful source of *social* threat that energizes these motivational processes. An ethnocentric reaction is then postulated to depend on the degree to which a cultural unit has clear boundaries and a coherence that distinguishes and distances it from the outgroup. This differentiation creates a social climate that allows the group to cope effectively with the threat. The end result will be an affective, emotional polarization between groups that depends only indirectly on cognitive on perceptual differentiation.

References

Billig, M., *Social Psychology and Intergroup Relations,* London: Academic Press, 1976.
Boulding, K.E., *Conflict and Defense: A General Theory,* New York: Harper, 1962.

Brewer, M.B. and Campbell, D.T., *Ethnocentrism and Intergroup Attitudes: East African Evidence,* New York: Wiley, 1976.

Burnstein, E. and McRae, A., Some effects of shared threat and prejudice in racially mixed groups, *Journal of Abnormal and Social Psychology,* 1962, *64,* 257-63.

Campbell, D.T., Ethnocentric and other altruistic motives. In D. Levine (Ed.), *Nebraska: Symposium on Motivation.* Lincoln, Nebraska: University of Nebraska Press, 1965.

Campbell, D.T., Stereotypes and perception of group differences, *American Psychologist,* 1967, *22,* 812-29.

Coser, L., *The Functions of Social Conflict,* New York: Free Press, 1956.

Deutsch, M., *The Resolution of Conflict: Constructive and Destructive Processes,* New Haven: Yale University Press, 1973.

Dion, K., Cohesiveness as a determinant of ingroup-outgroup bias, *Journal of Personality and Social Psychology,* 1973, *28,* 163-71.

Dion, K.L., Intergroup conflict and intragroup cohesiveness. In W. Austin & S. Worchel (Eds.), *The Social Psychology of Intergroup Relations,* Belmont, California: Brooks/Cole, in press.

Eiser, J.R. and Stroebe, W., *Categorization and Social Judgement,* London: Academic Press, 1972.

Fiedler, F.E., The effect of intergroup competition on group member adjustment, *Personnel Psychology,* 1967, *20,* 33-44.

Hamblin, R.L., Group integration during a crisis, *Human Relations,* 1958, *11,* 67-76.

Hamilton, D.L., Illusory correlation as a basis for social stereotypes. Paper presented at the meeting of the American Psychological Association, San Francisco, August 1977.

Heider, F., *The Psychology of Interpersonal Relations,* New York: Wiley, 1958.

Holmes, J.G., Group reactions to perceived threat, *The Canada Council,* 1974.

Holmes, J.G. and Miller, D.T., *Interpersonal Conflict,* New York: General Learning Press, 1976.

Jones, S.C., Self and interpersonal evaluations: Esteem theories versus consistency theories, *Psychological Bulletin,* 1973, *80,* 185-99.

Julian, J.W., Bishop, D.W. and Fiedler, F.E., Quasitherapeutic effects of intergroup competition, *Journal of Personality and Social Psychology,* 1966, *3,* 321-7.

Kahn, A. and Ryen, A.H., Factors influencing the bias towards one's own group, *International Journal of Group Tension,* 1972, *2,* 33-50.

Korten, D.C., Situational determinants of leadership structure, *Journal of Conflict Resolution,* 1962, *6,* 222-35.

Lamm, H. and Myers, D.G., Group-induced polarization of attitudes and behavior. In L. Berkowitz (Ed.), *Advances in Experimental Social Psychology,* Vol. 11, New York: Academic Press, in press.

Lanzetta, J.T., Group behavior under stress, *Human Relations,* 1955, *8,* 29-52.

Lerner, M.J., Miller, D.T. and Holmes, J.G., Deserving vs. justice: A contemporary dilemma. In L. Berkowitz & E. Walster (Eds.), *Advances in Experimental Social Psychology,* Vol. 9, New York: Academic Press, 1976.

Levine, R.A. and Campbell, D.T., *Ethnocentrism: Theories of Conflict, Ethnic Attitudes and Group Behavior,* New York: Wiley, 1972.

Lott, A.J. and Lott, B.E., Group cohesiveness as interpersonal attraction, *Psychological Bulletin,* 1965, *64,* 259-301.

Miller, E.J. and Rice, A.K., *Systems of Organization,* New York: Tavistock Publications, 1967.

Mulder, M. and Stemerding, A., Threat, attraction to groups, and need for strong leadership, *Human Relations*, 1963, *16*, 317-34.

Newcomb, T.M., The prediction of interpersonal attraction, *American Psychologist*, 1956, *11*, 575-86.

Rabbie, J.M., Differential preference for companionship under threat, *Journal of Abnormal and Social Psychology*, 1963, *67*, 643-8.

Rabbie, J.M. and Horwitz, M., Arousal of ingroup-outgroup bias by a chance win or loss, *Journal of Personality and Social Psychology*, 1969, *13*, 269-77.

Rabbie, J.M., Benoist, F., Costerbaan, H. and Visser, L., Differential power and effects of expected competitive and cooperative intergroup interaction on intra-group and outgroup attitudes, *Journal of Personality and Social Psychology*, 1974, *30*, 46-56.

Sales, S.M., Threat as a factor in authoritarianism: An analysis of archival data, *Journal of Personality and Social Psychology*, 1973, *28*, 44-57.

Schachter, S., *The Psychology of Affiliation*, Stanford, Calif.: Stanford University Press, 1959.

Schachter, S., The interaction of cognitive and psychological determinants of emotional states. In L. Berkowitz (Ed.), *Advances in Experimental Social Psychology*. New York: Academic Press, 1964.

Sherif, M., *Group Conflict and Cooperation: Their Social Psychology*, London: Routledge & Kegan Paul, 1966.

Spence, K., *Behavior Theory and Conditioning*. New Haven: Yale University Press, 1956.

Stein, A.A., Conflict and cohesion: A review of the literature, *Journal of Conflict Resolution*, 1976, *20*, 143-72.

Sumner, W.G., *Folkways*, Boston, Sinn, 1906.

Tajfel, H. and Billig, M., Familiarity and categorization in intergroup behavior, *Journal of Experimental Social Psychology*, 1974, *10*, 159-70.

Wilson, W., Reciprocation and other techniques for inducing cooperation in the prisoner's dilemma game, *Journal of Conflict Resolution*, 1971, *15*, 167-95.

Wright, M.E., The influence of frustration upon the social relations of young children, *Character and Personality*, 1943, *12*, 111-22.

Discussion

BODALEV: My first question is, "How do you define intergroup conflict from a social psychologist's point of view?"

HOLMES: This is not a model of intergroup conflict — it's a model of intergroup emotions and attitudes; such attitudes can result in behavioural conflict. This theory might suggest a context in which real conflict is going to occur, but the behaviour, that is, conflict behaviour, may be constrained by other factors, as well.

BODALEV: You seem to differentiate between the real and not a real intergroup conflict or psycho-social conflict. Could you give a definition of a real psycho-social conflict?

HOLMES: I don't understand what you mean by "psycho-social conflict".

KIESLER: Social psychological conflict.

ANDREEVA: Maybe you feel there is a difference between social intergroup conflict and social aspects of intergroup conflict, and social psychological aspects of conflict. What are specific social psychological aspects of intergroup conflict, in comparison with social aspects of intergroup conflict? Can we study intergroup conflict from the point of view of social psychology?

HOLMES: We're getting back to an issue we talked about before. Some of these variables are sociological variables, such as status for example . . . .

BODALEV: Putting it in another way, when you talk about conflicts, what is the social psychological content which must be present to conform to the definition of conflict?

HOLMES: The social conflict itself is not defined in terms of social psychological content. If one wants to say that conflict is occuring, one can create a syndrome of behaviours and attitudes to define conflict. The social psychological aspects relate to the *causes* of these changes in attitudes and behaviour. For instance — the cause might have to do with economic competition; this theory tries to show how economic conflict would have social psychological consequences.

STROEBE: How do you tie it in with Tajfel? You seem to be talking more about conflict of interest than its consequences, and not really taking into account what Tajfel and his collaborators later called "social conflict", that is the phenomenon by which, because you want to belong to the superior group and status is only there in limited quantities, you may downgrade the other group in order to belong to the superior group.

HOLMES: Is that what I said or is that what Tajfel said?

STROEBE: That's what Tajfel said.

HOLMES: That's also what I said, exactly.

STROEBE: Yes, but it would then follow that you would always or nearly always have outgroup downgrading . . . .

HOLMES: No, only if we have the social threat, and the group is already differentiated from the other group. Maybe one problem is that most Canadians and Americans have not seen Tajfel's theory.

KIESLER: Nor the Holmes theory.

HOLMES: What I depended on were his articles with Billig and with others that were in the *European Journal of Social Psychology* up to a year ago. There, the motivational component of his model was a generic norm in its first statement; this I didn't believe in and I didn't understand. Because of limitations of my own, I really do not understand his theory yet — I'll have to read it again. But from his earlier statements, I would feel he's susceptible to some of the same criticisms, that is, for not having a motivational component to his theory — that it's too cognitive.

ANDREEVA: The question about the cohesiveness of the ingroup, was that your own definition or is this what you are citing common in the literature?

HOLMES: It's derived from Cartwright and Zander and Lott and Lott, *Psychological Bulletin*, 1965.

ANDREEVA: In this definition, cohesiveness has three characteristics: a syndrome of attraction, and then conformity pressures, and finally the feelings of solidarity. When an ingroup perceives a threat from an outgroup, do all three factors which indicate cohesiveness undergo a change, or only one or some of them?

HOLMES: The evidence would suggest that all undergo change, but much recent research has simply used attraction to fellow members as a definition for cohesiveness. These studies are not yet informative on that point.

ANDREEVA: How long does the effect of increased cohesiveness exist after the real or perceived danger has passed?

HOLMES: In many of the studies, the threat is a persistent one, the threat continues over a period of time. In other studies, such as natural disasters, the cohesion exists for only a short period of time after the threat is removed. I think because status differences between people start to re-emerge.

ANDREEVA: Did you study, or are there studies on, the *significance* of factors causing the threat? Does that have an influence? Dependence on the significance of factors may be different in different instances, if for example the threat concerns very meaningful factors for the life of the group, as opposed to less meaningful factors.

HOLMES: I have not seen any direct comparisons between them. Maybe John Berry will know some from the cultural records. I don't.

BERRY: The only one I know of is the Harvey Campbell and Levine cooperative ethnocentrism proposal of ten years ago. That was published, I think, in the *Journal of Conflict Resolution,* and there is now a series of twelve to fourteen field studies published by Human Relations Press at Yale. Maybe if you were to do a comparison across those field studies, you might find some answers to your questions.

The Socio-psychological Approach to Personality

E. V. SHOROKHOVA

Man is the supreme value in the world and the sole creator of his own personal life. Man's essence, and the social prerequisites and conditions for the development of his personality, are the central research problems of philosophy, sociology, economics, politics and ideology. Goethe once said that the main subject in studies of mankind is man himself. The Marxists deserve credit for elaborating the only true scientific theory which, while being a prescription for the liberation of the working class, is also a prescription for the liberation and development of personality.

Human individuals live and act in society, in conditions of necessary mutual relations, rather than in isolation, or spontaneously, or by mere chance. These necessary interrelationships, which are based on production relations, determine in the long run the character of human history itself.

On the basis of his activities (first and foremost on his production activities) man, while assuming his social essence, at the same time sets himself apart as a socio-psychological system. While he is a social being, man is, at the same time, a particular individual with his own inner world, with psychological qualities and properties inherent only in him. Marxism has revealed the social essence of man, and has elaborated the correct methodology for further investigations of man. Vladimir Ilyich Lenin pointed out that Marxism focuses on certain social relations, and, hence, it focuses on concrete individuals, whose actions create these relations.

The social essence of man is reflected in his personal qualities, and human individuality is social in character. It is impossible, however, to *equate* man as a personality with man as a social being. Every man is a unity of the general, the special and the singular, that is, of his social, anthropological, biological and psychological components. It is necessary to investigate man as an entity consisting of these components, constantly reminding oneself of their inseparable link with some concrete situation in his life. Many representatives of so-called philosophical anthropology regard man not as an integral personality, but as a being having several different spheres of existence. The essence of man is reduced to his individual, anthropological existence, while the social function of man is presented as something external, somehow in alienation to his real essence. Marxism, in its approach to the social essence of man, reveals the mutual bond of man and the medium he lives in.

In his notes on James Mill's book, Marx wrote that if the true community bond *(Gemeinwesen)* of people is their human essence, then people, in the process of the active implementation of this essence, create or produce community bonds (their social essence); this is not some abstract, universal force that is in some way in opposition to the concept of the single individual, but rather the essence of every separate individual — his own activity, his own life, his own delight, his own wealth.[1]

The classics of Marxism-Leninism repeatedly point to the fact that the essence of man became fully revealed only in society. "The actual spiritual wealth of an individual wholly depends on the wealth of his real relations . . . ."[2] The social determination of man's behaviour is primary. "Only in community with others has each individual the means of cultivating his gifts in all directions: only in community, therefore, is personal freedom possible."[3]

(1) See the above mentioned notes of K. Marx printed in Russian for the first time in: *Voprosy filosofil* (Questions of Philosophy), 1966, No. 2, p. 119.
(2) K. Marx and F. Engels, *Works* (in Russian), Vol. 3, p. 36.
(3) *Ibid.*, p. 75.

In the long run, everything in personality turns out to be socially determined. At the same time, the natural basis of man (the properties of his organism, the peculiarities of his higher nervous activity) forms the conditions under the influence of which (or against the background of which) social determination is implemented. It is necessary to take into account the heterogeneous aspects of social determination for the determinist approach to psychological phenomena. In nature transformed by man, and in society created by man, there exist various determinative factors; these are themselves changed in different ways depending on changes in socio-economic conditions. These factors include the development of nature which has been transformed by man, the social development of mankind and the individual history of man. These factors stipulate, in different ways, the different processes, properties, qualities of psychological phenomena, as well as different degrees and rates of the changeability of these phenomena in the course of the ontogenetic development of man.

The properties and processes which are subject to the greatest socio-historical changes in personality are those which reflect the social conditions of man's life, and his attitude toward the phenomena of social life. In the course of socio-economic development, changes occur in the content of motives and in the correlation of personal and social interests. Changes in the psychological makeup of people (which are stipulated by the social system), as well as in their behaviour and actions, are basically the same for all people living in a certain socio-historical epoch. In certain instances, general social conditions combine in different ways with the specific living conditions and the activities of a separate individual. The general acts only through the specific, and is revealed in the individual. The individual development of every man is determined by the peculiar correlation of external and internal conditions. In the individual history of man's development, stable properties and qualities are molded and those peculiar features are formed which determine the uniqueness of personality.

Science must promote the arrangement of social life; this

arrangement should correspond to the true essence of man, making it possible for him to assimilate and use the experience and knowledge accumulated by mankind; it must provide boundless possibilities for man's perfection. For this purpose, it is necessary to study and develop, in harmonious unity, both the common, socially significant properties of personality and the unique qualities of personality and the special form of their revelation.

The traits of personality, which are molded in the sphere of social relations, are generally manifested as its specific socio-psychological peculiarities. The task of social psychology in personality research is that of analysing the psychological peculiarities in which the social character of a person is manifested. It involves the analysis of the conditions which form him as a social being, giving rise to those common psychological peculiarities that become the national, occupational and class features which prevail in a given society, at a given time and under given circumstances.

In defining the specifics of socio-psychological knowledge, we proceed from the conceptions of certain Soviet authors (e.g., S.L. Rubinshtein, A.V. Brushlinsky) who argue that psychology in general, and social psychology in particular, ought primarily to study psychological processes. Political economy sees man primarily as the main productive force. For sociology, personality may be seen as the product of social relations, as the subject of social life, as an element of the social system, or as a member of a certain social community. Through certain of its social functions, personality becomes involved in the system of social relations. Sociology is interested in personality, Jadov states — "not as an individuality, but as a depersonalized personality, as a social type, as a deindividualized, depersonalized personality".[4]

(4) V.A. Jadov "O razilichnykh podkhodakh k knotsepsil lichnosti i swayazannykh s nimi razlichnykh zadachakh issledovaniya massovykh kommunikatsii" (On the different approaches to the conception of personality and the various tasks connected with them in the research of mass communications). In the collection *Lichnost i Massoviye Kommunikatsii* (Personality and Mass Communications), Issue III, Tartu, 1969, p. 13.

Borrowing from the general and specific laws of social development revealed by sociology, social psychology investigates the formation of the personality's inner world, which is manifested in its individual psychological peculiarities and specific content of its activity.

The characteristics of personality as a product of social circumstances, its structure, the role functions of personality and their influence of social life — these constitute the initial points for socio-psychological analysis of personality; all the forms of social influence over personality are investigated in the process of their inception, development and formation. The characteristics of a certain nation, class and occupation appear in the psychological makeup of the individual personality, in its motives, feelings and intentions. "The correlation between personal and objective class features is both complex and indirect, because it is obvious that there are socio-psychological distinctions among members of one and the same class; people who are objectively in the same set of conditions may react differently, at times in quite the opposite way to the same phenomena; people belonging to different social groups may display common consciousness and behaviour. If social functions and roles assigned to individuals are regarded impersonally, along with the sources of influence as elements of a social system, then socio-psychological vision presumes the analysis of how these functions, roles and influence are incarnated in the internal structure of personality."[5]

The socio-psychological aspect of the study of personality involves the analysis of laws governing the formation of its internal psychological structure and the function that the personality fulfills in controlling its own behaviour. These laws are revealed concretely in different psychological aspects of man and in the spheres of his vital activities. Among these spheres, however, there are some where socio-psychological and personal factors are very closely connected. Let us consider some of these spheres.

(5) Yu.A. Zamoshkin, "Sotsialnaya psikhologiya" (Social Psychology), *Filosofskaya Entsiklopediya* (Philosophy Encyclopedia), Vol. 5, p. 78.

In the process of personality formation and in the process of the ontogenetic development of man, the influence of social factors becomes especially noticeable. The process of the socialization of personality takes place in the constant intercourse between the person and society. The social roles of personality are learned. Both sociological and socio-psychological laws govern the process of the assimilation of social roles by personality, and the fulfillment by personality of its role functions; these laws also govern the assimilation of social ideas, culture, norms, and their influence on personality. Man occupies a specific place in the system of social relations. This objective situation is consciously realized by the personality. The personality's *sets*, and its subjective attitudes toward itself (as well as its assessments, its orientation, and the system of behaviour motives and convictions) constitute the nucleus of the socio-psychological characteristics of personality. On the one hand, the social status of personality, the totality of its social relations, are reflected in all these components; on the other, these components also reflect a certain kind of autonomy of the personality, its relative independence and its specific character in the system of social life. The study of the mechanism of the influence of social factors on both the shaping of the personality and the laws governing the functioning of personality as a socio-psychological formation constitutes the main aspect of the multifaceted socio-psychological investigation of personality.

In setting up personality as a separate object of socio-psychological research, we must regard both personality and the collective as two united, inseparable components. In actuality, they seem to be just two different levels of a socio-psychological investigation. In the long run there is no social psychology which would not be simultaneously the psychology of personalities in certain relations to one another. The social behaviour of man is stipulated by his belonging to a certain community. Changes in personality stemming from the influence of other people can be either transient or stable. A given social community — be it a class, collective or group — influences not only consciousness, attitudes and positions, but the concrete activities of man. Socio-psychological investigations have shown that, in a collective, a person demonstrates stronger will, discipline and persistence in attaining a goal than if he were to strive for it alone. Among factors intensifying the effect of collective activities on man is the collective's spirit of emulation and cooperation. The creation of a general psychological atmosphere in the collective is the result of the individual contributions made by separate personalities. This was pointed out by Engels when he wrote: "But from the fact that the wills of the individuals — each of whom desires what he is impelled to by his physical constitution and external, in the last resort, economic circumstances (either his own personal circumstances or those of society in general) — do not attain what they want, but are merged into an aggregate mean, a common resultant, it must not be concluded that they are equal to zero."[6] The more or less stable economic, political, cultural and other social conditions determine the class, national, and occupational peculiarities of personality, creating, in their entirety, a communal typology of personality.

The study of this communal typology, the actual position of the personality in the collective, the conscious realization by man of this position, and his interrelations with the collective as a whole and within the collective constitute the necessary prerequisite for solving any socio-psychological problems of personality.

Personality as "social being" is formed, and it functions in the process of its constant interrelations with other people. One of the mechanisms of these interrelations is social intercourse.[7] Social intercourse is a need of man. Together with productive work, it is a source of social development. Not only is the social essence of man formed and realized through social intercourse, but his individual characteristics are revealed. Intercourse constitutes the core characteristic of the collective

(6) K. Marx and F. Engels, *The German Ideology*, Progress Publishers, Moscow, 1964, p. 91.
(7) This is another translation of *obshcheniye*, discussed in this book by Andreeva (p. 57).

174   *E. V. Shorokhova*

activities of people and the activity of the personality in the collective. It is an important factor for developing personality. The assimilation of experience is implemented, not only in activity, but in social intercourse as a specifically human method of organizing activity. The study of mass media and their role in the cultural life of personality occupies a special place in investigating the problems of social intercourse. The investigation of the impact of mass media on personality is not limited merely to the enumeration of forms of information distribution and the description of information content, but it must include analysis of the psychological laws governing its impact on man. This means that the socio-psychological aspect of mass media must include attention to the problem of the development of personality with the help of mass media.

The perception of Man, i.e., Man's generalized "knowledge" about people, influences joint activity, determining its content, its process and its results. When a person consciously implements his attitude toward people, he thus influences their attitude toward him. The assessment standards, stereotypes and attitudes of these people come to life in interaction with the person they evaluate; in turn, they stipulate a peculiar impression which this person makes on each of them.

Socio-psychological aspects of personality investigation embrace all the phenomena of the so-called psychology of influence. Among these phenomena are suggestion, conviction, imitation, fashion and so on. Some bourgeois sociologists and social psychologists are of the opinion that, due to the scientific and technological revolution of modern society, with its elaborate means of mass influence, the patterns of mass culture make people conform to standards, eliminating the problem of the individualized personality or the specific features of personality's inner world. This, however, is only true of capitalist society. In the formation of communist society, socio-economic progress presumes the all-round development of personality, its cultural florescence. Under socialism, personality does not suffer the imperative pressure of stereotyped demands, or the dictate of fast-changing vogues, or the sharp changes of mass moods — phenomena which are so typical of bourgeois society. Social conditions under socialism promote the harmonious and integral development of personality with a rich spectrum of its individual peculiarities.

In describing the prospects for the development of social intercourse in conditions of communist society, Karl Marx stressed that one of the highest criteria for the perfection of human relations must be their adequacy at the level of cultural values, which individuals exchange among themselves in the process of their social intercourse. The genuine attitude of people toward each other should consist of one's association of each person with the values that correspond to his essence. Marx wrote that "If you are to presume Man as Man, and his relation to the world at large as the human attitude, then you can exchange love only for love, trust only for trust, and so on. If you wish to delight in art, you must be a person educated in art. If you wish to influence people, you must be a person really stimulating and encouraging other people. Every one of your attitudes to Man and to Nature must be definite, corresponding to the object of your will, a manifestation of your real individual life."[8]

Among the problems which social psychology considers in its concern with personality, a special place is accorded to the problem of value orientations. In relations between the individual and objective reality, one must consider the assessment by Man of whatever is taking place, and the correlations of personality needs with the objective possibilities for their satisfaction. The search for the meaning of things, phenomena, events, and interpersonal relations serves as a powerful stimulus for behaviour. On the one hand, value orientations express the social status of a person; on the other hand, they express behaviour stipulated by demands, needs, and personal properties. A hierarchy of values expresses the hierarchy of needs of a person, revealing the different sides, aspects and levels of his essence. The individual and the social, personal and communal

(8) K. Marx and F. Engels, *From the Early Works* (in Russian), Moscow, 1956, p. 620.

176 E. V. Shorokhova

merge in one tendency. "In everyday practice, however, we constantly come up against instances when the conscious intentions of people are far from being in agreement with their actual behaviour. A still greater contradiction is often seen in verbally stated 'programmes' of action, and real actions observed from aside in a certain situation. This unquestionable fact is the subject of investigation of sociologists, psychologists, pedagogues, and other specialists in social sciences investigating the mechanisms of the social behaviour of people."[9] Value orientations serve as a form of the interconnections of personality with social groups. Through them the problems of personality are included in the subject of socio-psychological research. Sociology investigates the real positions of a person, or the system of actions of a personality. The process of formation of value orientations and psychological mechanisms in controlling value orientations are investigated with respect to real behaviour of personality in specific socio-historical conditions and concrete socio-psychological situations.

In summary, the socio-psychological approach to personality is realized in research (1) on the social determination of the psychological aspect of personality; (2) on the social motivation of the personality's behaviour and activity in various socio-historical and socio-psychological conditions; (3) on class, national and occupational aspects of personality; (4) on the analysis of the laws governing the formation and manifestation of the social activity of personality, and the ways and means for increasing this activity; (5) on the problems of inner contradictions in personality and the ways for overcoming them; (6) on the elaboration of problems for the self-development of personality; and (7) on the establishment of the psychic cast of the personality of a new communist society.

Discussion

KIESLER: I'm still not sure I understand the Soviet use of the term "personality".

(9) See "Lichnost i eyo tsennostniye orientatsil" (Personality and its value orientations), *Informatsionny byuleten* (Information bulletin), IKSI AN SSSR i SSA, Moscow, No. 19, p. 2.

Sometimes it seems to mean simply individual psychology, or very close to what we would think of as cognitive psychology; other times it's close to character. It might be helpful if you could differentiate between "personality" and "character".

SHOROKHOVA: Soviet psychologists, probably as with most other psychologists, distinguish between "an individual" and "personality". When we describe an "individual", we ascribe to him many biological and social qualities of man (for example characteristics of temperament, physical height, colour of eyes, hair, and so on), those physical attributes which distinguish one particular individual from another. When we talk about "personality", we consider mainly social psychological qualities.

HOLMES: Is personality viewed as relatively stable across situations? Is there much attention in Russian social psychology as to the predictive power of stable characteristics of the person compared to the predictive power of temporary or situational aspects of the person?

SHOROKHOVA: Personality is a stable formation which is formed in the context of varying social conditions and thus it appears as a stable formation in its relationship to the surrounding environment.

LOMOV: I think I might paraphrase that question, by offering an example; take a particular quality or attribute of the personality, say courage or bravery — would it remain with a person under all circumstances?

SHOROKHOVA: Personality is a complex of particular mental qualities, on the whole stable under different circumstances. According to certain specific parameters, "bravery" will appear in a way appropriate to that personality; but if conditions change radically, the manifestation of such personality qualities might undergo a change. Under certain very considerable changes of environment, the person might manifest a behaviour which is in apparent contradiction with his usual personality.

HOLMES: Am I to assume, then, that Russian psychologists have been successful in predicting behaviour from measures of individual personality? In North America, psychology has not had that distinction.

SHOROKHOVA: We try to predict the *development* of personality by studying the personality traits and the conditions in which personality is formed. The whole system of education is based on a model of this type, that is, to develop desirable personality traits. But Russian psychologists do not have too much experimental work, and the operational model itself is not too clear, much as it is in your own case.

BODALEV: I would like to tell Professor Holmes that Professor Jadov is working exactly on those questions that you have asked. He and his colleagues are trying to determine the most significant situations for any particular person, and they want to establish correlations between the situations and the most important personal characteristics in value orientations of people. And given knowledge of a particular person's value orientation, they predict with great accuracy the behaviour of that person in any particular situation.

ANDREEVA: May I briefly describe this schema of Jadov? He calls it the "dispositional conception of the regulation of social behaviour" and it is a hierarchy of four different levels of personal dispositions. Uznadze shows that each disposition is situated between a need and a corresponding situation. At the lowest level Jadov puts "set", in the sense that Professor Uznadze has used it — it's an old notion in Western social psychology, too. "Attitudes" are higher level dispositions. At the lowest level, a man meets only his simplest needs and acts in simplest situations. At the second level — the level of more complex attitudes, he has other higher needs, and acts in different kinds of situations. Next, at the third level, Jadov puts "value orientation" as a higher kind of disposition. Finally, Jadov posits a "general orientation ot personality". This disposition is between the highest level of social needs and the highest level of situations in which the personality acts. Jadov tries to explain each case of personality behaviour not only with the help of *set*, or not only with the help of *attitude*, but with the help of this entire system of dispositions. This attempt resembles those of Western social psychologists such as Rokeach or Fishbein, but Jadov came in another way to the same things, and it was the Marxist orientation of Jadov that helped him to develop this system or this hierarchy as a whole. Each action of man involves the influences of all kinds of dispositions, and the result of this action can be understood only if we interpret it within the whole context of social activity of this man.

MARSHALL: This question refers to a previous discussion as well as to the present one, and also to a comment by Dr. Lomov about the puzzlement in Soviet psychology about the place of subjective experience — the mental event. You also describe personality as a complex of characteristics, and you describe these as co-determined by biological and social variables moving through space. Here is a puzzle for any nation: how do you get from the one set of phenomena to the other? What interests me very much is to learn what concepts within current Soviet philosophy of science, philosophy of psychology, address themselves to this very problematic relationship.

LOMOV: Could you perhaps ask something a little easier?

MARSHALL: Yes, sir — what is the relationship between mind and body?

LOMOV: Of course, this is a difficult problem. In Soviet psychology mental pheno-mena are considered as different forms of subjective reflection of objective reality. But in general it is easier to put this question than to answer it.

MARSHALL: I understand your response.

BUEVA: I specialize in the *philosophical* aspects of personality and I would like to say something about discussions that exist in this field. A first problem involves the parameters which determine the whole personality. If we were to look only at value orientations or only at the system of needs, or at any other qualities we would fractionate personality, and study only parts of it in our laboratories. In order to understand the integration of these qualities, then we have to address ourselves to the study of the various levels and to the effects of introduction of certain other systems into the level at which personality is being studied. We believe that personality consists of a system of personal qualities and that the biological base gives us the dynamics of the system.

   We have a very unique natural demonstration which shows that the personality system is formed socially, and this involves experiments by Professor Mescherikoff with deaf, dumb and blind children. This experiment is particularly important because it shows the importance of *activity* in the formation of consciousness. The primary level of human mentality is determined not by verbal communication, but by the acquisition of values through contact with objects in the physical surroundings. A person must master human activity with objects. Unfortunately, we still do not have materials for comparative analysis of the formation of mental processes in children. In cases where children were born with deformities from thalidomide, they were incapable of forming their processes through physical activity, through interacting with the objects surrounding them. Thus, it would be interesting to make a comparative study of the development with those that are available.

MARSHALL: To what extent has the work of Jean Piaget been influential in the development of such ideas in Soviet psychology? It seems to me that the notion of interaction with the environment in the formation of personality is, in a sense, very much a Piagetian concept, and I wonder historically what the relationship has been.

ANDREEVA: The works of Piaget are well known in the Soviet Union and we have a number of our own specialists, for example Vycutsky, Leontiev and Galperin, who have done similar or parallel studies.

ABOUD: About the issue of personality *vs.* situational factors, I think North American social psychologists have had a problem in resolving that, primarily because they see situational factors as variable; they never look at social or situational factors that are stable. I get the feeling that the Soviet study of personality looks a lot more at those class or ethnic factors that are stable.

SHOROKHOVA: You are both correct and incorrect — dialectics should be applied to your answer. When we study personality, we begin with the premise that personality reflects general and social conditions of its existence, that personality possesses traits which are determined by one's belonging to a particular class, to a nation, to a profession. In contrast, it appears that when North Americans speak about the role of personality in a particular environment or situation, what is meant is only the immediate environment. Although I might be wrong, it appears that when you consider the immediate environment, you are not aware of the wider factors that determine personality. It seems you should consider a wider environment, an environment which is wider than the sum of its parts, when you study personality in a particular situation. But when you study personality in a particular situation, it is important to choose a situation that has a social significance.

C. THEORY, METHODOLOGY AND ETHICS

Damned if We Do — Damned if We Don't

PAUL G. SWINGLE

Every year I have the opportunity to offer a few workshops on the subject of behavioral science to groups of senior level managers. During the course of the introductory material I usually describe a couple of relatively straightforward experiments demonstrating manipulation without awareness. I ask the course participants to put themselves in the position of manager of a large store or restaurant. I then explain the relationship between arousal and performance. Namely, that as we increase the level of arousal of an organism we increase the probability of occurrence of the most probable response of that organism. Hence, if a person is shopping and we can increase the level of that person's arousal, that person should shop more rapidly. Presumably, there should be no important influence upon the actual nature of the behavior taking place, but simply that the behavior will take place more rapidly.

Similarly, diners in a restaurant should eat more rapidly, or more leisurely, depending upon whether we increase or decrease their level of arousal. After discussing the relationship between arousal and performance, I then comment upon why the manager of a large supermarket or restaurant might wish to influence the speed of behavior. Spreading out shoppers during peak periods, increasing the number of diners one could serve

181

on busy evenings, or encouraging more leisurely dining on slow evenings are the usual examples offered.

The procedure for accomplishing this is contained in the study by Smith and Curnow (1966) and in some of the architectural and environmental literature. Basically, one simply varies the level of background stimulation by manipulating sound and illumination. There are, of course, many factors other than background illumination and sound which influence behavior, such as the arrangement of furniture in a room, the degree of openness of the interior of a building, the peripheral inventory of interior thoroughfares, and so on. For the purposes of the management workshop, however, I suggest only the manipulation of background sound and illumination.

The proposal that I offer these people, again following the scenario of managers of busy supermarkets or restaurants, is to install a number of counting devices such as photo-electric cells and a couple of micro-processors which will keep track of the number of people in specific areas of the store or restaurant. When it becomes desirable to speed up or slow down behavior of persons in those areas, the background stimulation in the designated areas is gradually increased or decreased depending upon how the manager has decided to program the unit. The people in those areas increase or decrease their performance speed and they are unaware of any manipulation.

I indicate that our expectations for this traffic control system would be of the order of 5-10% of the person's operant speed. Further, the evidence indicates that there are no changes in the buying behavior of people exposed to such treatments, their evaluation of the pleasantness of the environment appears to be unaffected, they do not seem to buy any more or any less, they simply do what they were going to do but they do it more rapidly. I also point out that due to the technological revolution in the microprocessor and integrated circuit fields, the cost of such a system would be trivial, assuming, of course, that they already possess lighting and background music systems which would not have to be drastically modified to accomplish our ends. The question I then put to the managers is, "May I have the contract to proceed?"

The purpose of this exercise, of course, is to stimulate a discussion addressed to the problem of the ethics and morality of managing and controlling people. The responses I received from the managers are highly predictable and normally cover such things as disbelief that the system will work, at which time I offer them a guarantee that if not satisfied we will take the system away at no charge; to the question, "Won't the customers be offended by this system?" I emphasize that customers will never have to know that a control system is in use because the increase in ambient stimulation is extremely gradual and is not perceived by the individuals. Concerns and comments more relevant to the ethics of the situation include the "worse peril argument" (i.e., this manipulation is trivial relative to the kinds of controls upon behavior that we are all exposed to every day), the problem of controlling excesses in the use of such technology without informed consent, the realization that in general it is the person who is capable of paying for the technology who determines its use, and finally, a concern about just how far people could go in terms of the application of behavioral control technology. The workshop session generally concludes with a discussion about the likelihood of some sort of technological explosion which will render behavioral science technology dangerous to individual freedom and dignity. That, of course, is an extremely complex issue and one of very great contemporary concern.

In the above example, the application of the behavioral principle is dependent not upon any great advances in psychology, for we knew about the arousal — performance trade-off for some time, but rather rests upon the enormous explosion in electronic technology which rendered the cost of the development of such a system economically feasible. According to Toong (1976) the cost per bit of data processing capability has gone from approximately $20.00 in 1962 to about 1¢ in 1976. This technological explosion has, of course, generated its own set of concerns which varies from the development of electronic goliaths which simply befuddle those people who are supposed to be responsible for them to the problem of privacy.

The Crisis of Confidence in Social Psychology

However, with respect to the potential for technological explosion in the area of behavioral science, social psychologists at present seem to be in an era of self-questioning and lamentation. In fact, we are fatigued of being exposed to hand-wringing articles discussing the crisis in social psychology, and how our best scientists are floundering about, attempting to find meaningful paradigms and research methodologies. Many social psychologists have pointed out that it is all a game in which one simply determines what trivia one can readily publish and then assuming the attitude that such trivia are important and meritorious. Others have pointed out that we really do not have a behavioral technology of any value and hence, other than taking precautions for the problems associated with unchecked power and cultural pollution, the question of ethics in social psychology is quite beside the point. Others have pointed out that we do not really have a science, but rather that social psychology might be more reasonably conceptualized as social history and thus we can never make any lasting or generalizable discoveries (Gergen, 1973). In short, we seem to be in a period of depression and eroded confidence which stands in marked contrast to the infectious enthusiasm and self-confidence which characterized the field only a score or so years ago (Elms, 1975).

It is important to note that social psychology is not the only discipline which seems to be going through an era of self-questioning and self-doubt. In fact, it is not difficult to encounter hand-wringing articles lamenting the lack of meaningful progress in other disciplines. Medicine has been recently chastised as being a serious threat to health, the destructive impact of technology upon our environment is extensively documented and commentators on the other social sciences have questioned the value of their disciplines (Elms, 1975). North American society seems to be in a self-questioning stance, with some evidence of a resurgence of interest in religion, more primitive lifestyles, the occult, etc.

It is no coincidence, I think, that coincident with the era of self-questioning and lost confidence, we have a large body of prophet-of-doom literature. In short, social psychologists, like many other people, see hunger, environmental destruction, slavery, and a multitude of other forms of human pain and suffering, and realize that we have 50,000 tons of destructive capability for every man, woman and child on earth. Such a realization may lead one to conclude that we must be the lunatic asylum for the galaxy, if not the universe. The despair and lack of confidence expressed by many social psychologists, then, may simply reflect the fact that they believe that the situation is so far out of hand as to be hopeless, and that no discipline is likely to make much of a contribution towards setting things straight.

There is a tendency for such discontent to be converted into radicalism, the belief that the problems we face must be dealt with politically. We are slowly beginning to realize that the lack of application of knowledge need not indicate theoretical bankruptcy in the social sciences. We have decidedly fallen victim to the fallacious belief that knowledge implies control. The application of knowledge, as Rapoport (1975) has pointed out, depends upon the existence of institutions to carry out such applications. For example, the problem facing peace researchers is that no agency exists for the application of such technology. Hence, if we assume that war is structural, in that war-making agencies deliberately plan and execute wars, then satisfying the peace researchers' goal may require that such agencies be undermined, or something tantamount to a Pentagon for Peace be developed.

The primal scream for relevance gave rise to many interesting responses by social psychologists. The diversity of the responses supports the principle that we must include person parameters in our paradigm (Hampden-Turner, 1971). Many of the reactions to the demands for relevance are not threats to society. The tendency for laboratory-based researchers to preface talks, books, articles and so on with statements about time donated to human rights groups, royalty donations to charity and the like are generally designed to ward off attack by those who feel that using public money for issues which seem irrelevant to society's needs contributes to the maintenance of the exploitative *status quo*. Social psychologists are natural targets for such attacks because we have not heeded the advice to label variables with Roman numerals rather than with terms to which the laity attach significance.

A serious consequence of the disquiet which overcame some social psychologists when confronted with the demand to demonstrate their worth was to scurry into the field. Ethology had become fashionable, and prophets of doom achieved positions of considerable prominence. Recognizing that we were prone to disparage the more qualitatively oriented social sciences, the furtive whisperings of social psychologists about the sorry state of our preparedness to deal with socially important issues gave way to emigration from the laboratory to the world at large. The dashing about in the real world in search of research sanctuaries from the Zeitgeist gave rise, in my judgement, to serious cultural pollution. That pollution derived from the unsophisticated transference of the laboratorians' methodological armamentarium to field situations. Rather than confronting the serious epistemological and ethical issues surrounding natural field experimentation, some social psychologists tore part of a sheet from the clinician's handbook and asserted that good intentions and a desire to cure justified certain indignities. The second part of the torn sheet, that dealing with the obligation to demonstrate the cure or benefit, and the requirement of shared goals, was frequently ignored.

It comes as no surprise to experimental social psychologists that control is the only discontinuity of any import between the laboratory and the field. However, although control and manipulation are, in my judgement, acceptable in laboratory contexts, they decidedly are not methods of choice in field situations. Unsophisticated application of our powerful research capabilities represent serious threats to the freedom and dignity of social psychologists as well as to society at large. We have subjected unsuspecting people, who are simply carrying out their day-to-day activities, to indignities which violate canons of ethical behavior, if not the law (Silverman, 1975; Wilson and Donnerstein, 1976). The argument that control agencies in our society are engaged in unobtrusive surveillance, and that marketing and advertising people systematically attempt to manipulate our behavior to such an extent that our feeble efforts do not constitute a peril is, I think, erroneous.

In this era of blame attribution it has become fashionable to denounce various sources of knowledge. The experimental methodologies tend to be subjected to considerable criticism and we have been warned that reliance upon such techniques is teleological; linear, causal models have been attacked as being inconsistent with the state of the world at large, and if we are not cautious, the theories built upon such models can seduce us into developing Ptolemaic systems complete with elegant epicycles which a Copernicus with his 105 IQ (Cox, 1926) can upset.

Hence, social psychologists have good reason to be cautious. We are accused of playing games (Ring, 1967), breaking the law (Silverman, 1975), polluting the social environment (Kelman, 1968), developing theories which are inconsistent with the essential nature of the social environment (Hampden-Turner, 1971), or not having any major theoretical basis at all (Arrowwood, 1975). We are told that we do not understand the concept of social issues (Rappoport and Kren, 1975) much less being able to do something about them. In fact, some have stated that areas of research must be "rescued" from scientists (Mann, 1974), and that relative to the truths of novelists, what we have to offer are fictions (Čook, 1977). We have been repeatedly told that we do not have a powerful paradigm (Secord, 1977), and we have been advised to cut back on our publishing rate (Elms, 1975). Our funding becomes suspect when we accept money from institutions involved in activities which are considered socially unacceptable. We are told that we are often deluded into thinking that what we do makes any difference at all (Boulding, 1976), or conversely, that any really relevant research is crushed by vested interests (Goodwin and Tu, 1975).

Finally, we are told that we do not read or recognize the truths which appear in books or journals other than those in our own very narrow fields of interest.

Ethics

There is pretty good evidence that Cyril Burt falsified data. This dishonesty had serious implications since his contention that 85% of an individual's performance on IQ tests was attributable to inherited characteristics influenced immigration and educational policies which seriously disadvantaged countless thousands of people (Kamin, 1974). Dishonesty in the sciences is widely known, there are many examples in parapsychology, medicine, physiological psychology and so on, and I suspect that many, if not most of us, have discovered a graduate student or two who has massaged data in one form or other.

Unfortunately the serious problems associated with developing an ethical code for social psychology are not as simple as the straightforward question of dishonesty. We have problems associated with incompetence, professionalism, indifference, the pathological effect of the meritocracy, as well as the problems associated with beneficent social interventions, either for research or therapeutic purpose, which threaten the freedom and dignity of people in our society.

Although concern with ethics is fundamental to much of the self-questioning extant among social psychologists today, no ethical statement is ever complete. Hence, the following remarks represent the author's response to the growing commentaries surrounding these issues.

In my judgement, the problem of informed consent is central to much of the squabbling that is going on in social psychology presently. There are those who maintain that no violations of the principle of informed consent are tolerable in a socially responsible science of human behavior. There are others who feel that there are conditions which justify exceptions to this rule. Someone has written that someone who steals from a thief is guilty of no crime and one hears many psychologists arguing that research and/or therapeutic activity designed to understand or reduce the incidence of socially destructive behavior need not be hampered by the obligation to obtain informed consent.

The APA committee which addressed itself to this issue concluded that they could not establish a "Thou shalt not" commandment but rather suggested that "Thou shalt worry deeply, consult with others sincerely, and be prepared to justify thy decision to thy peers and the public", if considerations of scientific gain seem to justify a limited compromise of ethical ideals (Smith, 1975).

The Risk/Fun Model

Many have taken exception to the above position, arguing that most cost/gain analyses are inappropriate for determining ethical issues. The only risk/benefit model acceptable to most every researcher is that the knowledge gained must be converted into benefit to the person who is the subject of investigation (Rommetveit, 1972; Baumrind, 1975).

The principle problem with risk/benefit models is generally not the estimation of risk, but rather the estimation of benefit. In the scramble to be relevant many social psychologists went into the field with poorly conceived, sensationalized research sanctioned by the incantation of the scientists' creed, "I am working on the frontiers of knowledge and I am mandated to find out things about social behavior". The mantle of scientific respectability has been thrown over much regrettable field research because scientists have agreed to cant that caring is as important as curing, and that knowledge gained can justify imprudent compromises of ethical ideals.

If we modify the risk/benefit model somewhat, I think the problem can be solved. The new model would be of a risk/fun type. A researcher must be able to justify risk to subjects on the basis of personal enjoyment. We would immediately bring a screeching halt to many of the infringements upon human dignity brought about by sanctimonious social scientists claiming to be working for the betterment of humankind.

The Demise of the James Bond Myth

The following research project was conceived and executed because it was fun. I have had occasion to speak with many people who work for control, force, and security agencies. The extent of the hardware side of control technology which these people have revealed to me I find frightening. Horowitz (1970) has discussed the problem of expanding police hardware and my exposure to the people using these techniques has convinced me that behavioral technology is not only alive and well, but extremely powerful. The application of this technology is our ethical responsibility. However, as many activists are quick to point out, one cannot assume responsibility for changing the whole system. Hence, one should start in one's own sphere of influence.

Before relating the research project, I should like to review my feelings about the ethics of this enterprise given that I was receiving information from people who might not have been aware of the type of person they were talking to. You recall earlier I pointed out that Cook (1977) recommended that one consider the truths of novelists rather than the fictions of social scientists. Hence, I feel that it might be appropriate to adopt the ethical stance of a novelist who claims to be writing about true situations. For example, Forsyth (1972) points out in the author's note to his book *The Odessa File* that he does not name his informants for three reasons:

> Some, being former members of the SS, were not aware at the time either who they were talking to or that what they said would end up in a book. Others have specifically asked that their names never be mentioned as sources of information about the SS. In the case of others still, the decision not to mention their names is mine alone, and taken, I hope, for their sakes rather than for mine.

It was brought to my attention that a number of force and security agencies are using subliminal auditory persuasive communications for the purposes of controlling behavior in natural field environments. My initial response to this revelation was to invoke what I like to call the James Bond myth. Namely, if we see some remarkable feat of behavioral science in a psychological science fiction film, we make the assumption that bona fide psychology cannot accomplish anything of comparable magnitude. However, a scan of the literature revealed that such subliminal auditory influences upon behavior were in fact documented. Henley (1975) demonstrated that when the words "happy" and "sad" were presented at subthreshold auditory levels, subjects' judgements of the degree to which suprathreshold, visually presented, neutral faces appeared cheerful or morose were influenced. Further, she points out that the effects of the subliminal cues were found to carry over to trials on which the faces were presented without concurrent auditory stimulation. Henley and Dickson (1974) found that imagery evoked by music presented to one ear was influenced by words arriving below threshold at the other ear.

Fisher (1975, 1976) reports that subliminal messages such as "Lonely, all by myself, I feel sad, sad, sad, and low, I have the blues, lonely, the world is a dreary place, no hope at all, bleak, what's the use, no hope" (Fisher, 1975, p. 92) can influence responses to the Holtzman Ink blots (scored for "Barrier Index"). The effect is prominent for males, is dependent upon priming the subjects, loses effectiveness for males with repetition, can be blocked by a flashing light and is unaffected by the subjects' awareness of the subliminal message, although the effect is not found for supraliminal messages. The stimulus intensity in Fisher's studies was set as 42.5 db in a room with 40 db ambient noise. The message source was 1 meter from the' subject. Three independent judges familiar with the message content were unable to discriminate the presence or absence of the message and no subjects were found to be aware of the message presentation, unless made aware by the experimenter for purposes of the research design.

Enhancement of judgements of stimuli presented in the auditory or visual modality by subliminal sound has been demonstrated by several investigators. Bevan and Pritchard (1963) report that judgements of the loudness of a stimulus can be increased by introducing a tone below auditory threshold. Hardy and Legge (1968) found that visual or auditory thresholds

for neutral stimuli were raised by the presentation of emotional
stimuli at a subliminal level in the other modality. A change
in sensory sensitivity resulting from subliminal auditory emotional and neutral words has also been reported by Broadbent
and Gregory (1967). Finally, Zwosta and Zenhausern (1969)
report the surprising finding that the effects of sound energy
on detection rates for a spot of light in an illuminated masking
field is curvilinear. The maximum effects were found for white
noise presented at 15 db below and 15 db above threshold with
minimal effects at −5, +5, and +10 db.

This finding is in agreement with Dixon's (1971, p. 315)
observation that the "effects of subliminal stimulation are
greatest . . . when the stimulus is well below rather than just
below the awareness threshold . . .".

The question, however, is not so much whether one can
demonstrate the effects of subliminally presented auditory
stimulation in a laboratory context with constrained subjects,
but rather whether one could find evidence of such influence
with unrestrained subjects.

To this end, 18 experimentally sophisticated subjects were
asked to rate 40 slides of paintings borrowed from the Art
Department of the University of Ottawa. Subjects were asked
to rate each painting on six bipolar adjective scales: beautiful-
ugly, dull-exciting, strong-weak, bad-good, warm-cold and
awkward-graceful. Each bipolar adjective set was separated by
a 100 mm line. Subjects were asked to indicate their ratings by
simply drawing a line through the 100 mm line at the point
which corresponded with their assessment of the picture.

Slides were presented for 30 seconds during which time the
subjects were asked to look directly at the picture followed by
30 seconds in which the screen went blank during which time
they were asked to complete the scales. The auditory message
was simply a repetition of either the positive or the negative
adjectives from the above-mentioned scales, or a set of neutral
words. For positive influence, a female voice simply repeated
"beautiful", "exciting", "strong", "good", "warm", and
"graceful". For the negative manipulation, the female voice

repeated "ugly", "dull", "weak", "bad", "cold", and "awkward". The neutral words were "slide", "room", "projector", "student", "desk", and "table". This list of positive, negative or neutral words was repeated continuously at approximately 1 second intervals during the course of the 30 second slide presentation. During the 30 seconds in which the screen went blank and subjects were required to complete their scales, white noise at a comparable db level was presented. The auditory stimuli were presented through a single speaker mounted in the centre of the ceiling of the classroom. The taperecorder was in another room and hence, subjects were unaware of the fact that auditory stimulation was being presented. Five increasing sound levels of background stimulation were presented. The maximum average sound level at ear level below the ceiling speaker was 73 db with peaks to 92 db. The added sound levels measured at the speaker were 61.0 db, 63.3 db, 65.6 db, 67.9 db, and 70 2 db. The level of ambient noise in the empty room was 66 db. The sound levels were determined by having the present investigator stand under the speaker and adjust the sound until the final level was just audible.

Subjects rated 8 pictures at each one of the five levels. Two pictures were presented with the positive auditory cues, 2 were presented with negative auditory cues, 2 were presented with comparable levels of white noise, and 2 were presented coincident with the presentation of neutral words. The presentation order was randomized.

Subjects were asked to guess what the experiment was about and to indicate the slide number when they became aware of any manipulation of an independent variable. I would like to again repeat that these were very sophisticated subjects. Every one of them had conducted at least one full-length social psychological research project. Hence, they were very suspicious.

The earliest indication of any awareness of an auditory presentation was Slide 25. Hence, our analysis will be limited to the three first sound levels.

Eliminating the six subjects who stated that they were aware that sound was being manipulated, the ratings of the six slides at each one of the three sound levels were averaged. This brute force analysis indicated a trivial difference between positive and negative conditions (negative $\overline{X}$ = 54.48; positive $\overline{X}$ = 57.15; $t(11)$ = 1.30, $p < .15$). The difference between positive and negative ratings being about 5%, which incidentally is comparable to the Smith and Curnow (1966) finding, encouraged me to relax until I recalled that Henley (1975) reported that such subliminal cues maintained an influence over time and shadowed later judgements.

Hence, the data for only the first sound level were analyzed with rather startling results. The mean ratings for the 2 slides in each condition for the non-suspicious subjects were 64.62, 57.73 and 53.82 for the positive, neutral and negative conditions respectively. The positive condition differs from the negative $(t(11)$ = 3.60, $p < .005$) and the neutral $(t(11)$ = 1.99, $p < .05$). The difference between the neutral and the negative conditions is not reliable $(t(11)$ = .98, $p < .20$). The pattern for the six suspicious subjects is exactly the same with means of 55.76, 52.05 and 50.62 for the positive, neutral and negative conditions respectively.

These pilot data lead me to lend credence to the aforementioned revelations regarding the influence of behavior in non-laboratory settings. One can easily imagine the number of potential applications of such a technology. The influence upon behavior seems to be between 5 and 12% and hence, is certainly an economically sound application of our technology.

It is interesting to note Dixon's (1971) comment, that because of differences in individual thresholds, position and distance of persons from stimuli sources, and the like, it is unlikely that an effective stimulus level could be found for a mixed group. While it is undoubtedly true that wide individual differences are likely to occur, the above data suggest that stimulus levels can be found which will influence aggregate levels of behavior.

Encouraged by the above data, a second study[1] was addressed to determining the effects of subliminal auditory messages on

(1) Study two was conducted in collaboration with Kerry Lawson and Louis Renaud.

behavior in a two-person, two-choice power game situation (Swingle, 1970).

Three groups of 15 and one group of 16 female college students played the weak position in the power game shown below:

Player B
(powerful)

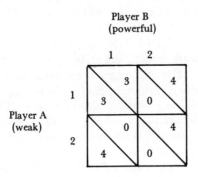

Subjects played the game for 100 trials against an opponent programmed to respond cooperatively (response 1) on 80% of the trials. On each trial, signalled by a "GO" light onset, the subject and the computer made response choice 1 or 2. After both responses were registered, a light came on behind on one of the four quadrants of the matrix indicating the results of that trial. Hence, if both choices were 1's, the top left quadrant would light up indicating that both the subject and the other player (computer) received 3 payoff units. The payoff points were accumulated automatically on two impulse counters on the console. Subjects were kept unaware of the fact that the opponent was programmed and were told that points would be redeemed at 2.5 cents per point for subjects whose names were drawn in a lottery of the subjects who participated in the project.

This game is a power game in which player B is in absolute control. By playing response 2, 100% at the time, player A would receive zero payoff whereas player B would receive four payoff units per trial. Previous studies (Swingle, 1970) have indicated that highly cooperative opponents tend to be exploited by weak opponents.

Three subliminal Sound conditions and one No Sound condition were included. The sound levels for all conditions varied from −2.5 to −30.0 db −2.5, −5.0, −7.5, −15.0 and −30.0) as measured at the speaker. The subject was seated over 1 meter from the sound source and the ambient sound level in the room was 70 db. The decision to use multiple sound levels was guided by research reports indicating effects of subliminal sound as low as −30 db. The messages were recorded through a gain control circuit which reduced peaking db levels.

For condition one (Plus C) a male voice repeated "Be nice, be kind, do not be selfish, your opponent is wise, your opponent is strong, your opponent is successful, your opponent is realistic, push 1, hit number 1, press 1".

For condition two (Plus D) the subliminal message was "Your opponent is failing, your opponent is foolish, your opponent is naive, your opponent is weak, she is stupid, get her now, you've got her, push 2, hit number 2, press 2".

The third subliminal sound condition (WN) was a white noise control. The white noise was presented at the same average db levels as the above messages.

The fourth condition (NS) was a no subliminal sound condition.

Probes of the subjects after the game indicated that no subjects were aware of the subliminal messages when asked what the experiment was about, whether they had noticed anything, etc. Judges could not discriminate between the presence or absence of any of the subliminal presentations.

The average number of response-two choices (noncooperative) for the Plus D, Plus C, WN and NS conditions were 70.0, 47.5, 58.8 and 69.4 respectively. The plus D differed from the Plus C ($Z = 3.26, p = .0007$) and the WN ($Z = 2.31, p = .0104$). The Plus C and the WN conditions differed at a marginal level of reliability ($Z = 1.60, p = .0548$). The NS control differed from the Plus C ($Z = 2.14, p = .0162$), but did not differ either from condition

WN ($Z = .993, p = .1611$) or condition Plus D ($Z = .237, p = .407$).

The evidence from the above preliminary studies, as well as from the few reported studies in the literature, is compelling. It does appear as though choice behaviors can be influenced by subliminal auditory messages and certainly warrant systematic study. One can easily imagine the number of potential applications of such a technology.

Conclusion

It is difficult to say sensible things about ethical principles in social psychology. One is tempted to proseletyze one's personal values, or to accuse others of being unacceptably indifferent to issues of moral import.

Social psychologists and other social scientists have interfered with the day-to-day activities of unsuspecting people in natural field situations to an ethically reprehensible extent. Part of the problem, in my judgement, stems from the erroneous belief that our technology is weak and inconsequential, and that this encourages many to dash about the "real" world demonstrating that they are studying "real" social behavior.

It is becoming more obvious to me that our technology is in fact disquietingly powerful and is being used and can be further utilized in ethically questionable ways. We must acknowledge our responsibility for the use of that technology. It is, of course, not a new problem.

The issue of the moral and ethical responsibilities of the social psychologist is extremely complex and any set of guidelines we establish for professional conduct is, like all other things in society, ever-changing. We are also vulnerable to the demoralizing insights of one's grandmother, to borrow one of Stanley Schacter's concepts, in that some feel, in agreement with Moore (1963), that what is good is good, and that is the end of it.

198   *Paul G. Swingle*

References

Arrowwood, A.J., Theory in social psychology, Paper presented at the Canadian Psychological Association meeting, June 1975.

Baumrind, D., Metaethical and normative considerations covering the treatment of human subjects in the behavioral sciences. In E.C. Kennedy (Ed.), *Human Rights and Psychological Research*, New York: Crowell, 1975.

Bevan, W. and Pritchard, J.F., Effect of "subliminal" tones upon judgement of loudness, *Journal of Experimental Psychology*, 1963, *66*, 23-9.

Boulding, K.E., Panel paper presented at roundtable discussion entitled *Alternative Approaches to the Management of Conflict*, International Studies Association, Toronto, February 28, 1976.

Broadbent, D.E. and Gregory, M., Perception of emotionally toned words, *Nature*, 1967, *215*, 581-4.

Cook, B., Tune in, turn on, drop out; The plug-in drug, *Saturday Review*, 1977, *3*, 27-28.

Cox, C.M., Early mental traits of 300 geniuses. In L.M. Terman *et al.* (Eds.), *Genetic Studies of Genius* (2nd ed.), Vol. II, Stanford, Calif.: Stanford University Press, 1926.

Dixon, N.F., *Subliminal Perception: The Nature of a Controversy*, London: McGraw-Hill, 1971.

Elms, A.C., The crisis of confidence in social psychology, *American Psychologist*, 1975, *30*, 967-76.

Fisher, S., Effects of messages reported to be out of awareness upon the body boundary, *Journal of Nervous and Mental Disease*, 1975, *161*, 90-9.

Fisher, S., Conditions affecting boundary response to messages out of awareness, *Journal of Nervous and Mental Disease*, 1976, *162*, 313-22.

Forsyth, F., *The Odessa File*, New York: Viking, 1972.

Gergen, K.J., Social psychology as history, *Journal of Personality and Social Psychology*, 1973, *26*, 309-20.

Goodwin, L. and Tu, J., The social psychological basis for public acceptance of the social security system. The role for social research in public policy formation, *American Psychologist*, 1975, *30*, 875-83.

Hampden-Turner, C., *Radical Man*, Garden City, New York: Anchor, 1971.

Hardy, G.R. and Legge, D., Cross-modal induction of changes in sensory thresholds, *Quarterly Journal of Experimental Psychology*, 1968, *20*, 20-9.

Henley, S., Cross-modal effects of subliminal verbal stimuli, *Scandinavian Journal of Psychology*, 1975, *16*, 30-6.

Henley, S. and Dickson, N.F., Laterality differences in the effects of incidental stimuli upon evoked imagery, *British Journal of Psychology*, 1974, *65*, 4, 529-36.

Horowitz, I.L., *The Struggle is the Message*, Berkeley, Calif.: Glendessary Press, 1970.

Kamin, L.J., *The Science and Politics of IQ*, Hillsdale, N.J.: Erlbaum, 1974.

Kelman, H.C., *A Time to Speak*, San Francisco: Jossey-Bass, 1968.

Mann, R.D., The identity of the group researcher. In G.S. Gibbard, J.J. Hartman & R.D. Mann (Eds.), *Analysis of Groups*, San Francisco: Jossey-Bass, 1974.

Moore, G.E., The subject matter of ethics. In R. Abelson (Ed.), *Ethics and Metaethics. Readings in Ethical Philosophy*, New York: St. Martin, 1963.

Rapoport, A., Peace research and ideational climate. Paper presented at the Canadian Peace Research and Education Association meetings, Edmonton, Alberta, May 31-June 2, 1975.

Rappoport, L. and Kren, G., What is a social issue? *American Psychologist*, 1975, *30*, 838-41.

Ring, K. Experimental social psychology: Some sober questions about some frivolous values, *Journal of Experimental Social Psychology*, 1967, *3*, 113-23.

Rommetveit, R., Language games, syntactic structures and hermeneutics. In J. Israel & H. Tajfel (Eds.), *The Context of Social Psychology: A Critical Assessment*, New York: Academic Press, 1972.

Secord, P.F., Social psychology in search of a paradigm, *Personality and Social Psychology Bulletin*, 1977, *3*, 41-50.

Silverman, I., Nonreactive methods and the law, *American Psychologist*, 1975, *30*, 764-9.

Smith, M.B., Psychology and ethics. In E.C. Kennedy (Ed.), *Human Rights and Psychological Research*, New York: Crowell, 1975.

Smith, P.C. and Curnow, R. "Arcusal hypothesis" and the effect of music on purchasing behaviour, *Journal of Applied Psychology*, 1966, *50*, 225-56.

Swingle, P.G., Exploitative behavior in non-zero sum games, *Journal of Personality and Social Psychology*, 1970, *16*, 121-32.

Toong, H.D., Microcomputers, unlimited horizons. Paper presented at the Mini and Microcomputer Conference, Toronto, 1976.

Wilson, D.W. and Donnerstein, E., Legal and ethical aspects of nonreactive social psychological research, *American Psychologist*, 1976, *31*, 765-73.

Zwosta, M.F. and Zenhausern, R., Application of signal detection theory to subliminal and supraliminal accessory stimulation, *Perceptual and Motor Skills*, 1969, *28*, 699-704.

Discussion

SEGALOWITZ: I have a question for some of our Soviet friends. There's been much discussion in North America about ethics in research, particularly social psychological research. I wondered if there are similar discussions, and what form they take in the USSR.

ANDREEVA: Soviet psychologists are fully aware of the existence of ethical problems. I would like to divide ethical problems into two categories. I will first mention the one which I consider less important. It is that the social psychologist of necessity interferes with the personal life of the person he is observing, if he carries out his experiment or observation in the field. We do stress observations and experiment in real life situations. This means that we will study workers in their factory or other people in their place of work, or athletes in their team. We question ourselves about our right to put our questions to real people about their real feelings, their goals, etc. Very often our experimental subjects are quite reluctant to answer the type of questions they are asked. They object largely because they consider these questions too personal. And the social psychologist must have very strong qualities of personal and moral responsibility, in order to formulate this type of question correctly. But this type of ethical difficulty can be overcome with respect to our society. When we do field experiments in an industrial setting, we stress that the aims of our research are not in any contradiction with the aims of any particular social group which is being investigated. So, at this level, ethical problems which arise appear to be capable of solution. I would like now to touch on more complex ethical problems.

The question can be put this way: what can social psychology do, and what is it that it cannot do or may not do in society in general? We take the point of view that social psychology is not allowed to manipulate a person under any circumstances whatsoever. We would not manipulate a person or personality, but we would assist in the process of management of personal interrelationships. There is a difference between intruding on an individual's personal life and an attempt to ameliorate relationships in a social context. The goal of social psychology is seen as an attempt to improve the ability of social interaction in groups. But when it comes to the question of debate on the subject there is quite a considerable amount, especially in the field of applied psychology. The Soviet literature contains now a number of articles discussing Skinner's book, *Beyond Freedom and Dignity,* because this book seems to represent an example of manipulation of people. That behavioral technology is not acceptable for me, nor for any social psychologist.

SEGALOWITZ: I'm curious too about the question of deception and informed consent — about the amount of information one gives to a subject in an experiment, in a laboratory.

ANDREEVA: When we conduct an experiment in a group setting, we absolutely insist on giving full information about the goal of the experiment. This does not mean that the last technical detail will be explained, because in order to understand some of the technical details, one needs more information or background than a lay person is likely to have. In this respect, the instructions to one's analysed subjects, and the way the instructions are formulated, become very important. Before we embark on an experimental project, we conduct considerable informational work. If we are to do the study in a work place, we will have discussions and explanations of what is being contemplated with management, with representatives of the working group and so on.

THORNGATE: I am reminded of some recent criticisms of learning theory and behavioral manipulation, these techniques that are supposed to have come out of behavioral science, and be of use in clinical and other settings; these critics say that these techniques were known long before psychologists studied them. Animal trainers in Rome used them very well. Is it really that the behavioral scientists have discovered these techniques, or have we only codified them in words so they could become more popular?

SWINGLE: Bertrand Russell pointed out that all scientific progress is simply a stage of rediscovery. I don't think it matters much whether we rediscovered it recently or whether we discovered that somebody else discovered it. The question I think is the application of this technology and what kind of threat that is to society. The application of the technology may not be something we are aware of, and I believe we are under some obligation to find out what's being done.

Methodological Problems in Social Psychological Research

DMITRI P. GRIBANOV

My original intention, honoured colleagues, was to speak on something else. But having listened to some of the papers that have been presented here, I thought that the most useful thing for me to do would be to discuss problems of general methodology, and certain methodological problems one encounters in studying man.

It is well known that in recent years, interest in studying man has heightened, to become one of our most complex and most absorbing problems. Many sciences are engaged in this study: these include molecular biology, biochemistry, social and political sciences, and so on, and there is an enormous amount of factual material. Considering that man is being studied by many and various disciplines, disciplines sometimes *very* different one from the other, we naturally have to consider the complex relationships between these sciences. Many books and articles have been written about the study of man, and if we were to study them carefully, we might come to the conclusion that there is no unifying scientific methodology; there is no single approach. Each science seems to create its own approach and its own methodology. This is not a simple issue — it's very complex. And things are not the way they were in the 17th or 18th century; we now have a lot of money being spent on science, and therefore it behoves us to look for correct pathways, which correspond to realities. If we consider the literature with

detachment, we come to the conclusion that the approaches
and methodology do not essentially differ from those in the
17th and 18th centuries, when solutions of the social problems
of man were proposed through the application of classic "mechanical" concepts and methods. History can justify what was
being done then, because sciences such as biology and chemistry
had not been developed; only classical mechanics and its laws
had been adequately studied. And scientists believed that events
could be explained only in terms of the motion of matter.
This methodological principle was even applied to the study of
man and society.

Something similar — and I mean only similar and not exactly
the same — is happening now. In the literature, we read that
certain scientists reduce chemistry to physical laws. They try to
explain heredity by resorting to chemical and physical laws.
There are theories which attempt to apply quantum mechanics
to the study of man. Some people who work in the field of
cybernetics equate man with a computer. Sometimes, biological
laws are applied to the study of society, and, in reverse, sometimes social laws are applied for the explanation of biological
phenomena. This type of problem points to the need of a
philosophical solution. One of the methodological strategies
which would help us eliminate deficiencies in our study of man
would be the study of dialectical materialism as it relates to the
classification of the forms of motion of matter.

We divide the varieties of motion of matter into five types.
The first is the mechanical form of *movement*. By "movement"
we mean the change of a material body in space from point A
to point B, and the laws for studying this are mechanical laws.
This form of motion is philosophical, an abstraction, and it
incorporates all forms of mechanical movement. It incorporates
the laws of Newton, of Kepler, of Galileo, and so on. The second
form of motion is physical. This form of motion incorporates
laws of molecular physics, quantum mechanics, etc. The material
vehicle of this form of movement are elementary particles,
nuclei, and various fields, such as electromagnetic fields, and so
on. The third form of motion is chemical. The chemical form

of motion includes all organic and inorganic forms, and its manifestations are all around us. The fourth form of motion is biological. This unifies all the motion of biology, physiology, the study of man, of flora and fauna, and the materials to be observed are plants and animals, including man. Finally, there is the social form of movement, and here science studies the forms of social movement and the development of man and society, as with political and economic science, and so on.

With respect to forms of movement, man deserves particular attention, because he differs considerably from the rest of the animal world, in terms of three factors: the first is speech, the second one is the ability to produce tools, and third is consciousness — the ability to form abstract notions. The specific form of motion here is social, and is characteristic only of man. It is characterized by social laws, and we feel that these laws are objective and are not dependent upon human consciousness.

The basis of all society is the collectivity of relations that are based on man's productivity. These economic relationships determine man's behaviour in society. The highest form of relationship is the social form, and it is followed in descending order by the biological, chemical, physical and mechanical. Each of the higher levels includes within itself the lower ones. The biological form includes the chemical, physical and mechanical, and so on. But the reverse is not true — the biological form does not include the social one in itself, and so on. Dialectical materialism distinguishes between basic and accessory forms of movement. For the study of biology, the biological form of movement is basic. Chemical and physical movement are accessory or subordinate to the biological ones. The biological being lives according to the laws of biology. If the biological movement were deprived of biological laws it would then revert to chemistry. A dead body is chemistry, and laws of biology do not apply there. The biological form of matter determines biological laws, although the biological form is dependent on the subordinate such as chemical and physical. Biological laws are important when the biological form of movement is functional; but when it is not functional any more, then the given form of matter disappears.

Presently science is in such a state that the adequate study of a particular object on only one level, namely its basic level of the movement of matter, cannot be done. We cannot study man or any other form of life by applying biological laws alone. We must descend to lower levels of study. This leads to the creation of new forms of science by scientists, and as you know such sciences have come into being — such as biochemistry, biophysics, physical chemistry, and so on. But we must ask ourselves the question, how legitimate is it to apply the methodics of the lower form to the higher form?

As I said, a full picture of the object, its essence, can be disclosed on two or three levels: the basic one and the accessory ones. The study of a single form of movement deprives it of its essential basis. We cannot study man on the biological or social level alone because chemical laws play an important role in man. The reverse is also true — inclusion of only the subordinate forms in the study of higher forms may answer the question of *how* this movement takes place, but does not answer the question *why* it occurs this way and not some other way. We cannot fully transfer the laws of one system to another. As I have said earlier, there have been attempts to study man by applying laws of chemistry alone, neglecting the laws of physics and the social laws, and it is true that the lower form always helps the study of the higher one. But we must remember that the higher form, which contains itself all the lower ones, distorts the laws of the lower forms. For instance, a biological species such as man reflects the functioning of chemical laws, but these pure chemical laws have been distorted by the biological nature of man. The necessary chemistry is not the same pure chemistry that we can study in the laboratory, in isolation from biology, and we must keep this in mind when we study biological forms. When we transfer chemical methodology to the study of biology, we must remember that in doing so we are in effect changing the nature of the material object itself, and therefore the methodology will have to be changed. This is an important point which often escapes attention: the methodology for the study of lower forms of motion must be correspondingly altered for the study of the higher one.

We may state the following general conclusion: that the main form of movement in any particular instance is in a unified relationship with the lower ones, and this relationship should not be ignored; the different forms interreact, and they find themselves in cause-and-effect relationships with one another. But the determining role in the study of a particular object belongs to the basic form of movement. The accessory of lower forms only help to study the higher, but their principles cannot be transferred in any absolute sense to a higher form of movement.

Discussion

KIESLER: It's nice to know that social science ranks so high in the Soviet view.

GRIBANOV: If you're going to study the development of science historically, it is the most recent to arrive on the scene.

ZAJONC: I wonder if you could illustrate where information and information processes fall into the system of categories?

GRIBANOV: This is a very concrete question. Where any object "fits" depends on the level of study of the object. If you are studying chemical matter, information comes in at one level, and if you do a study of biological matter, then information comes in at a different level.

LOMOV: I think it depends on how information is defined.

ZAJONC: I would like to hear that definition.

LOMOV: But there are different levels of information.

ZAJONC: I am simply trying to understand how information processing at *any* level is conceptualized in this framework. Your framework deals with movement, namely change of objects or entities in space, and information is an additional property of this movement. It is not the movement itself, nor some physical property of this movement that gives it information content, and information does not obey the same laws as energy; for example, there is no conservation of information while there is conservation of energy. I'd like to know how you treat this concept.

GRIBANOV: If you are talking about cybernetics information, then one can find similarities in terms of physics in every material vehicle. Each one of these levels has similar "currents". Accepting this helps us to study each one of these levels, and there is no inconsistency. All levels have something in common. They all exist in time and space. They all move. They all have similar laws; and these notions must be utilized. It would be another thing completely if we were to "absolutize" some physical law, and then try to imagine that the biological forms existed according to that physical law, and that biological laws were not important for the biological forms. We would then commit a serious methodological error.

KIESLER: Consider the classical areas of social psychology such as attitudes, interpersonal attraction, or group interaction. How can a conception that is as abstract as the one you have described be any help at all in our research in these basic areas of social psychology?

GRIBANOV: The point is that into this scheme, it *is* possible to introduce concrete examples. What I have outlined is the most general scheme of all, relevant to the study of the universe. We also have a number of levels in our methodology. We have a general methodology of general science, which is applicable to a number of levels, and each concrete science has its own methodology, and these different methods are not contradictory. This classification is a global one, and in the study of subjective processes such as awareness, it might not even be particularly useful. But when we do a general, wide study of an object considering its particular form of movement, then this classification is useful.

KIESLER: I have psychologist friends who believe in God, and others who don't, and they write very similar books on science.

GRIBANOV: Newton wrote good laws of physics being a religious man.

LOMOV: Chuck, in your opinion, when you study attitudes and intergroup relationships and personality — all the points that you brought up — in your opinion, is it important to use biological methods, and to understand biological features of human being? Is that a problem or not? What do you say?

KIESLER: Sometimes — but knowledge of how biological, mechanical, physical and chemical aspects of human beings relative to the psychological aspects is at best imperfect — at *best* imperfect. We attempt in some implicit way to take these related aspects into account, but I don't think that expressing my view on these "levels" of motion and my philosophy of science necessarily affects my research at all, or makes me more knowledgeable. It's too far removed from what I know.

LOMOV: All right, but regardless of philosophy — take just concrete research — let's say you are studying group dynamics — do you find that you need in some cases to study biological features, or mechanical qualities of the members of the group that you are studying?

KIESLER: We *have* studied them, but only in the sense that you have to study fingers to design airplanes. It's implicit but it doesn't affect our research very much. Consider pragmatically all the literature on group dynamics. There were perhaps 3000 experiments in the 1950s. In not 1% of those was there any explicit role of chemical, physical, or mechanical factors.

GRIBANOV: But suppose one were to describe life in terms of basic physical processes and ignore the laws of biology, because one felt that they are not necessary. If we were to follow this approach, we would then have to liquidate the sciences of biology and chemistry, and make you unemployed.

KIESLER: I think I'd better recognize someone else to join in the discussion, or I'm going to be unemployed sooner.

THORNGATE: You say that this classification derives from dialectical materialism. And yet in our libraries in North America, we divide the sciences just like that. For example, we have one area for social sciences, one for biology, and so on. Are you saying then that our architects and librarians are dialectical materialists?

GRIBANOV: It is quite obvious that *anyone* who studies concrete sciences can assume the standpoint of dialectical materialism by the very nature of his work, but it does not happen automatically. Consciously or unconsciously the scientist should accept certain methodological principles (in the broad sense).

THORNGATE: Do you see a difference between your classification and Western or North American classification, and if so, what is it?

LOMOV: There is no special Western or Eastern classification of science. There is no such thing. There is only one classification, and this is the result of historical development of our knowledge. But the understanding, interpretation and use of the principles and content of sciences might be different.

BAREFOOT: I think there may be some differences in the way different forms relate to one another, though. And I would like to ask a question about the problem of "distortion". How, say, might a biological law be distorted by a social law, or a chemical by a biological?

GRIBANOV: Take the gene, for example. It is a molecule. If you would isolate a gene from biology, it is then a chemical. But if a gene is looked at in its biological context, it is not a purely chemical form any more; the activity of the gene is subordinated to the activity of the organism as a whole. It carries out certain functions of the organism, and in some measure loses part of its chemical specificity.

LOMOV: At one level, of course biological regulators control our behaviour. Right? But we can control our biological dispositions by social means. Right? I think that Bob Zajonc gave a very good example of this when he showed how part of the social system affects intelligence.

KIESLER: I have the feeling that no matter how long we discuss this we will never quite agree.

LOMOV: Not in our lifetime.

PART III

Theory and Research: Reciprocal Implications

A. THE USSR

Mental Processes and Communication

BORIS F. LOMOV

When mental functions and processes came to be subjected to a concrete-scientific (and, more particularly, to experimental) analysis, investigators understood their task to be one of clarifying the "purified" regularities and characteristics of these functions. The experimental methods being worked out at the time were aimed at achieving the utmost detachment of particular perceptive, mnemonic, intellectual, etc. functions from the whole system of psychic phenomena, at neutralizing their influence upon this system, and at investigation of the function as a natural, unique quality in itself. Thus at the initial (analytical) stage of experimental psychology, psychic functions and process were being approached as abstract categories.

The development of activity theory in Soviet psychology was a critical point in overcoming abstract functionalism. Psychic processes and functions came to be considered in the context of a real subject's activity, which made possible discovery of their regulative role in the activity. This approach has laid the basis for re-evaluation of the system of psychic functions and processes; within its bounds there has been investigated the development of sensory-perceptual processes and sensitivity, of mnemonic functions, of imagination and thinking.

It should be noted that most experimental work dealt with

the "subject-object" relations only, and that the person's activity (as a rule, the "practical", object-oriented one) was considered as a separate problem. His communication with others was seen as beyond the field of investigation. On the contrary, we now see that we should bear in mind that communication is an undetachable part of human life and thus, as data show, psychic processes performed under conditions of communication differ from those of individual activity. Our point of view is that for the further development of research on mental processes, it is essential to take into account the dependence of dynamics of psychic processes on forms, ways and means of communication.

We shall now consider the results of some simple experiments aimed at establishing the particular dynamics of certain psychic processes under conditions of direct communication. At present, there exists neither an adequate theory of communication nor ideal methods for the investigation of psychic process dynamics under conditions of communication. Their ultimate development is a future task; hence the investigations described should be seen as a step in that direction.

Joint activity of subjects, which necessarily requires the process of communication, was one of our research foci. The subjects — students and senior pupils — formed basic two-man groups or dyads.

The experiments conducted were "natural" ones, i.e., the subjects did not know they were taking part in an experiment. The process of verbal communication between them was recorded on tape — another fact about which the subjects did not know — and their problem solving behaviour was observed (unfortunately we lacked the means of exact recording of subjects' behaviour).

We conducted three series of experiments. In one of them the subjects were to perform a joint visual search for a barely distinguishable object (the activity of observation). In another they were to depict the plan of some locality. In the third, the subjects were to reproduce the text of a verse.

Series 1. Peculiarities of Visual Search for Objects under Conditions of Direct Communication

Two-man groups observing a picture of natural urban landscape were asked to find a barely distinguishable object, which had certain specific characteristics (colour, form). The experiment was carried out as a game. The subjects were told verbally the name of the object and of its specific characteristics. Sometimes they were shown pattern pictures depicting either the form or the colour of the object. Sometimes the pictures depicted both the colour and the form. We were interested to know how the communication process between the subjects would develop in the course of joint observation.

Several types of joint problem-solving were demonstrated. In some cases the subjects found the object independently and almost simultaneously. They entered into communication only to check the results of one another's search, that is, "to coordinate the images". Such cases were rare and, in fact, they took place only if the task appeared to be rather simple for both of them.

In cases when the task was found to be difficult for both of them, communication infiltrated, so to speak, the whole of the search process. The subjects settled on common initial points for observation, outlined a common strategy, and they sometimes came to agreements about a search zone division. In the process of joint observation, different hypotheses were suggested, checked and corrected and the search pattern became specified. As it happened, such instances also were rather rare in our experiments.

The most typical pattern of the joint search in tasks with an average level of difficulty was when one of the subjects found the object before another one and then entered into communication with him, in an attempt to contribute to his success. In words and gestures, he began to control his partner's attention, narrowing the zone and limiting the route of the search.

As a rule the main problem of the first stage of communication was the location of reference-points. It was not the case that the reference-points were always set by the one who had found the object; quite often they were suggested by the one who had not yet solved the problem. As a rule, objects with some specific colour, form or location in the zone of joint search were selected to be the reference-points. There were cases when subjects took for reference-points similar (but not the same) objects. This disrupted coordination of the joint search, and led to difficulties in the "image exchange".

As soon as common reference-points are singled out, subject A begins to "construct" the route of subject B. It should be noted that A would never try to give to subject B the route he had followed in his own search; indeed, it can be seen from subjects' reports that as a rule they are not able to give a full reconstruction of their own search route, but they can be very exact in the reconstruction of the route formed in the joint search. When the object is located, subject A constructs a new, more rational (in his opinion) route to give to his partner. When he controls subject B's search actions, he not only shows the location of the object in accordance with the common reference-points, but sometimes also establishes some methods for B's performance. (For a more detailed investigation of the search route peculiarities under conditions of communication, it would have been very informative to make a comparative analysis of eye-movement trajectories of individual and joint search).

In the event that A has found an incorrect object, his partner as a rule would discover the mistake. Then the subject would come back to the pattern, specify it and start a new cycle of joint search. In other words, a joint search suggests mutual correction of the object pattern.

The search ends by *coordination of perceptive images and mutual decision making*.

It should be noted that out of all the spectrum of means and ways of interaction during joint visual search, verbal communication plays an auxiliary and subsidiary role. Speech in these cases has a situational character; its structure is elementary and vocabulary is poor. The main means of communication here are gestures. Three types of gestures can be pointed out: indicating, depicting and simulating ones.

With the help of the *indicating* gesture, the direction of the partner's gaze is set and the search zone is narrowed; i.e. the indicating gesture is used as a means of *regulation* of *perceptual selectivity* that is singling out the figure against the background. It is interesting to note that, when resorting to the indicating gesture, the subject seems to match his field of vision with that of his partner; that is, his gesture gives the direction from the partner's standpoint.

The *depicting gesture* is used as a means of form reproduction of one or another object (reference-point), and it also contributes to perceptual selectivity in that it helps the partner to single out the indicated object.

With the help of the *simulating gestures,* the partner's visual search route is regulated. The gesture reproduces certain elements of the route, as well as some methods for one or another distance estimation action.

The extent of communication during joint visual search depends on the complexity of the problem being solved and the level of coordination of actions (the level of synchronization, primarily). The more complex the task, the less coordinated the actions of the partners, the more extensive is the process of communication.

Series 2. Some Peculiarities of Topographical Concept Dynamics under Conditions of Direct Communication

The subjects were asked to draw a plan of Leningrad's Dvortsovaja Square and its surroundings. The task did not require a high level of drawing skills. The subjects were Leningrad residents or frequent visitors to the city. At first the task was given to each subject separately and then, a few days later, they were to perform it together.

We shall consider results of one of our experiments, focusing on joint task performance.

216   *Boris F. Lomov*

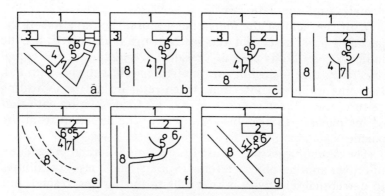

Figure 1. Joint and separate composing of a plan of Palace's Square.

(a) — plan of Leningrad Palace's Square
(b) — a plan composed by examinee
(c) — a plan composed by examinee
(d, e, f) — consecutive versions of a
    plan under joint composition
(g) — final version of a plan

1. Neva river
2. Winter Palace
3. The Admiralty (building)
4. General Staff
5. Arch of General Staff
6. Pillar of the Alexandrine order
7. Gertsen Street
8. Nevsky Prospect (avenue)

Figures 1-a, 1-b and 1-c show, respectively, the correct plan, and the plans drawn by subjects A and B when performing the task separately. It can be easily seen that both latter plans are erroneous. Neither subject *had any doubt* that his plan was correct in principle; only some details of it seemed questionable. It was in the process of communication that blunders were discovered; this created the problem-solving situation and the need for communication. In instances where plans drawn by each of the subjects were identical, or nearly so, the process of communication was short and, in fact, consisted in the statement of their identity.

The goal of the initial communication stage was the same as in the first series of experiments, that is, to clarify common reference-points (common coordinates). In the record of the experiment chosen for illustration, subject A took for an initial reference-point the outlet of the Nevsky Prospect to the Admiralty; subject B chose the Headquarters Arch. The process of communication was aimed at clearing up the relations between these two reference-points. During the process of communication, hypotheses were being suggested by each of the subjects and then jointly checked. It is interesting to note that the correct decision was given not by the subject A who, one might think, would know Dvortsovaja Square pretty well (he was a Leningrad inhabitant) but by his partner (subject B was a Muscovite). But at any rate, the correct decision had been developed in the process of joint discussion of hypotheses, that is, in the *process of communication*.

In those cases when both subjects had more or less similar conceptions of the surroundings, their communication was aimed at perfection of the scale, location and specification of certain details, and elimination of blanks in the plan. Meanwhile the details were approached in accordance with common reference points.

At this stage of communication, hypotheses were being suggested, checked and then either rejected or accepted by both of the subjects.

Since subjects reproduced (with one or more mistakes) the plan of the surroundings as a whole, their topographical concepts could be defined as a sort of "full scale map". In the process of communication, some elements of their topographical concepts were developed and subjects proceeded to operations with a "route-map". Concurrently, the development of actions was performed by each of the subjects with the orientation to the common system of reference-points.

In topographical task performance, means of verbal communication play a more significant role than in the process of joint visual search. Nevertheless, subjects resort to a broad use of gestures which serve here as a kind of means for image *exteriorization*. Due to gestures, particularly to depicting and simulating ones, an image of one of the subjects becomes clear and available to another subject. (Comparison of cyclograms of a real action and a simulating gesture show that the gesture gives only a schematic and general representation of the action). The process of communication leads to a certain transformation, perfection and enrichment of subjects' images. It results in a certain image unification for both subjects.

The data of the experimental series show that the degree of *exactness and completeness* of topographical plan reproduction under conditions of communication is higher than that under conditions of individual activity.

Series 3. Some Peculiarities of Verse-text Reproduction under Conditions of Direct Communication

In a preliminary investigation, subjects were separately asked to reproduce the beginning of the first chapter of Pushkin's *Eugene Onegin*. It allowed us to get some background performance data on, and then to select for the main series, the subjects who remembered the beginning of the first chapter only partially.

A few days later we held the main session and asked two-man groups of subjects to reproduce the same text under conditions of direct communication. In both cases the performance was being recorded by a concealed tape-recorder.

Recordings of separate (individual) performance gave us the "classic" data found in many publications on memory: that is, an exact recitation of the beginning (and sometimes of the end) of some stanzas; substitution of some words; transposition of some words, lines and stanzas; substitution of meaningful summaries instead of word for word recitation, and so on.

The picture was quite different in the situation of text reproduction under conditions of communication. In this case, shifts of roles, mutual correction, joint search for forgotten words and phrases in connection with hypotheses formation and evaluation were recorded.

One of the characteristic peculiarities of joint reproduction was that the extent of word for word recitation was greater than the total sum of both subjects' individual recitations. Furthermore, both the level of accuracy and confidence in this level was higher as well. It would be wrong to construe the results of reproduction under conditions of communication as a simple sum of what was remembered by one of the subjects and that which was remembered by another one. The erroneousness of this interpretation is illustrated by Figure 2. As a result of joint recollection, the material being reproduced first of all is the material memorized by both subjects solidly and exactly. These portions of text play the role of common "coordinates" (a "skeleton"), which form a system of foothold images and helps reproduction of the other images. An important feature of the construction of the foothold image system is a mutual reinforcement and correction of the reproduced material. The reserve for correction in joint reproduction is much greater than in individual ones; a "common memory fund", so to speak, from both of the subjects is formed.

The process of recollection includes some elements of recognition which stimulates reproduction: A recognizes what B has reproduced and this "elicits" new text portions out of his memory. Processes of self control of each of the subjects are more active under conditions of communication.

In joint reproduction, "gaps" and "doubtful places", i.e. text portions that cannot be reproduced exactly by either of the subjects, are more clearly identified. Text portions that are well remembered and text portions that are badly or not at all remembered are singled out and defined with better precision and certainty. It is with respect to the badly remembered portions that the joint search is performed. This kind of a search is performed in individual reproduction as well, but in a joint reproduction it is much more intensive.

It should also be noted that the very strategy of search under conditions of communication is different. In the process of individual reproduction, the subject who has found a "gap" follows the principle of multiple returns to the beginning of the text (stanza) followed by new "runs" through the text. This kind of a strategy can be called a scanning one. Rather often subjects who find a "gap" are not able to overcome it, and refrain from further attempts at reproduction.

In the process of communication, these gaps (reproduction

220   *Boris F. Lomov*

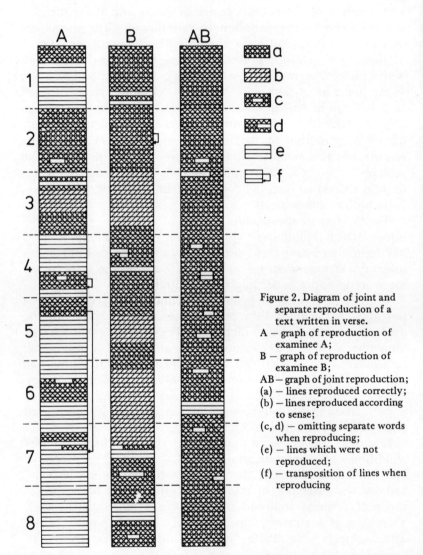

Figure 2. Diagram of joint and separate reproduction of a text written in verse.
A — graph of reproduction of examinee A;
B — graph of reproduction of examinee B;
AB — graph of joint reproduction;
(a) — lines reproduced correctly;
(b) — lines reproduced according to sense;
(c, d) — omitting separate words when reproducing;
(e) — lines which were not reproduced;
(f) — transposition of lines when reproducing

"blockades") become a kind of focus of joint efforts. It is in the zone of gaps that the joint search is being organized. Having discovered the gaps the subjects actively propose hypotheses, discuss and correct them. Also, in the process of joint reproduction, correct recall happens more often than in the individual process.

Finally, it should be noted that the process of joint text reproduction (as with the drawing of a plan of locality) is more active and emotional in general; this also contributes to its greater effectiveness.

The data of these experiments allow us to formulate certain judgements concerning the conditions, functions and structure of communication, as well as of the dynamics of the psychic processes involved. The results demonstrate that a problem situation is one of the most significant preconditions for a need for communication to appear. Of course, it is not the only precondition; the need to communicate also appears, for example, when a person wants to change his emotional state ("to unburden his heart") or in a system of interpersonal relations, to cooperate with somebody, etc. But it should be a problem (or a task) which for one or another reason cannot be solved by some ready skills, abilities or knowledge of a single person, involved in concrete activity.

The main functions of communication in our experiments were the exchange of the results of each subject's cognitive activity, the resulting mutual regulation and correction of performed actions and the formation on this basis of a group "community", that is of an "aggregate subject of the activity".

The dynamics and structure of communication are determined in every case by the conditions under which it takes place. It depends on the type of the problem being solved, on individual characteristics of communicators and on their relationship (we did our best to neutralize this factor by selecting those subjects who would enter into joint activity on an equal footing).

On the basis of our experimental data, it is still difficult to suggest a complete model of communication structure. Nevertheless, we would like to mention some of its most significant aspects, from our point of view. The first stage of the process of communication is selection of common "coordinates" of joint activity (reference-points, foothold images). They play the role of certain determinants in relation to which the whole process of communication is being built, and to which the distribution and coordination of actions for every member of the group is being performed. Sometimes in the process of the coordinate formation, certain contradictions arise, hampering the agreement about joint actions. This problem of sources of contradiction requires separate study.

The process of communication develops like a spiral, so to speak. It includes an alternating exchange of functions of both communicators. Thus the communicators have two-way and reversible relations. Significant aspects of communication are synchronization of the communicators' actions, their reciprocal stimulation, regulation, correction and supplement. Common programs and common strategies of joint activity are being formed in the process of communication. The strategy formed under conditions of communication differs qualitatively from the individual one.

In comparison with an individual activity, the effectiveness of every joint problem-solving endeavour was higher in our experiments. This finding is not new; it was known to social psychologists long ago. But it should be also noted that social psychology obtains contrary facts as well. The effectiveness of joint activity obviously depends on many factors. Relations of communicators, the way the activity is organized, the group structure, etc. should be noted among them. Nevertheless, the data obtained allow us to suggest that formation of a certain "common fund" of concepts, ideas, methods of problem-solving, i.e., the formation of a kind of interpersonal psychological "community" is a condition which increases effectiveness of activity.

Different types of psychological activity have been studied in our experiments. In one of them the leading role was played by sensory-perceptual processes (visual search); in another by processes of concept formation (depiction of locality), in the third, by mnemonic processes (verse text reproduction). As our data demonstrate, the dynamics of these processes are significantly dependent on communication. Thus, communication can be considered as one of the most significant determinants of these dynamic processes.

Finally, it should be noted that the correlation of different means of communication is determined by the problem's being jointly solved. In some cases, speech plays the leading role; in others, gestures (which are most characteristic of the tasks requiring space orientation and reproduction of spatial characteristics of objects). We think that in the process of communication related to an exchange of emotional states, the leading role is probably played by facial expressions.

As has already been mentioned, we view our experiments as preliminary ones. The data obtained may be considered as an outline for further research. It is necessary to apply serious effort in order to work out more precise experimental methods, and better means of data and communication model description.

Discussion

SEGALOWITZ: I find this talk extremely interesting, particularly because we're just beginning some research in which we look at similar things, but where the people in the dyad have to speak in their second language. Now — it seems to me that when people are communicating, there are two things which are very different for them than when they are alone. One is that the level of motivation might be different.

LOMOV: That's right.

SEGALOWITZ: And the other is that there's feedback, which might improve the subject's performance.

LOMOV: Right.

SEGALOWITZ: Now each of these could, individually or together, affect at least three things I can think of: one is the subject's sensitivity to the stimulus characteristics. That is, if he's better motivated or if he gets constructive feedback, he might become better at picking up the pattern. In a signal detection sense, he might have a different criterion for making a perceptual decision; and terms of evaluating the outcome of his perception, or deciding whether to report the results to the experimenter, he might change his evaluations. I'd like to know whether you've done any work, or are thinking of doing work, that would look to see which of these factors are affected — either alone or in combination — in communication. And secondly, do you think some sort of social situations might produce worse decisions rather than better decisions, and whether the number of subjects and the social relationships between subjects might affect this?

LOMOV: Our research programme envisages the study of the things you mention, but the first level of investigation is concerned only with the structure and dynamics of communication. We do not yet have an adequate model for the study of the phenomena you mention, and moreover we have in fact tried to ignore them so far, but they will be examined gradually.

ABOUD: You say that people could not re-construct their own thoughts individually, as opposed to when they were in a group. I wonder if you would get the same results if you made people think by themselves the way they are thinking with the group. So, if they were doing this task by themselves, make them verbalize, or make them draw the picture *as if* they were drawing it for someone else.

LOMOV: You are absolutely right, and this can be done. You must remember that in our experiments our subjects did not know that they were taking part in an experiment. And they did not receive any specific instructions when they were acting individually. The important question is why, when he is acting individually, a subject just *cannot* recall his thinking process, but when he's in communication, he does recall it. This suggests that memory works differently in the two settings. He is the same person — he still has his own characteristics — but once he's in communication with another, he performs differently.

ABOUD: I have been working with that difference as well, but I have been thinking of it in terms of a difference in thought processes. In one situation, one uses intuitive thought, and in the other one, analytic thought.

LOMOV: But the choice of process is determined by the situation of communication.

KIESLER: I find that these results are interesting as a model of social behaviour — what you call the spiral of dyadic interaction. This has been a problem historically in social psychology. That is, how does one represent or study social behaviour in its natural context, in its sequence of A to B, B to A, etc.? I wondered how you are trying to tackle your data, statistically. Do you try to investigate phases of the process? Do you try to represent the communications from A to B and B to A?

LOMOV: So far we have refrained from using statistical and mathematical methods, because the basis is not sufficiently clear. But some initial attempts have been undertaken; in psychophysical laboratories we have started work in this area, as Dr. Nosulenko will show.

KIESLER: That's one kind of lead — the psychophysical approach is one way to tie a handle to such data. Another would involve Markov processes.

LOMOV: Some experience would remind us that mathematics and statistics often serve to confuse a problem rather than to clarify it. This doesn't mean that I am against these methods, but it is very important, first of all, to clarify things, and only then to apply mathematical procedures.

THORNGATE: It struck me that you are attempting in some way to develop methods for improving the productivity or judgement of collectives. And that seems to be quite admirable. What happens in your country if you discover a very good technique for doing this — how does it get implemented throughout the culture? And lastly, do you meet, as we do in our culture, strong resistance to change?

LOMOV: There are two parts to my answer. The first will concern our research. The essential objective of the Academy of Sciences is basic research. In our experiments we are at the stage when we are not thinking of the possibilities of practical application of what we are going to discover. And the aim of our experiments is *not* to increase the effectiveness of the collective. Social psychologists carry out their work at various levels — macro-, middle- and microlevels. We want to have a look first at the picture as a whole and also to try to connect experimental and social psychology.

Now about implementation of discoveries in general and resistance to change.

This question is sometimes complex for us as it is in Canada. The main problem is to provide good scientific arguments to prove the necessity or desirability of a change. Then many of our psychologists are called upon to deliver psychological knowledge to officials and we observe that respect for our science is tending to grow. This is also a more easy way to prepare our officials to accept proposed changes.

KIESLER: You should keep in mind that the education of ministers is in itself a social psychological process.

LOMOV: This is certainly so.

The Estimation of Sound Intensity when Subjects Communicate

VALERIY N. NOSULENKO

In recent years, according to Lomov and others, problems of communication which were first developed and studied in social psychology have become part of the general field of psychology. Research on the details of cognitive processes, and in particular on variations in such processes when subjects communicate between themselves and share some activity in common, have a particularly great value.

One of the fundamental problems in psychophysics is that of sensory scaling. Such research yields understanding of how sensory processes are organized during the subjective estimation of sensations. It is remarkable that subjective estimation of sensation, as opposed to the estimation of sensory sensitivity, involves extremely complex processes of measurement and decision. The various paradigms for studying estimation usually involve the subject in evaluating a stimulus, with respect to a standard or a unit which he has chosen himself, or which was given to him by the experimenter. In such experiments, as we now know, many factors can influence the scale developed by the subject. These factors include details of the decision making process, specific features of the choice of sensory units or standards, details of stimulus organization, specific features of the experimental method and the character of the subject's own activity.

227

Zabrodin, in his work of 1972 and 1976, noted that when subjects communicate between themselves during the performance of a sensory task, they receive supplementary information. At least two sorts of qualitative modification to the whole sensory system seem to be possible. First, shifts in sensory standards or in the unit of the subjective scale could be a source of variance when subjects communicate between themselves. Second, modifications could occur to the structure of the decision-making process, which would be linked to a reorganization of decisional mechanisms themselves. We shall present some results today from an experiment devoted to the study of both kinds of modification and to the details of the structure of decision processes when subjects communicate, in as natural a way as possible.

Experimental Technique

In the first part of each experiment, subjects were tested in the following manner: auditory signals differing in intensity were presented binaurally, and the subject was asked to estimate the level of intensity with respect to a standard chosen in advance by the subject. The second part of the experiment was similar to the first, but now subjects were able to communicate between themselves.

We suggested the same unit to each subject and instructed them to evaluate each stimulus with respect to this unit. To both subjects we simultaneously presented the same signals and asked them to evaluate these signals. To examine the effects of the process of communication, we instructed subjects to make two evaluations of sound intensity level. The first estimation was made immediately after hearing the stimulus. The second estimation was made following discussion between the two subjects.

The stimuli were 1000 Hertz pure tones with a continuous duration. The set of stimuli consisted of six equally spaced sound intensity levels in a total range of 0 to 10 decibels. Each signal was presented twice for two seconds, with a two second inter-signal interval. Following presentation, the subject had five seconds to make his evaluation. The total set of stimuli was made up of 150 signals, with the probability of presentation of any given intensity level held constant. For each subject pair we presented at least two such stimulus sets. In the present experiments, we have studied six subjects, individually and in various combinations of communicating pairs. Let us examine qualitative details of sensory processing and of the subject's use of psychophysical scales with and without communication.

Results

(1) From the subject's own reports and indirectly from our results, we can verify that, in communication conditions, the subject was likely to evaluate the signal with less care since he could correct his estimation at any time, either so as to correspond with the estimation of his partner or simply after discussion of his partner's estimation.

(2) In communication conditions, we can obtain psychophysical scales which are common to both subjects, although there is always some modification to the nature of the scales when compared with those developed without communication.

(3) Analysis of subject's strategies shows that for most subjects, it appears to be easier to work with a standard chosen from the lower end of the stimulus range. However, it is not possible to say that all pairs of subjects can achieve a common standard.

(4) Despite the fact that most subjects felt the communication conditions to be easier, we found that some subjects could not or would not correct an original estimation. These subjects preferred to make a single estimation of signal intensity.

Let us now consider quantitative aspects of experimental data.

(5) Comparing results from communication and no-communication conditions, we observe shifts in mean estimation

which differ both in magnitude and in direction for each pair of subjects. We find an important shift in mean estimation in the direction of partner's estimation. The most important difference in mean estimation is between second estimations and those estimations made without communication.

(6) There are important differences in magnitude and in direction of shifts in mean estimation as a function of the particular partner. Additionally, subjects are capable of changing from one type of scale to another. For example, they can shift from ordinal to interval scales, or the reverse.

(7) In communication experiments, differences between estimates made by two partners are always less than differences between within-subject estimates obtained without communication. During the course of the experiment, the difference between second estimates diminishes in absolute magnitude with respect to initial estimates.

When we analyse the difference between means as a function of sound intensity level, we find that in all cases the difference between second estimates is less than the difference between initial estimates. At the same time we cannot demonstrate any clear functional relationship between differences in estimation and sound intensity.

(8) Variation in estimation is also significantly affected by the change from no-communication to communication conditions. The greater the change or correction of mean estimate, the greater the difference in variability between no-communication and communication conditions. In almost all cases, variability of estimates in the communication condition is no lower than the smallest variability obtained in the no-communication condition. For those subjects who show considerable variability in the no-communication condition, we see a tendency for variability to diminish in the communication condition and for estimates made by these subjects to approach the best observations made by the partner. In particular, we notice the simultaneous increase in variability which occurs for both subjects whenever there is a sudden modification of the type of scale used during the communication condition.

Summary

With respect to the results as a whole, it is useful to note that two kinds of change occurred in the communication condition: firstly, changes in mean estimate, i.e., changes in the nature of the psychophysical scale; and secondly, changes in variability, i.e., in the stability of estimates. At the moment, we cannot completely explain these results, but we can attempt some preliminary conclusions. Communication seems to serve either to increase the efficiency with which a particular scale is used, or to change the nature of the scale. When such changes do not occur, there is an increase in variability.

Our results show that communication between subjects plays an educative role. We have not presented the results here, but we have carried out experiments without communication following completion of the experiments described here, and have found that from practically all subjects we obtain psychophysical scales which parallel those obtained from the same subjects in communication conditions. In other words, subjects develop an estimation strategy during the communication condition which remains invariant in subsequent experiments.

The process of communication of shared activity changes various aspects of sensory processing in itself. Our experiments have demonstrated the possibility of changing the subject's basic sensory unit or standard which is common to two subjects. Moreover, the choice of a common standard can serve to reduce variability between subjects.

Essentially, communication produces variations in decision making and in the processing of sensory information. Such variations result in changes in the nature of the psychophysical scale used by the subject.

Finally, the effect of communication is essentially dependent upon individual differences between subjects. This finding requires a more detailed analysis using methods more appropriate for experimental social psychology. If we find consistent relationships between individual characteristics (personality variables) and the subject's efficiency in subjective estimation, we could then employ quite simple psychophysical scaling techniques in order to estimate or control for personality variables during shared activity.

Discussion

ZAJONC: I think there are some very interesting possibilities in doing this sort of psychophysical work in the context of social psychology. I think there are two categories of social psychophysics. One type is what you have been doing, namely the attempt to see how intersubjective estimations develop, and I think this is important, not only for social psychology, but it's also important for psychophysics. Magnitude estimation is not really an individual test: magnitude estimation depends to a large extent on the social context, from which the subject derives his category judgements, his numbers, his magnitudes. It is not something which is unique and purely individual. And I think there are also other especially good possibilities in your laboratory, because I have seen the work of Zabrodin and others and I'm much impressed with the very high level of your research. The possibilities which are open are really vast. For example, one could use the methods of estimation as you have done, take the resulting scale, give it to another subject, and let him use the method of production to see whether there is a transfer of these scales through different subjects by these various methods. That is, try going from estimation to production, but changing subjects in the meantime. I also think there is a different type of psychophysics, which is the psychophysics that social psychologists would be very interested in (I won't say "would", I should say "should" — they aren't) and this involves the sort of psychophysics that follows in the tradition of social judgement. There have been a number of attempts here, such as by Hovland and Sherif, another is Stroebe and Eiser, but now I'm talking more about a judgement that is closer to psychophysical work. Normally, when we know something about the stimulus that is being judged, we very often find in social judgement work that the "physics" part of the estimation is not very elaborate. What are the prospects for a psychophysics of interpersonal relationships, or of social structure? Can we scale, for example, degree of liking for a person or commitment to a group? Is it possible to do this? Much work in social psychology — impression formation for example — is work which tries to describe the way people combine trait labels in their minds. But there is very little work in which we are trying to assess the degree to which an impression might be correct; what might be the relationship between perceived intelligence and actual intelligence? We have the possibility of making comparisons between judgements about qualities of the social stimulus; we can do it with power, we can do it with status, we can do it with competence, we can do it with all sorts of qualities which are important in social interaction. This sort of psychophysics seems very promising.

KIESLER: I think this work is interesting because it adds something to social psychology which social psychology needs, that is, the precision of measurement; you're quantifying primary dependent variables, things that we are accustomed to use all the time, but which are not usually measured precisely. A second issue is the point that Dr. Zajonc was making. We know very little about the measurement of the object, social or otherwise, that the person interacts with, perceives. Such work provides an important context which will be a big step toward a better understanding of what we've always done.

STROEBE: There is one old problem, and I'm never quite sure whether it's a real problem or simply a problem we have posed for ourselves. It is the question of whether these shifts which you find are shifts in the frame of reference, or are they real shifts, reflecting some real change in perception? I wonder whether you could try, for example after the discussion, to use a different scaling method, like magnitude production or something as Bob Zajonc suggested. You could get at the basic question of whether or not it's just a different use of numbers that you observe after the discussion.

NOSULENKO: We have done many experiments individually, without communication. And the scale of dispersion obtained with one subject without communication was always significantly smaller than in the communication process. Therefore, we conclude that the shifts we observe are due to the introduction of the communication element.

STROEBE: I agree that the *effect* is due to the communication. My question was, is it merely a shift in the reference table? Do we see the same length, for example, but agree after communicating that we will call it three centimeters instead of five centimeters and therefore start using different numbers? Or is it that after we discuss the stimulus we somehow really *see* it differently?

LOMOV: This is an interesting remark and maybe it should be checked.

STROEBE: Or could you show the effect with a different measurement technique?

LOMOV: That's a good idea.

B. CANADA

Self: An Identity, a Concept, or a Sense ?

FRANCES E. ABOUD

Abstract. The social psychological perspective on "self" is examined in terms of three restrictions it has imposed on theory and research: analyzing groups and ignoring individuals, evaluating behaviour by comparing it with a social norm, and relying mainly on explicitly verbalized content. Alternative strategies for studying the self are discussed: attending to individual responses which deviate from the average, evaluating behaviour in terms of some "ideal" developmental standard, and developing techniques to explore the more intuitive levels of self-awareness and the structural characteristics. The term "sense of self" is elaborated on and is used as the focus for describing studies which investigate three structural characteristics: internal consistency, uniqueness, and constancy.

A recent and popular textbook of social psychology introduced a chapter on "The Self" by remarking that "you may not be able to remember a time when you did not possess a feeling of self-awareness" (Middlebrook, 1974). This statement, in a simple way, resolves a dilemma which has confronted psychologists throughout the century: Is the study of "self" a feasible or meaningful one for a psychologist ? Or is the self merely an artifact (Lowe, 1961) or a theory (Epstein, 1973) to be debated as a philosophical issue, not as an empirical issue ? My own belief is that this "feeling of self-awareness" is a component of human functioning, and for this reason alone merits further study. It may turn out to be a figment of our imagination, an illusion with no basis in physical reality. But so may be the feeling of personal control (Lefcourt, 1973) or freedom (Skinner, 1971) or love (Rubin, 1973). The value of these subjective

experiences can only be determined after careful study from
many different psychological perspectives.

Social psychologists have been most successful in providing
empirical data on what people mean when they refer to their
"self". They have defined self as the labels used by a person to
describe or evaluate their own experiences (Gergen, 1971).
But the framework for this research has, to my mind, been a
narrow one. It has served its purpose of providing a paradigm
for empirical research, but must now be opened up. In a sense
it has been limited to a "lay" definition of self, rather than to
a scientific definition of self. Maybe we would benefit by revers-
ing Kelley's (1973) claim that naive attribution can be seen as
analogous to a scientific process, and start analyzing the scientific process as analogous to the lay process.

The analogy can be drawn more clearly by looking at three
characteristics of naive psychological functioning which have
tended also to characterize the social psychologist's approach
to the study of self. One of these is the tendency to stereotype
or to dwell on group averages. A second is the habit of evaluating behaviour by comparing it with a social norm. And a third
is the concern with content as it is explicitly verbalized rather
than with underlying patterns or structures.

With respect to stereotyping, research has demonstrated that
when asked to describe an individual, people rely heavily on the
fact that the individual belongs to certain categories, such as to
a gender or ethnic group (e.g. Aboud and Taylor, 1971; Aboud,
1976; Peevers and Secord, 1973). They will consequently
describe the individual in terms of the stereotyped characteristics which apply to the group as a whole. This is fine as a first
approximation, but it does not allow for variation between
individuals.

The attitude of social psychologists to their research subjects
is not much different. The individual being studied becomes
part of a group and his individual thoughts and feelings are
understood or explained only if they are similar to those of the
group as a whole. We generally attempt to explain only the
group mean; we rarely dwell on variances. As is the case with

the lay stereotyping process, the social psychologist's stereo-typing strategy for analyzing and explaining his data may be functional and accurate, to a limited extent. But it limits the amount of information available to us, so that neither our descriptions of people nor our theories about the causes of behaviour are complete. It also leads others to believe that this particular outcome is the only alternative available to them; that, for example, we are all doomed to resolve inconsistencies in ourselves by dissonance reduction.

The second process in which "naive" people engage frequently is the process of social comparison. When evaluating either themselves or another person, people tend to compare the target person to a social standard, and on that basis evaluate him as good or bad. Evaluation of a person is based entirely on his status relative to the norm or to another person. Relative comparisons eventually get translated into absolute evaluations; for example, "the same" means "good" and "different" means "bad".

Social psychologists have likewise adopted this manner of evaluating the behaviour of groups relative to the social norm. The assumption is that to be similar to the norm is good and to be different is bad; or the more socialized one is (in the sense of having adopted the values, attitudes, and behaviours of the group), the better. This assumption has resulted most clearly in invalid and irresponsible conclusions in studies which compare, and on that basis evaluate, different cultural groups. As a response, many Canadian minority groups have demanded an "equal but different" status within the Canadian multicultural framework. Similarly, it is assumed that if a male identifies with "masculinity" less than the norm, he is in trouble. Perhaps we should consider the idea that not all normative behaviour is good. We have already realized this in the areas of conformity and aggression, but have not yet extended this critical viewpoint to the areas of attraction, independence, responsibility, or self-perception.

If we do not compare people with a norm, how can we evaluate behaviour? Eiser and Stroebe (1972) provide a strong case for the insistent use of one standard or another when people make judgements. Many experimental social psychologists avoid this dilemma by using for comparison purposes a control group which was created to experience everything but the critical variable, and not to reflect any value standard. The assumption is that it is important to study whatever exists. But an increasing number of people want to know what *can* exist, not just what does exist. In response to this need, a number of psychologists attempted to provide a description of the "ideal" or "fully functioning" person (e.g. Allport, 1961; Maslow, 1954; Rogers, 1959). To my mind, these descriptions provide an excellent alternative to the social standards we usually use. Although one can criticize the content and the lack of specificity or empirical support for some of these descriptions, I feel that they are worth pursuing.

Why are many social psychologists reluctant to consider an "ideal" as an alternative standard? Perhaps they are so resistant partly because they want to see their discipline as being value-free. A more probable explanation is that as persons they are used to inferring negative evaluations whenever behaviour is discrepant from a standard. If they were to select an ideal to be the standard for comparison, all or most behaviour would be negatively evaluated. The real problem therefore lies with our process of evaluation, not with the standard.

The value of an ideal standard has become more apparent to me while studying the social development of young children. Take for example the typical findings on adult self-evaluation. Weiner and Kukla (1970) and Riemer (1975) demonstrate that success results in high self-evaluation and failure in low self-evaluation. Additional knowledge that many other people also succeeded or that many others failed attenuates the evaluation. Success plus high norms leads to lower self-evaluation than success plus low norms. Children up to the age of eleven do not seem to use the normative information when evaluating themselves. Success leads to high self-evaluation regardless of a high or a low norm, and conversely, failure leads to a low self-evaluation regardless of a high or a low norm (Ruble, Parsons and

Ross, 1976). How might psychologists evaluate the children's behaviour?

There are three alternative standards one could use depending on the conclusions one wants to make. Using a peer standard, one would conclude that the children are functioning in the same way as most children their age — they do not use social comparison information (e.g. Ruble, Feldman and Boggiano, 1976). Using an adult standard, one would conclude that the children do not have a complete understanding of social evaluation processes. Underlying this conclusion is the assumption that the more closely a person's response resembles the average adult response, the more socially developed he is. Using an ideal standard (as proposed by Maslow, 1954 or Rogers, 1959) one would conclude that ignoring social comparisons in favour of an internal standard of evaluation may be a very good thing. Adults are often unaware of their own aspirations or sense of mastery and so tend to rely on external norms or consensus to evaluate themselves. Thus, in terms of the ideal, children may be using a better strategy for evaluating themselves. Before I push this conjecture too far, I should say that both the ideal and the adult standards are necessary to give the complete picture. In other words one would want to show that children were cognitively capable of understanding and using both outcome and social norm information, but for meaningful (to them) reasons chose not to do so when making self-evaluations. To be socialized into the ways of unreflective adults (Nisbett and Wilson, 1977) is not always beneficial.

The third limiting characteristic of social psychological research on self is its concern with content rather than structure. The content of the description or the positiveness of the evaluation is focused on, but not the degree of differentiation, integration, or stability of this description and evaluation. Each item of the content is viewed as an isolated but equally important part of the self-concept; no one characteristic is regarded as more essential than another. This probably stems from an overemphasis on the social determinants of self-identity; that is, the theory that the nature of a person's self-identity is a direct reflection of the feedback given him by others. According to this view, the self is nothing more than the sum of various reactions and labels provided by other people about oneself (Cottrell, 1969; Mead, 1934). Furthermore, this view of self reflects only the content which resides at the most explicit, verbalized level of thought. This is very similar to Nisbett and Wilson's (1977) description of the "naive" person's attempts to explain his personal behaviour. Instead of looking for underlying causes or patterns in one's own behaviour, most people do not look beyond the superficial level of stereotyped traits.

These, then, are three characteristics which seem to pervade most (but not all) of the social psychological research on self. They have limited our thinking on the topic of self to that which resides at a verbalized level of awareness, which consists of isolated and often superficial items of description, which reflects mainly information from external social forces, and which is to be evaluated in comparison with a social norm.

In an attempt to overcome these limitations, I chose as the focus for my research the concept of a "sense of self". By "sense of self" I mean an awareness or consciousness of the presence of an entity which is essential to one's psychological existence. It differs from self-concept, which denotes a description of oneself, and it also differs from self-esteem, which denotes an evaluation of oneself. Both one's self-concept and one's self-esteem may change without affecting one's sense of self, just as the content of a group may change without radically altering the structure. It *is* possible that certain major changes in content such as those that occur during adolescence (Erikson, 1968) do precipitate a break-down of the structure. But the essential independence of structure from content provides a basis from which we can study those circumstances in which changes in one lead to changes in the other. Three structural characteristics which seem to contribute to a sense of self are internal consistency, uniqueness, and constancy. These characteristics are mentioned most often by "self" theorists such as Allport (1961), Duval and Wicklund (1972), Gergen (1971), and Mead (1934). One issue that needs to be considered in research on self is the relative importance of structure *versus* content, and the relationship between the two.

A second issue arising from the concept of a "sense of self" is the level of awareness where such a sense resides. You can ask a person to describe his self-concept and you will most likely get a list of traits or experiences. But you cannot ask a person to describe his sense of self and expect to get a coherent answer. Psychologists need new measures from which to infer the nature of this sense of self — whether it exists, and to what degree it shows coherence, distinctiveness, and constancy. Such measures should tap into various levels of awareness: the sensory or experiential awareness of being a unified entity, the intuitive or perhaps imaginal level of awareness, as well as the verbal analytic level. I suspect that for most children and for many adults, their sense of self resides at the sensory or intuitive thought levels. They have a sense of self in one form or another, but are unable to articulate the components which contribute to it.

The third issue is the extent to which a sense of self necessitates a social framework, within which we as psychologists define and evaluate such a concept and within which the "naive" person develops and maintains such a sense. Certainly psychologists do not need to limit themselves to studying only the norm or average response to their measures. Nor do they need to assume that this average response is the only appropriate standard against which to compare and evaluate other responses. They can also study the extremes, and thereby work out the ideal direction for growth and development. Given our present knowledge on the lack of self-reflective thought in the average adult (Nisbett and Wilson, 1977), we can be certain that the norm will not coincide with what is ideal or even possible. We might also try to determine what is desirable.

The more difficult question is whether a person needs a social framework within which to develop and maintain a sense of self. I found it interesting that one of the few social psychology textbooks which devotes a whole chapter to the self (Middlebrook, 1974) justifies its inclusion by stating that the process of self-development is determined by the social environment. Most social psychologists still view the self very much as Mead did in 1934. According to Mead, the sense of self exists only as a result of social experiences, specifically the feedback on how other people react to you. Presumably, the more feedback the stronger one's sense of self. Middlebrook allows for only two occasions when the self is not dependent on others: when one's self-esteem is so high that external standards can be dispensed with, and when one wants to avoid discrepant information coming from others. This type of theorizing excludes the important factors of cognition, motivation, and development.

Duval and Wicklund (1972) have added some alternative views of the self which seem plausible. The first is that one can have a sense of self without feedback from other people, simply by directing one's thought toward oneself. The second is that a sense of self exists as soon as one can be conscious of internal stimuli. The responses of other people, or the ability to take the role of another in order to view oneself as an object are reduced to secondary importance — they are only two of many factors which contribute to cognitive development of a sense of self.

My own view is that, in the early stages of development, what one thinks about oneself is not dependent on information from other people. Later on, it becomes very dependent on social information for both definitional and evaluative purposes. It is possible to have a stage beyond this when once again social factors do not contribute very much. This sequence is supported by other research in the area of gender identity (Block, 1973), self-evaluation (Veroff, 1969), moral development (Kohlberg, 1969), and ego development (Loevinger, 1976). The advantage of this sequential view is that it can deal with individuals as developing along a continuum with the direction of change being toward the "ideal". At any one point in the sequence, one may be more or less influenced by social information, cognitive limitations, or motivational factors. Since normative adult behaviour represents only one point somewhere in the middle of this continuum, why use it as the basis for a theory? To be more specific, I will relate this discussion to research on the three structural characteristics of a sense of self mentioned previously: internal consistency, uniqueness, and constancy. The critical issues, as I see them, are: Do these characteristics exist and in what form? Do they contribute positively or negatively to one's sense of self?

Internal Consistency

Internal consistency refers to the integration of psychologically different aspects of oneself. This presumably provides a feeling of unity. Much of the dissonance research suggested that people felt uncomfortable with and therefore avoided awareness of psychological inconsistencies in themselves. There are many possible explanations for the consistency-oriented behaviours that we find. According to Kiesler and Pallak (1976) we may be motivated to reduce the arousal associated with our own novel or incongruous behaviour. A more superficial explanation is that both the demands of an experimental setting and the demands of a question such as "Who are you?" pressure the subject into giving a consistent response. A third intriguing possibility is that the nature of language is such as to restrict the speaker to a logical sequence of expression. If a person were trying to describe himself verbally, his answer might be constrained by the sequential, rule-following demands of speech. More importantly, since analytic thinking has many characteristics in common with speech (e.g. explicit, sequential), thoughts about oneself may likewise be constrained. However, some interesting experiments by Cvetkovich (1978) demonstrate that most self-directed thoughts are intuitive rather than analytic. Intuitive thinking is characterized as implicit, nonsequential, and not easily retrievable.

We are still left with the question: What do these consistency-oriented behaviours reflect — a need to *feel* internally consistent, to *think* about oneself in terms of consistent attributes, or to *present* oneself to others as a consistent person? In addition to separating these three levels of awareness, I think we need to look closely at what is being integrated. One can hardly talk about an internally consistent sense of self when the facets that are being integrated are few in number or only superficially different. A more ideal state would be integration of highly differentiated facets of oneself. Differentiation as well as integration should be considered. Gergen and Morse (1967) attempted to incorporate both of these concepts in a measure of internal consistency by having students choose five positive and five negative traits which described themselves, and then had them rate the degree of compatibility of all possible pairs of the traits. Out of a possible score of 135 (high inconsistency), the mean for 209 students was 36.64 with a large standard deviation of 21.33. Since the students were told to choose both positive and negative traits, ability to differentiate was not really tested. But the measure of integration is a good one.

Some research I have been involved in was initiated by John Christian (1976). He wanted to find out the number of different dimensions people were able to use and to integrate when thinking about themselves and people who were significant to them. All possible pairs of stimuli were judged by the person to be similar or dissimilar, and these judgements were entered into a maximum likelihood multidimensional scaling program (Ramsay, 1977). Each individual's set of judgements could be described as integrating one, two, three, or more dimensions. Among the university population tested, the number of different dimensions used ranged from one to five. In a subsequent study we found that 37% of the students in grade II used one dimension and 63% used two dimensions; for grade IV students the figures were 28% and 72% respectively (Aboud and Christian, 1977). In this case, looking at individuals located on an open-ended dimensionality continuum was more profitable than comparing them to the adult norm which was three dimensional. Because this technique does not rely on verbalized thought, many children were found to be integrating the same number of dimensions as some adults.

Uniqueness

The second characteristic I mentioned was uniqueness. Uniqueness refers to the feeling that one is different from any other person. It presumably provides one with a sense of self that is separate and distinctive. Social psychological research has shown us both sides of the uniqueness variable: on the one hand people are attracted to similar others (Byrne, 1969) and they seek out group affiliations (Turner, 1975); but on the other hand they feel uncomfortable and will change their attitudes when faced with other people who have very similar attributes (Fromkin, 1973). This paradox might be resolved if we could demonstrate that group uniqueness can also satisfy needs for individual uniqueness, or that groups provide mechanisms for achieving uniqueness within the group. Although most self theorists believe that uniqueness contributes positively to one's sense of self, I do not think that all forms do.

We have found in our research that many five- and six-year-old children will describe themselves by highlighting the difference between themselves and others. Briefly, we asked them to talk about themselves by pointing to pictures of other people and saying in what way they were similar or different. They came up with an average of eight self-descriptors using this recognition technique, a figure quite a bit higher than that found by using spontaneous verbal production techniques (e.g. Secord and Peevers, 1974). One-quarter of the children described themselves by pointing only to pictures of people who were similar, one-quarter pointed only to people who were different from them, and the remaining half used both similar and different characteristics but the different ones were mentioned first (Aboud and Ruckenstein, 1977). Highlighting differences may help the child to develop a sense of himself as being unique. On the other hand, it is often an inaccurate exaggeration (as when the child points to a picture of someone who is similar in every observable way except for the one characteristic on which he chooses to focus). Fromkin (1973, p. 96) provides support for this inaccurate exaggeration of uniqueness in a study with college students. It seems that females rated their sexual beliefs as most unique about themselves, but in fact these beliefs were not very different from those of their peers. Furthermore, sexual beliefs were not often discussed among these women. This suggests a need to maintain a feeling of uniqueness despite its inaccuracy.

I have been trying to research this feeling of uniqueness using a more indirect approach. Modifying some questions developed by Guardo and Bohan (1971), I asked students "Could you be a French Canadian and still be the person that you are?" On one level, this is a question about uniqueness; it is asking, could you be someone else and still maintain whatever is essential to your "self". Some people say that they could *not* be another person; that whatever they are is unique to themselves and this would preclude adopting another role. Others feel that they are unique in a psychological sense, and that whatever makes them unique could not be lost despite the role change. Still others feel that they are not unique, that their essential characteristics could be found in a French Canadian.

This is a complex question. The fact that it was perceived as more and more complex as we moved from kindergarteners, to second graders, fourth graders, and finally university students, implies that an older person has a more sophisticated view of what is essentially "himself". Younger people tend to describe themselves and others with concrete observable characteristics. Only later are the psychological subjective characteristics used, and even then not substantially so (Secord and Peevers, 1974; Livesley and Bromley, 1973). This suggests that there is another level to the question "Could you be a French Canadian and still be the person that you are?" besides uniqueness. It is also asking, would your sense of what is essentially you remain unviolated despite the "superficial" changes of place, context, or ethnicity. This is really the third characteristic of a sense of self that I mentioned earlier: constancy or continuity. Even though social psychological research has shown that people change their descriptions of themselves as a result of time, place, and social context (e.g. Gergen and Wishnov, 1965), we would not think of this as contributing positively to one's sense of self. The problem with most of the research upon which this conclusion is based is that the changing attributes are often peripheral rather than central to the person's psychological existence. Such studies reveal little about a constant sense of self.

The "Could you be..." question allowed people to express whatever characteristic they felt made them "the person that you are" and to say whether this would persist despite an ethnic change. In fact I asked them about seven ethnic members, their own plus six others: Jewish Canadian, English Canadian, French Canadian, Black Canadian, Chinese Canadian, Indian Canadian, and Eskimo Canadian. The kindergarten children overall were more concerned about uniqueness than either second or fourth graders if we accept as an index the percentage of children who said they could be no more than one ethnic member and still be themselves (34% *vs.* 8% and 0% respectively). It is interesting to note that 8% of the university students felt this kind of uniqueness — similar to second graders.

When we categorized their reasons as referring to concrete or psychological characteristics of themselves, an overwhelming proportion of 94% were concrete. Further analyses revealed that those who said "no" were viewing their concrete characteristics as essential and unchangeable. They would say, "I couldn't speak their language" or "I don't play with bows and arrows" or "I can't change my skin colour". Children who answered "yes" to the question referred to the same concrete characteristics but saw them as changeable and/or unessential. They would say "I could learn to speak their language" or "I could get a suntan". Sometimes a second or fourth grader would hint at an internal entity that would remain unchanged despite external behavioural or appearance changes: "I would be speaking French but I would still be me on the inside."

The answers given by adults to these ethnic change questions differed from the children's data in only one respect: more of the adults referred to psychological characteristics such as traits, abilities, and values. Those who did not describe themselves in psychological terms responded no differently from fourth graders. Those who did use psychological descriptors had to decide whether they were essential or unessential, and transferable or nontransferable. Most of the time they concluded that the self-descriptors were essential and nontransferable, so the average number of "yes" responses was as low as it was for the grade II and IV children (4.46, 4.27 and 4.52 respectively).

Although I could never hope to categorize all the thoughts generated by these questions, I think they point out that certain forms of uniqueness do not contribute positively to a sense of self. If uniqueness is based on a concrete characteristic which can easily be lost or acquired by anyone, or if it is based on a characteristic which is obviously not unique, then the sense of self will continually be threatened by other people's similarities. However, if uniqueness is based on simple separateness, then I see fewer problems for the individual. Once again I do not feel that normative adult behaviour which is described in the social psychological literature as seeking uniqueness provides a very good standard for evaluating behaviour. At this point, however, I cannot give strong logical or empirical support for an alternative.

Constancy

The question of constancy or continuity, like internal consistency, is somewhat more clear-cut. Most "self" theorists feel that having a definition or evaluation of oneself which remains relatively constant despite fluctuations of time, place, and social context contributes positively to a sense of self (Allport, 1961; Rogers, 1959). Constancy here does not mean inflexibility; it means that although changes are made in self-concept and self-evaluation, these changes do not disrupt the essential aspects of one's self-definition or one's feeling of worth.

Block's (1973) definition of sexual identity contains the same idea: being secure enough in one's own gender to be able to express attributes regarded as more appropriate for the opposite sex. When I asked kindergarten children and university students if they could be someone of the opposite sex and still be the person that they were, only 25% of the children and 63% of the adults said they could. The developmental direction is toward saying "yes", but nevertheless many of the adults are saying that they would be essentially different if they were a member of the opposite sex. The adult norm, then, does not represent a mature sexual identity in Block's terms.

Using similar reasoning, we assumed that when a child was asked "Could you be a French Canadian, and still be the person that you are?" he would first consider what was essential to himself and then weigh this against the change required to be a French Canadian. Since most children defined themselves and French Canadians in terms of language, the difference between a "yes" and a "no" response lay in whether or not language was perceived as changeable and superficial (in the sense of being not essential to one's psychological existence) or fixed and essential. When one defines oneself in terms of the external social characteristics of an ethnic group, any suggestion of changing this role would be tantamount to changing one's self.

Contrary to this ideal standard set forth by self theorists, social psychological research demonstrates that adults evaluate themselves relative to other people (Festinger, 1954) and consequently fluctuate according to the social context. For example, Morse and Gergen (1970) found that adults evaluated themselves more negatively when in the presence of a "socially desirable" other, and *vice versa*. The internally inconsistent adults changed their self-evaluation more than the internally consistent ones. My own research with young children has shown that they too vary more or less when evaluating themselves in association with a variety of significant others. The structural measures of amount of variability in self-evaluation ratings, variation as a function of the value assigned to the other, and undifferentiated self-evaluations all loaded highly on one factor. This factor emerged independent of a content factor on which measures of goodness loaded highly. Thus some children showed a great deal of variation from one self-evaluation to the next and varied consistently as a positive or a negative function of the significant other. Other children did not show this kind of variability, but the difference was unrelated to age. Those who were constant showed less interest in social comparison information after performing a task.

Although these results are very similar to the results of adult research, I would not want to say that this kind of variability contributed positively to a sense of self. We have evidence from both the child and the adult data that not all people fluctuate with the social context, and furthermore that this constancy is associated with internal consistency, a characteristic which also contributes to a strong sense of self. The fact that this constancy can be found with young children leads me to wonder whether children may be better off if they were not socialized into considering other people as standards. Many people (Rogers, 1959; Veroff, 1969) feel that children have their own internal standards to start with, but then become socialized into accepting external standards.

To summarize, by discussing research on the development of a sense of self, I have tried to make several points about social psychology. The first is that we need to do research and analyze data in a way that will help us understand individual functioning. Group averages do not provide all the information necessary to establish what does and can exist. Most research will allow for an ideographic as well as a nomothetic approach. Secondly, we are limiting the area of social psychology and the study of self if we exclude aspects of functioning that are not entirely determined by social forces. I suspect that it is this overemphasis on social determinants that has led to measures which tap only the verbalized and analytic content of thoughts. It may be more useful to look at structural characteristics and at intuitive and sensory forms which contribute to a sense of self. Even if we were to find that cognitive, motivational, or developmental factors determine the sense of self more than do social factors, it is clear that there is still a great deal for social psychologists to study about the relationship between self and others. The third point is that evaluating behaviour by comparing it with the norm may not be very enlightening. As an alternative, I have suggested the so-called "ideal" standards proposed by people such as Allport, Rogers, and Maslow. Many of their ideal characteristics need to be questioned and tested. But the idea of having a goal toward which individuals are developing seems to me to be a better strategy for understanding what exists and what is possible.

References

Aboud, F.E., The effect of stereotype generalization on information seeking, *Canadian Journal of Behavioural Science*, 1976, *8*, 178-88.

Aboud, F.E. and Christian, J.D., Development of ethic identity: a multi-dimensional scaling analysis, McGill University, Montreal, Canada, 1977.

Aboud, F.E. and Ruckenstein, S., Sense of self and social curiosity, McGill University, Montreal, Canada, 1977.

Aboud, F.E. and Taylor, D.M., Ethnic and role stereotypes: Their relative importance in person perception, *Journal of Social Psychology*, 1971, *85*, 17-27.

Allport, G.W., *Pattern and Growth in Personality*, New York: Holt, Rinehart & Winston, 1961.

Block, J.H., Conceptions of sex role: Some cross-cultural and longitudinal perspectives, *American Psychologist*, 1973, *28*, 512-26.

Byrne, D., Attitudes and attraction. In L. Berkowitz (Ed.), *Advances in Experimental Social Psychology*, Vol. 4, New York: Academic Press, 1969.

Christian, J.D., Ego development, psychological differentiation, and definition of self. Doctoral dissertation, McGill University, 1976.

Cottrell, L.S., Interpersonal interaction and the development of the self. In D.A. Goslin (Ed.), *Handbook of Socialization Theory and Research*, Chicago: Rand McNally, 1969.

Cvetkovich, G., Cognitive accommodation, language, and social responsibility, *Social Psychology*, 1978, *14*, 149-55.

Duval, S. and Wicklund, R.A., *A Theory of Objective Self Awareness*, New York: Academic Press, 1972.

Eiser, J.R. and Stroebe, W., *Categorization and Social Judgement*, New York: Academic Press, 1972.

Epstein, S., The self-concept revisited: Or a theory of a theory, *American Psychologist*, 1973, *28*, 404-16.

Erikson, E.H., *Identity: Youth and Crisis*, New York: Norton, 1968.

Festinger, L., A theory of social comparison processes, *Human Relations*, 1954, *7*, 117-40.

Fromkin, H.L., The psychology of uniqueness: avoidance of similarity and seeking of differentness, Purdue University, December 1973.

Gergen, K.J., *The Concept of Self*, New York: Holt, Rinehart & Winston, 1971.

Gergen, K.J. and Morse, S.J., Self-consistency: Measurement and validation, Proceedings of the American Psychological Association, 1967, 207-8.

Gergen, K.J. and Wishnov, B., Others' self-evaluation and interaction anticipation as determinants of self-presentation, *Journal of Personality and Social Psychology*, 1965, *2*, 348-58.

Guardo, C.J. and Bohan, J.B., Development of a sense of self identity in children, *Child Development*, 1971, *42*, 1909-21.

Kelley, H.H., The process of causal attribution, *American Psychologist*, 1973, *28*, 107-28.

Kiesler, C.A. and Pallak, M.S., Arousal properties of dissonance manipulations, *Psychological Bulletin*, 1976, *83*, 1014-25.

Kohlberg, L., Stage and sequence: the cognitive-developmental approach to socialization. In D.A. Goslin (Ed.), *Handbook of Socialization Theory and Research*, Chicago: Rand McNally, 1969.

Lefcourt, H.M., The function of the illusion of control and freedom, *American Psychologist*, 1973, *28*, 417-25.

Livesley, W.J. and Bromley, D.B., *Person Perception in Childhood and Adolescence*, New York: Wiley, 1973.

Loevinger, J., *Ego Development*, San Francisco: Jossey-Bass, 1976.

Lowe, C., The self-concept: Fact or artifact? *Psychological Bulletin*, 1961, *58*, 325-36.

Maslow, A.H., *Motivation and Personality*, New York: Harper & Row, 1954.

Mead, G.H., *Mind, Self and Society*, Chicago: University of Chicago Press, 1934.

Middlebrook, P.N., *Social Psychology and Modern Life*, New York: Alfred Knopf, 1974.

Morse, S. and Gergen, K.J., Social comparison, self-consistency, and the concept of self, *Journal of Personality and Social Psychology*, 1970, *16*, 148-56.

Nisbett, R.E. and Wilson, T.D., Telling more than we can know: Verbal reports on mental processes, *Psychological Review*, 1977, *84*, 231-59.

Peevers, B.H. and Secord, P.F., Developmental changes in attribution of descriptive concepts to persons, *Journal of Personality and Social Psychology*, 1973, *27*, 120-8.

Ramsay, J.O., *MDS Manual. Version I*, Psychology Department, McGill University, Montreal, January, 1977.

Riemer, B.S., Influence of causal beliefs on affect and expectancy, *Journal of Personality and Social Psychology*, 1975, *31*, 1163-7.

Rogers, C.R., A theory of therapy, personality and interpersonal relationships. In S. Koch (Ed.), *Psychology: A Study of a Science*, Vol. 3, New York: McGraw-Hill, 1959.

Rubin, Z., *Liking and Loving*, New York: Holt, Rinehart & Winston, 1973.

Ruble, D.N., Parsons, J.E. and Ross, E., Self-evaluative responses of children in an achievement setting, *Child Development*, 1976, *47*, 990-7.

Ruble, D.N., Feldman, N.S. and Boggiano, A.K., Social comparison between young children in achievement situations, *Developmental Psychology*, 1976, *12*, 192-7.

Secord, P.F. and Peevers, B.H., The development and attribution of person concepts. In T. Mischel (Ed.), *Understanding Other Persons*, Oxford: Basil Blackwell & Mott, 1974.

Skinner, B.F., *Beyond Freedom and Dignity*, Toronto: Bantam, 1971.

Turner, J.C., Social comparison and social identity: some prospects for intergroup behaviour, *European Journal of Social Psychology*, 1975, *5*, 5-34.

Veroff, J., Social comparison and the development of achievement motivation. In C.P. Smith (Ed.), *Achievement-related Motives in Children*, New York: Russell Sage Foundation, 1969.

Weiner, B. and Kukla, A., An attributional analysis of achievement motivation, *Journal of Personality and Social Psychology*, 1970, *15*, 1-20.

Discussion

KIESLER: Data indicate that people don't have very well articulated ideas about themselves; our attitudes and concepts of self change situationally, and self-esteem changes situationally. You're making an assumption that there's some core beyond a dynamically changing self concept and self esteem — but what's beyond it?

ABOUD: I don't know whether anything exists, but I'm not talking about whether there is anything that exists.

KIESLER: You have a hope that there is. What makes you distinguish between the "hope" of a Maslow and the empirical data which fail to indicate that something goes beyond that hope?

ABOUD: I'm not concerned about whether a self does exist. I'm concerned more about what a person senses phenomenologically — if he has a sense that there's something continuing. There may not be, but it doesn't matter to me whether there is or isn't. Even though I have changed over the past thirty-odd years, I may still consider that I am the same person. The idea that there isn't any stability — that the self concept changes or that self esteem changes — is still very compatible with having a stable sense of oneself. The kind of concept that I'm talking about refers to an essential "thing" that a person *thinks* remains the same.

KIESLER: OK, you're speaking of something phenomenological; is it something that exists at one time, like a perceived sense of self, or are you speaking of my perception that I have been the same person, *over time?*

ABOUD: Either. It could even be a sensory feeling, as for example, when a young infant pinches his toe and realizes that it's part of him. That's very rudimentary sensory perception. So yes, I am talking about a perceived feeling that there is something essential.

KIESLER: Which does or does not change?

ABOUD: Which does not change even though superficial things, like my answers to "Am I intelligent?", or "Do I look pretty?" — those answers may change, but there's something that does not.

ANDREEVA: If you compare the different ways of forming the sense of self, in different groups (among children, among adults) do you think these different ways of forming a sense of self can be determined? Can you study not only the age of subjects, but maybe also the type of their activity,[1] the type of performance of

[1]See discussion of "activity" in body and discussion of Bueva's paper (pp. 111-18) (Ed.).

different groups? Have you done anything like this? Have you tried to compare different groups of adults who shared different kinds of activity? Can we interpret this factor, activity, as a determinant of the different ways of forming the sense of self?

ABOUD: I have not studied that, but it would be possible. There are certainly some children — very young children — who have a sense of themselves, and some children who do not. And there are probably many social reasons why some do and some do not, and it may be the group activity. It is probably how the group directs attention of that child.

BUEVA: Would you consider that the value of the individual in society depends on social structures and the type of education adopted in the society?

ABOUD: I think both of those factors are important in helping people to think of themselves as individuals, and to think of other people as individuals. But it's the way the education system proceeds, how it treats individual children, that would determine the importance they place on individuality.

ANDREEVA: Would it be more correct, Dr. Aboud, to say the process of socialization rather than the educational process? Is that what you mean?

ABOUD: No — I mean both.

BUEVA: Are there works available on comparative studies of various social structures and the values placed on the individual in those various social structures?

ABOUD: There is some research in climates where the teacher evaluates the child relative to other children, or in climates where each child is evaluated by himself.

KIESLER: We're having a problem here. We do not all mean the same thing by "social structure".

Social Psychology and Community Psychology: The Case of the Police

DONALD G. DUTTON

Abstract. The following paper examines social psychological contributions to an understanding of the police as a social sub-group. These contributions include non-verbal communication between police and citizens as effecting police-citizen contacts, attribution theory analyses of conflicting views of crime causation, occupational authoritarianism and the police working personality, intragroup influence and intergroup conflict theory as applied to police and other sub-groups, research on helping for police-community sharing of responsibility, theories of aggression such as the frustration-aggression hypothesis and its relevance for domestic violence. An attempt is made to show both how an understanding of the police benefits from social-psychological perspectives and theories and how thinking and research in social psychology benefits from real-world testing.

Many community psychology graduate curricula taught in North American universities draw their theoretical orientatiohs from clinical psychology and, more specifically, from a systems-behaviour modification approach. In this presentation I am going to describe how a social psychological orientation can contribute to an understanding of a highly visible community group: the police. By implication, the point I wish to argue is that the same theoretical orientations can provide invaluable adjuncts to a community psychology curriculum dealing with a variety of social groups and that a clinical-social orientation should provide the bases of such curricula.

My own interest in the police as a social group evolved initially from a doctoral minor in criminology as a compromise between aspirations to become both a lawyer and a psychologist.

My initial interest in the police centered around their use of specific interrogation techniques described by Zimbardo (1967) and investigated by Bem (1966) and Douglas and Dutton (1974). The central question of these investigations was whether such techniques could induce a belief in a false confession by a person being interrogated. As such the orientation of such investigations was in keeping with the police-social scientist polarity of the late 1960s which often cast the police into a "bad guy" role and led as a consequence to the infamous "blue curtain" being dropped before the inquiring eyes of would-be scientific investigators. Those investigators who "got themselves behind the arras", including such people as David Bordua (1967), Irving Piliavin (1964), Paul Chevigny (1969), Arthur Niederhoffer (1967) and Albert Reiss (1971) presented a bleak picture of police authoritarianism, corruption and abuses of power.

That both police and criminals commit acts which are violent and destructive is an acceptable premise. That social scientists turned their attention toward a sympathetic understanding of the social situational causes of such behaviour for criminals but not for police belies a value orientation of the late 1960s in which the police were viewed by social scientists as social control agents for the establishment, and social scientists were viewed by themselves as critics of this same establishment falling somewhere in a dimension between liberal and radical poles.

With the detente in North American society in the 1970s between formerly polarized groups, a corresponding shift in posture has developed in the approach taken by social scientists investigating the police, and, as a result, an increased receptivity to such study has developed on the part of the police.

My early interests in the police led me to three working propositions that have guided my later work. These are:

(1) That the police as a social group are a striking, glaring, neon example of many of the social processes that we are interested in as social psychologists: intergroup conflicts, intra-group solidarity and influence processes, non-verbal miscom-

munication, role conflict and stress. The set of relations between police and community presents an excellent opportunity for naturalistic study of these processes, as well as providing an altered perspective for our views on pro- and anti-social behaviour; the net effects of these social structural factors on police attitudes, attributions of crime causation and responses to job stresses constitute another example of such behaviours "writ large". Recently other writers have shared these views. Ezra Stotland devoted an entire issue of the *Journal of Social Issues* (1975) to the study of police and community. Jerome Skolnick (1967), Michael Banton (1973), Rodney Stark (1972), and Brian Grosman (1975) have all contributed insightful volumes on the police as a social group.

(2) The second working proposition was that such attempts to make sense of or understand police behaviour had not occurred because of the value orientation mentioned above. The investigative tools existed and had been applied to other organization groups by Kurt Lewin (1948), Warren Bennis (1976) and Chris Argyris (1974). What remained was to apply them to an understanding of police behaviour.

(3) The third working proposition was that by bringing the theories and orientations of social psychology to bear on a real world group in an applied research setting, an improved awareness of the strength and limitations of such theories could be developed. I viewed this as a real world panacea for the ills of social psychology which have developed from an overreliance on laboratory experimentation, and a resulting hermeticism. This last working proposition has proved to be somewhat naive (see Helmreich, 1975).

Having said these things I am now faced with the task of demonstrating to you how social psychology can contribute to an understanding of this social group. To do this, I will confine my comments to five areas of social psychological study of police behaviour: proxemics and non-verbal communication, attribution theory, attitudes and stereotyping, intragroup influence and intergroup conflict and pro- and anti-social behaviour.

Proxemics and Non-verbal Communication

The burgeoning research area of proxemics and non-verbal communication has provided some interesting analyses of communication problems in police-citizen contacts. Building upon some seminal studies in intergroup differences in non-verbal behaviours (Jones and Aiello, 1973; LaFrance and Mayo, 1973), James Baxter and Richard Rozelle (Baxter and Rozelle, 1975; Rozelle and Baxter, 1975) have studied non-verbal communication problems developing between white police officers and black citizens in the US.

Baxter and Rozelle have found that ethnicity, status differences and differential task orientations would all operate in such an interaction situation to produce a desire on the part of the black citizen for greater personal distance from the white police officer than the officer desires. As a result the officer "crowds" or "invades" the citizen's personal space, thus producing a constellation of nonverbal gestures (gaze aversion, head activity, protective arm and hand behaviour, trunk rotation and foot activity) plus a series of attempts to increase personal distance. The series of "invasions" (by the officer) and "evasions" (by the citizen) are interpreted by the citizen as another example of police bullying and by the officer as signs of the citizen's guilt. The officer, being unaware that his "crowding" produces the very symptoms that he takes as signs of guilt may make an error in judgement in such situations, since the nonverbal gestures produced by crowding are the same gestures that police officers interpret as guilt-indicators as part of their "street-psychology".

Of special significance here is the role played by differential interpretations of nonverbal behaviours of members of two different racial, cultural or social groups. Intergroup differences in eye contact could feed into the same matrix of misinterpretation. LaFrance and Mayo found that blacks tend to gaze avoid while listening and to gaze engage while speaking. The opposite is true for whites who gaze avoid while speaking and then make eye contact with a listener to signal the listener's turn to speak. If we envisage a black youth stopped for questioning in a high crime area by a suspicious white officer who has, in stopping the youth and asking for ID, already "invaded" his personal space, made him feel bullied, and produced a collection of non-verbal gestures which have aroused the officer's suspicions even more, we can see a potentially volatile situation developing. If, on top of this, the officer gives the youth a long lecture on avoiding that particular area of town and which he ends with a typically white gesture of gaze-engaging only to find the youth gaze-avoiding, it can clearly be interpreted by the officer as indicative of insolence and disrespect for authority.

Conversely, if the youth, in responding to the officer's questions, gaze-engages to a listener who in a black group would gaze-avoid, he finds the white officer staring right back at him. This intergroup nonverbal difference may be interpreted by the youth as further evidence of bullying. To a certain extent non-verbal miscommunication is feeding directly into the reciprocal negative stereotypes each hold of the other. Modern police training curricula include workshops on such issues to sensitize officers to these problems and to the more general problem of personal space in dealing with emotionally upset citizens. While studies by Kinzel (1970) on body buffer-zones in violent prisoners and by Dabbs (Dabbs, Fuller and Carr, 1973) on personal space requirements of students and prisoners in room centers and corners are instructive, the necessary studies on personal space requirements under varying conditions of emotional arousal are lacking. Such studies would be of great practical utility for police officers who have to control citizens in family disputes and other volatile situations.

Police Attributions of Crime Causation

In 1974 a criminologist by the name of George Kirkham published an article entitled *A Professor's Street Lessons* in which he rejected his own smug "ivory tower" view of crime causation and police work on the basis of a 6 month stint of duty with the Jacksonville, Florida, PD (Kirkham, 1975). While Kirkham's article highlighted the discrepancies between the police and criminologist's view of the world, it also read like the breathless and naive testimonial of a recent convert who had abandoned his former "real" world view for his present real world view. Such an approach fails as an attempt to come to grips with an explanation for "separate realities" based on different perspectives, differential access to information or information processing tendencies.

Some beginning steps in this direction have been taken by the writings in attribution theory by Kelley (1973) and by Jones and Nisbett (1973). Jones and Nisbett, for example, demonstrate how, on purely cognitive grounds, an actor and an observer of the actor's behaviour could arrive at widely differing causal attributions for the actor's action. Part of the reason for these differing attributions comes from the different referents or comparison points that the actor and the observer have. Actors, according to Jones and Nisbett, attribute unique behaviour on their part to the current setting or situation in which they find themselves while observers attribute unique behaviour to a pre-disposition in the actor. Years of research in social psychology (e.g., Jones and Harris, 1967; Milgram, 1963; Latané and Darley, 1975) demonstrate the underestimation of situational pressures by observers outside the situation. Conversely, years of clinical observation demonstrate the underestimation of personal responsibility for selecting social situations (relationships, etc.), which are eventually "blamed" for personal problems. By showing how different attributions can derive from different roles' access to information, frames of reference, etc. attribution theory can perhaps contribute toward an understanding of mis-understandings and hence to conflict resolution.

If we apply an attributional analysis to police-criminologist discrepancies, we begin to see how this might work. Police traditionally hold "radical free will" views of crime causation (Stark, 1972), which invest responsibility for illegal action in the person caught committing that action, regardless of that person's past experience in the cultural, societal, or other external forces acting on him. Criminologists, social workers, probation officers and other professionals in the criminal justice system tend to hold deterministic views of crime causation which view background factors as major determinants of crime causation. Needless to say, these differing world-views contribute in no small part to conflict between professional groups within this system.

Criminologists (Stark, 1972) tend to dismiss police views of crime causation as due mainly to ignorance on the part of the police. That is, although they eschew predispositional explanations for crime causation, they rely on these very explanations to account for the world views of a group with which they disagree. Stark, for example, dismisses the police free will view as reflecting a "widespread misunderstanding" of the logic of multiple causation and of statistical inference" (Stark, 1972, p. 143).

An attributional analysis of crime causation would consider the information that is both available to and utilized by police and criminologists. Police information processing of crime causation has to be decision or action oriented as befits a practitioner, especially a practitioner whose actions can have life or death consequences. Hence such processing largely precludes complex models of human action. A criminologist, it might be argued, can have a more complete model of crime causation, but not necessarily one that would lead to effective action under the limiting conditions that most police find themselves. A deterministic view of crime causation would constantly serve to remind the practitioner-officer that crime has broad social-origins that are effectively beyond his or her control, and that the person-oriented solutions in which they engage are short-term solutions which rarely have significant enduring effects in lowering a crime rate. To the extent that practitioner-officers want to think of their professional behaviour as relatively efficient and productive, they will possess a professional motive for viewing crime in free-will terms. Seeing the causes of crime as residing in enduring dispositional characteristics of criminals allows police to take some satisfaction in removing criminals from the streets. It gives a feeling of being able to control relevant events, a motive which White (1959) has termed "effectance".

In addition, police are regularly exposed to the kinds of actions which violate conventional social norms, such actions, as Jones and Harris (1967) have demonstrated, are the very actions which elicit dispositional inferences for the causes of the action from observers of the action. Both of the above factors could contribute to police attributions of crime causation. In addition police, unlike the criminologists whose role encourages a disinterested analysis of the situational origins of social problems, are required to take an active role in dealing with these problems. In so doing they become involved with individuals whose behaviour frustrates their efforts to be efficient. It may well be that behavioural outcomes which have unpleasant personal consequences for another person tend to elicit dispositional inferences from that person about the actor's behaviour. Such inferences may provide a cognitive form of justification for aggressive feelings toward a frustrating agent. Hence we would expect to find predispositional explanations held by groups about groups which frustrate them. Police hold such explanations about criminals. Criminologists hold such explanations for police world views and the behaviour derived from them, but do not hold such explanations for the behaviour of other groups.

Such an argument leads to the following contentions: (1) that the causal attributions of social groups can be better understood by examining the relevance of such attributions for group function, rather than by ascribing the attributions to a predispositional deficiency commonly held by all group members; (2) in attempting to make such an examination a social psychologist is leaning heavily on data and concepts of attribution theory, but he is also extending this theory by viewing attributions as arising within a complex of social roles and motives heretofore overlooked by attribution theorists, who have tended to be psychological-individual-cognitive rather than social in their orientation (Kelley, 1973; Ross, 1977; Monson and Snyder, 1977); (3) such an examination would itself raise further questions for empirical testing in the laboratory (e.g., what are the effects of social motives, group conflict, frustration, etc. on the tendency to make predispositional as opposed to situational attributions?).

Police Attitudes and Stereotyping

Early work in social psychology on the attitude constellation held by the "Authoritarian personality" (Adorno *et al.*, 1964) tended to attribute the development of such attitude constellations to treatment by the parents in the family setting. Later studies, however (Niederhoffer, 1967; Sales, 1973), have looked at authoritarianism as a response to present stress or threat in the adult life situation and in some cases (Stewart and Hoult, 1959; Niederhoffer, 1967) to occupational stress.

The sources of such occupational stress of police have been clearly described by Wexler (1974) and Skolnick (1967). Both writers describe an ambiguity or role strain as a central feature of the police job. There are several sources of this ambiguity. First is a lack of occupational autonomy. The police do not enact the laws that they enforce nor do they judge, pass sentence, or prescribe treatment. This results in a form of occupational alienation, where police feel like part of an assembly line (the criminal justice system) and often feel that other parts of the criminal justice system operate against them. Second, the legal framework divides police activities into two relatively distinct tasks: (a) "enforcing the law" which deals with consensually definable crimes which are illegal by definition and can be discerned as a specific behaviour (e.g., murder, speeding, assault); and (b) "order maintenance" which lacks the clarity of law enforcement and is based on an ambiguous notion of the public order as implicitly described by norms and mores (e.g., disputes between two parties who accuse each other of being at fault). The two tasks require widely different responses from police, creating a type of "double-blind" situation leading to occupational conflict and tension. A third source of strain is tension between the operational consequences of ideas of efficiency and initiative on the one hand and legality on the other.

These various ambiguities in the police occupational role have been viewed as producing a distinct police "working personality" characterized by extreme insularity and anti-intraception, coupled with feelings of social isolation and group solidarity, disdain for procedural legal restraints and a perceptual style shaped by persistent suspicion with particular attentiveness paid to signs of potential violence and law-breaking. In addition, evidence is beginning to accumulate to support the notion of increased authoritarianism with time on the job for police (Rokeach, Miller and Snyder, 1971; Macnamara, 1967; Niederhoffer, 1967; Teahan, 1975). Niederhoffer attributes the increase to feeling "justified and righteous in using power and toughness to perform his duties" and to the "macho" nature of a male subculture. However, it should also be mentioned that police, as a group, do not score significantly different from civilian groups (including college students) on authoritarianism (Lefkowitz, 1975). Strangely, many police researchers report that their observations of police behaviour reflect much higher rates of authoritarianism than the paper and pencil measures. Anti-intraception, ceiling effects on the scale and police mistrust of civilian testers may all operate to produce a middle range score that underestimates the actual score. Future studies may attempt to construct situational tests that look at trait relevant behaviour (e.g., compliance to an authority figure) rather than at paper and pencil measures.

Group Behaviour

Students of intragroup influence or intergroup conflict would again find the police interesting. Perceived outside threat (under estimations of community support, etc.) produce a tight solidarity that is most difficult to penetrate. The solidarity appears highest with new recruits (who as recent members subscribe to the group norm most assiduously) and tapers off with veterans. Standard indicators of a group standard exist (attitudes toward capital punishment homogenize with time spent on the job and are significantly different from the general population's). Both Stark (1972) and Westley (1951) character- ize the police as a minority subculture which tends to be "in conflict with and isolated from the community and in which the norms are independent of·the community" (Westley, 1951, p. 294). Such norms include militaristic conservatism and a strong emphasis on social order. Police spend more and more off duty time with other police as years on the job increase. Hence, this and other measures of group cohesiveness indicate a highly cohesive group that is somewhat isolated from the community at large. Team policing and other police-com- munity relations programmes are partial remedies for this isolation.

Several studies have looked at police intergroup conflict (Stark, 1972) or ways to reduce it (Diamond and Lobitz, 1973). Stark has examined conflict between police and students during the late 1960s and between police and blacks in the US. Lefkowitz (1975) and Rafky (1973), amongst others, have reported extremely high race prejudice in the police. Also, as Macnamara (1967) and Teahan (1975) have reported, racism increases with time on the job but independent of contact with the devalued racial groups, suggesting a form of socialization to a sub-culture value. In addition, Teahan found increasing polarization between black and white officers on the same police force with time on the job. While conflict between police and minority groups is largely a case of reciprocal negative stereotypes, unrelated sources of police frustration must also be viewed as affecting police hostility toward disadvantaged groups.

Pro- and Anti-social Behaviour

Research and theory in pro- and anti-social behaviours, as it has been developed since the seminal studies by Latané and

Darley (1975) can contribute in several ways to an understanding of violence as the police have to deal with it, and the helping response expected of the police by the public when such violence occurs.

One of the most striking realizations that comes from working with the police is just how much of the violence with which they have to deal is domestic violence, i.e., severe aggression occurring between two people who know each other, are living under the same roof, etc. About 40% of the homicides and assaults occurring in any North American or Western European city are "domestics" in this sense (Steinmetz and Strauss, 1974). Research on domestic violence has several implications for social psychological theory and *vice versa.*

First of all, some of the later theory and data from research on the frustration-aggression hypothesis (Kaufmann, 1974) indicate that targets for frustration-based aggression are selected because they are "accessible" and powerless to retaliate. These criteria are applicable to the victims of most domestic violence (women and children). The frustration-aggression research seems incomplete in two ways however: (1) much research on child-abuse indicates that one child gets selected as a target because of personal characteristics,[1] so that mere availability and powerlessness do not predict target selection; and (2) the sources of frustration are not formally or systematically addressed by the frustration-aggression hypothesis. Current key sources for frustration leading to wife beating include power losses by middle-class males (Whitehurst, 1974) leading to physical attempts to re-establish power. While domestic violence is a serious social problem, the public seem to ward off recognition of it as such. Public estimates of the extent and incidence of domestic violence are always too low. Theoretically, the public seem to adopt predispositional explanations for violent crimes which locate such crimes in a "criminal element" whose dealings occur in the streets. The result is sort of "we-they" distinction

(1) These might include exceptional intelligence which makes the child difficult to control, stubbornness or resemblance to a parent whom an abusing step-parent resents, etc. (Schneider, Pollack and Helfer, 1972).

that allows the public to avoid recognition of themselves as having criminal potential. Crimes between strangers are viewed as more serious than crimes between intimates even though incidence of violence indicates otherwise (Strauss, 1977).

Schotland and Straw (1976b) constructed and intriguing bystander intervention study which tapped this dimension. They staged man-woman fights that were made to appear as though they were occurring between strangers or between a married couple. Bystander intervention rates were perceived as more serious and where the woman was perceived as being in greater danger. Theoretically, this type of research paradigm could be further extended to use a variety of scenarios to indicate how background attitudes affect perceptions and behaviour toward domestic violence. Probably in no area so much as in violence do social psychologists need to get out of the lab and test their theories against real world phenomena. Bach and Goldberg's (1975) fascinating descriptions of the variety and forms of indirect psychological aggression have gone largely unnoticed by empirical researchers.

What I conclude from the foregoing review is that the discipline of social psychology has much to offer to the study of community groups. I have focused on the police. Kelly Shaver has done a similar review of social psychological contributions to the criminal justice system in general (Shaver, Gilbert and Williams, 1975). As such, social psychology can certainly make a conceptual and theoretical contribution to community psychology programmes.

Secondly, in so doing the discipline itself will be strengthened by testing its theories under real world conditions. This necessarily forces new foci and questions, and places narrow perspectives on behaviour on a new type of empirical firing line.

References

Adorno, T.W., Frenkel-Brunswick, E., Levinson, D.J. and Sanford, R.N., *The Authoritarian Personality*, New York: Wiley & Sons, 1964.

268   *Donald G. Dutton*

Argyris, C., *Theory in Practice: Increasing Professional Effectiveness*, Jossey-Bass, 1974.
Bach, G. and Goldberg, H., *Creative Aggression*, New York: Avon, 1975.
Banton, M., *Police Community Relations*, Collins: London, 1973.
Baxter, J.C. and Rozelle, R.M., Spatial dynamics related to perceiving the other person's intentions. *The Police Chief*, 1974, *61*, 66-9.
Baxter, J.C. and Rozelle, R.M., Nonverbal expression as a function of crowding during a simulated police-citizen encounter, *Journal of Personality and Social Psychology*, 1975, *32* (1), 40-54.
Bem, D.J., Inducing belief in false confessions, *Journal of Personality and Social Psychology*, 1966, *3*, 707-10.
Bennis, W.G., Benne, K.D., Chin, R. and Covey, K.E., *The Planning of Change*, New York: Holt, Rinehart & Winston, 1976.
Bordua, D.J., *The Police: Six Sociological Essays*, New York: Wiley & Son, 1967.
Chevigny, P., *Police Power*, New York: Vintage Books, 1969.
Dabbs, J., Fuller, J. and Carr, T.S., Cornered college students and prison inmates. Paper presented at the American Psychological Association, 1973.
Diamond, M.J. and Lobitz, W.C., When familiarity breeds respect: The effects of an experimental depolarization program on police and student attitudes toward each other, *Journal of Social Issues*, 1973, *29*, 95-109.
Douglas, R.L. and Dutton, D.G., Cognitive dissonance revisited: another look at the dissonance-self-perception controversy, *Canadian Journal of Behavioural Science*, 1974, *4*, 64-74.
Grosman, B., *Police Command*, Toronto: Macmillan, 1975.
Helmreich, R., Applied social psychology: The unfulfilled promise, *Personality and Social Psychology Bulletin*, 1975, *1*(4), 548-60.
Jones, E.E. and Harris, V.A., The attribution of attitudes, *Journal of Experimental Social Psychology*, 1967, *3*, 1-24.
Jones, E.E. and Nisbett, P., *The Actor and the Observer: Divergent Perceptions of the Causes of Behaviour*, General Learning Press, 1973.
Jones, S. and Aiello, J.R., Proxemic behaviour of black and white first, third and fifth grade children, *Journal of Personality and Social Psychology*, 1973, *25*, 21.
Kaufmann, H., *Aggression and Altruism*, New York: Holt, Rinehart & Winston, 1974.
Kelley, H., The process of causal attribution, *American Psychologist*, 1973, *28*, 107-28.
Kinzel, A., Body buffer zone in violent prisoners, *American Journal of Psychiatry*, 1970, *127*, 59-64.
Kirkham, G., Doc Cop, *Human Behaviour*, May 1975, 17-25.
LaFrance, M. and Mayo, F., Gaze direction in diadic interracial communication. Paper presented at Eastern Psychological Association meeting, 1973.
Latané, B. and Darley, J., *The Unresponsive Bystander: Why Won't He Help?* New York: Appleton-Century-Crofts, 1975.
Lefkowitz, J., Psychological attributes of policemen: A review of research and opinion, *Journal of Social Issues*, 1975, *31*(1), 3-26.
Lewin, K., *Resolving Social Conflicts*, New York: Harper & Row, 1948.
Macnamara, J.H., Uncertainties in police work: The relevance of police recruits, backgrounds and training. In D. Bordua (Ed.), *The Police: Six Sociological Essays*, New York: Wiley, 1967.

Milgram, S., Behavioural study of obedience, *Journal of Abnormal and Social Psychology*, 1963, *67*, 371-8.

Monson, T.C. and Snyder, M., Actors, observers and the attribution process: Toward a reconceptualization, *Journal of Experimental Social Psychology*, 1977, *13*(1), 89-111.

Niederhoffer, A., *Behind the Shield: The Police in Urban Society*, New York: Doubleday & Co., 1967.

Piliavin, I. and Briar, S., Police encounters with juveniles, *American Journal of Sociology*, 1964, *70*, 206-44.

Rafky, D., Police race attitudes and labelling, *Journal of Police Science and Administration*, 1973, *1*, 65-86.

Rokeach, M., Miller, M.G. and Snyder, J.A., The value gap between police and policed, *Journal of Social Issues*, 1971, 27(2), 155-72.

Ross, L., The intuitive psychologist and his shortcomings: Distortions in the attribution process, *Advances in Experimental Social Psychology*, 1977, Vol. 16.

Rozelle, R.M. and Baxter, J.C., Impression formation and danger recognition in experienced police officers, *Journal of Social Psychology*, 1975, *96*, 53-65.

Sales, S., Threat as a factor in authoritarianism, *Journal of Personality and Social Psychology*, 1973, *28*, 44-57.

Schneider, C., Pollack, C. and Helfer, R.E., Interviewing the parents. In C.H. Kemps & R.E. Helfer, *Helping the Battered Child and his Family*, London: J.B. Lippincott, 1972.

Shaver, K., Gilbert, M. and Williams, M., Social psychology, criminal justice and the principle of discretion: A selective review, *Personality and Social Psychology Bulletin*, 1975, *1*(3), 471-84.

Shotland, R.L., and Straw, M.K., Newsline, *Psychology Today*, Feb. 1976.

Shotland, R.L. and Straw, M.K., Bystander response to an assault: when a man attacks a woman, *Journal of Personality and Social Psychology*, 1976, *34*(5), 990-9.

Skolnick, J.H., *Justice Without Trial: Law Enforcement in Democratic Society*, New York: Wiley & Sons, 1967.

Stark, R., *Police Riots*, Belmont, California: Wadsworth, 1972.

Steinmetz, S. and Strauss, M., *Violence in the Family*, New York: Harper & Row, 1974.

Stewart, D. and Hoult, T., A social-psychological theory of the authoritarian personality, *American Journal of Sociology*, 1959, *65*, 278.

Stotland, E., Police and community, *Journal of Social Issues*, 1975, *31*, 1.

Strauss, M., Violence in the family: How widespread, why it occurs and some thoughts on prevention, United Way Symposium on Family Violence, Vancouver, B.C., 1977.

Teahan, J.E., A longitudinal study of attitude shifts among black and white police officers, *Journal of Social Issues*, 1975, *31*(1), 47-56.

Westley, W., The Police: A Sociological Study of Law, Custom, and Morality. Unpublished Ph.D. dissertation, University of Chicago, 1951.

Wexler, M.N., Police culture: A response of ambiguous employment, from C. Boydell, *The Administration of Criminal Justice in Canada*, Toronto: Holt, Rinehart & Winston, 1974.

White, R.W., Motivation reconsidered: The ·concept of competence, *Psychological Review,* 1959, *66,* 297.
Whitehurst, R.N., Violence in husband-wife interaction, from S. Steinmetz & M. Strauss (Eds.), *Violence in the Family,* New York: Harper & Row, 1974.
Zimbardo, P.G., The ₀psychology of police confessions, *Psychology Today,* June 1967, *1,* 16.

Discussion

ANDREEVA: Where is the difference between the social psychological approach and the pure sociological approach to the analysis of this special group?

DUTTON: I think part of the difference is in social psychology's emphasis on the individual, perhaps especially in the use of attribution theory to try and understand the individual's epistemology.

LOMOV: This relates to psychological aspects – but what about sociological aspects?

DUTTON: Well, I think social psychology stands between the two disciplines, as we have said. The main difference from sociology would be on the cognitive aspect of an individual's trying to make sense of his social world. The sociological aspect, I suppose, is in the way that group structure affects some of the dependent behaviours that we look **at.**

ANDREEVA: Would you agree that when we do an analysis of the purely social or sociological functions this should be left to sociology, and it should not be included in a socio-psychological analysis?

DUTTON: No – I think just the reverse.

ANDREEVA: You mean that you think social psychology itself can describe and explain the functions of a given social group?

DUTTON: I guess it depends where your emphasis is, but I think it's important to understand the individual's perception of the social factors that are affecting him, the social structures that are affecting him. And I think sociology has, to an extent, been guilty of leaving that out. You're concentrating mainly on the social structure and the effect that it has on the individual.

ANDREEVA: No – right now I'm not concentrating on anything. I'm asking you.

DUTTON: What we really need to do is look at the individual's perceptions, or what we sometimes call their causal attributions, their conception of what is affecting them; that, I think, means that you need to know something about the individual. You have to focus on the individual as a social unit of analysis to a certain extent, and I think that's something social psychologists ought to be doing.

ANDREEVA: But *what* you attribute to members of that social group, or *what* I will attribute to them depends upon the real social functions of this group, doesn't it?

DUTTON: It depends on the functions of that group, and it also depends on *your* position in the social structure, and what information *you* have available to you, and your roles and relations with that particular group. One thing that's been lacking in attribution theory in social psychology is that there hasn't been enough attention paid to the set of social structures and the contexts in which one person is viewing another. We have maybe been too cognitive. But if you consider sociology, the opposite is true; there hasn't been enough attention paid to some of these cognitive factors that operate at the individual level. I think probably that the two approaches need to be brought together somehow.

THORNGATE: Once we understand the relationship between the police and the public, what do we do then? At the beginning of your talk, I got the feeling that your emphasis was on making the police understand more about the public, and if police were better educated in social psychology, then their job would be more effective, etc. I see two problems with this approach. One – if you tell the police this information, they may simply reject it – "I don't care". And secondly, members of the public, if they knew that police were operating by this information, could exploit it to their own great benefit.

DUTTON: What do you do then? You do a lot of things. If it's information that you think has application, such as the work on non-verbal communication, then you can make it part of the police training programme, as we've done in British Columbia. Whether it's accepted or not depends on a lot of things – on how you put it across, on what support you have, and to what extent it becomes an integral part of the programme. I think it can be put across in a way that gets accepted. I'm not really concerned about public exploitation, I can't really see that as a major problem. Some of the other things in attribution theory clearly aren't anything that would ever be useful to the police. They're of more academic interest, but they're still valuable, because looking at this particular social group teaches you to ask questions you may not have asked if you spent all your time doing the research from a theoretical and lab-based point of view.

BODALEV: The paradigm that you have described – do you think it is the only one to describe police-community relations? Or do you visualize, at least hypothetically, other possible relationships between the community and the police?

DUTTON: If you mean different ways of looking at or viewing these relationships, I think other ways of viewing them are possible, too. For example, I don't know anything about the role of the police in Russia, or how they are viewed by the community, or how they are integrated into the community. That would be something that would be interesting.

BODALEV: In the laboratory from which I come, there has been an experiment studying the perception by the police of various types of criminals, and they studied policemen with various backgrounds in terms of their length of service and also their experience with various types of criminals. There were great differences found between various types of police officers – the longer they had worked, the more they seemed to understand. Also important was the type of attitude which they showed, whether it was a superficial attitude or a concentrated attitude. Depending on those, their own behaviour toward the criminal was very different. The ease of understanding the personality of the criminal and the different values assigned to the accused also varied very much with the type of crime.

ANDREEVA: We make a big difference between a purely sociological approach and a socio-psychological approach in this problem. Professor Bodalev has just stressed the socio-psychological approach. When you ask how the relations between the community and police force change in the Soviet Union, we feel that his is not a problem for socio-psychological study. In the Soviet Union, these problems would be studied primarily by sociologists as well as lawyers, within the general framework of studying the essence of social change in our country.

DUTTON: Here, they've been studied about 40% by sociologists, 40% by lawyers and 20% by social psychologists, but my feeling is that sociology is too important to be left to the sociologists, and law is too important to be left to the lawyers, so social psychologists have to step in.

BUEVA: There are two separate problems here. The relations between police and community should be properly the field of sociology, but I accept that the interpersonal relationship between an individual policeman and an individual criminal should be a field of study for social psychology. The third question is the influence of the solution of problem number one on problem number two.

DUTTON: Suppose you have a police officer who, because of role strain or of conflicting demands on him, begins to develop an ulcer, or a set of psychosomatic problems. The sociologist can perhaps tell you where the role strain comes from, but is he going to be able to tell you about the physical side, or how it manifests itself? A medical doctor might be able to tell you about the psychosomatic problems, or how the role strain is manifesting itself, but he might not think in terms of where the role strain was coming from. Perhaps a social psychologist drawing from either side can help to integrate the relationship between these two phenomena.

ZAJONC: I suppose it is very meaningful and proper to speak of divisions between social psychology and sociology when you are talking about some basic, fundamental principles, although even then it's perhaps difficult. But I think when you're talking about an applied problem, or a problem with special implications, then the boundaries of what is social psychological, what is sociological, what is anthropological, what's pure psychology, become very vague and diffused. I think that all forms of knowledge must converge toward the analysis of the problem. It's difficult to really decide if a specific aspect of the problem is sociological or social psychological.

LOMOV: Right.

The Social Psychology of Second Language Communication

NORMAN S. SEGALOWITZ and MICHELINE FAVREAU

In this paper we describe the "state of the art" as we see it in the areas of bilingualism and second language communication. In particular we focus attention on issues relevant to the attainment of bilingual skills by adults, especially non-nativelike second language skills. We also try to indicate where closer collaboration between cognitive psychologists and social psychologists might be fruitful for an understanding of the dynamics of cross language communication.

Perhaps the most appropriate way to begin a review in this field is to refer to a 1967 paper by Wallace Lambert of McGill University entitled *A Social Psychology of Bilingualism*. In this paper, Lambert articulated and identified four major concerns for social psychologists interested in bilingualism: (a) language choice; (b) dialect variation; (c) "social" motivations in second language learning; and (d) problems of social adjustment. This paper has been central in the literature of bilingualism and has led several researchers to turn their attention to these areas. We will, therefore, briefly review some of the recent research developments in these areas and suggest possible directions for future research in each of them.

Language Choice

The issue regarding language choice in interactions between

273

speakers of different mother tongues has been formulated in terms of bilinguals who sound nativelike or nearly so in their two languages. Since these bilinguals can pass as members of the ethnic group whose language they happen to be using at any given moment, a major concern has been with reactions toward them as representatives of the ethnic group associated with the language they are speaking.

The basic experiments developed to explore such questions are now well known. Typically, subjects hear a series of recorded passages in English and French which, unknown to them, contain samples of French and English speech by the same bilingual individuals. The French and English speaking subjects are then asked to rate the speakers on personality trait or other scales. Under these conditions the same recorded speaker is judged to have one set of characteristics when speaking English but a different set when speaking French (see, for example, Lambert, Hodgson, Gardner and Fillenbaum, 1960). The findings imply that the choice of language that is used in a cross linguistic communication can evoke perceptions in the listener that are to a large extent colored by stereotypes about ethnic groups.

Much of the work that followed focused on the relationship between the listener's own experience in learning a second language and his readiness to perceive bilinguals in stereotyped terms. A major concern was what impact, if any, does second language training have on the learner in terms of broadening the way he perceives others, or in terms of loosening his affiliations to his own primary ethno-linguistic group. For example, Lambert, Gardner, Barik and Tunstall (1962) assessed American students attending a French summer school for changes in attitudes toward French people and culture, as well as their own feelings of identity. They reported that positive attitudes toward France and the French language correlated with success in learning, but that attitudes did not change as a function of the experience in the school. They did find, however, that feelings of "anomie" increased with experience at the school, indicating that the learners were feeling more culturally marginal between

French and American reference points (there is no indication how long such feelings lasted).

Although such research has dealt primarily with the fluent or near fluent speaker and with reactions to language choice stemming from ethnic attitudes, more recently the topic of language choice in bilingual communication has taken a somewhat different turn. One example of the kind of study we have in mind is by Simard, Taylor and Giles (1976) concerning language choice and interpersonal accommodation. They were interested to see whether a listener's reactions to a communication from a bilingual is a function of the language *actually used* or of the *attributions* the listener makes to account for the speaker's choice of language. In their study, Francophones listened to French and English communications from Anglophones. In one condition the listeners were led to believe the Anglophone speakers knew how to speak French but were prevented from doing so by the experimenter. In another condition the Anglophone speakers were made to appear to have both the capability and the option to speak French but nonetheless deliberately spoke English to the Francophone listener. The results revealed that when the Anglophones spoke English — that is, did not accommodate by speaking the listener's language — the French listeners' knowledge of whether the speaker used English through choice or compulsion influenced their judgment about the speaker's French language capabilities. This perceived cause of the nonaccommodation also affected the listeners' own choice of language when returning the communication. There was also evidence that it affected their comprehension of the message. Together these results suggest that the implications of language choice are not simply a matter of stereotyped impressions of ethnolinguistic groups, but are very much a matter of the attributions listeners will make to account for the behaviour of the interlocutor.

The finding that success in comprehending the message can be influenced by the listener's beliefs about why the interlocutor spoke in a particular language is especially interesting. Two interpretations of this result come to mind, either or both of which may turn out to be true. Consider the listener's reaction to the speaker where the speaker appeared to deliberately avoid using French. This reaction may have been one of emotional upset or preoccupation with the speaker's apparent noncooperativeness. As a consequence the listener was not able to process the message very well and hence misunderstood it. In signal detection terms we might say he became less sensitive to the signal presented. A second possible interpretation is that the listener, seeing how little effort the speaker made, correspondingly reduced his own effort in decoding the message. In this case the listener might have decided upon an interpretation of the message only when he was absolutely sure of himself; if further thought or analysis was required to comprehend the message, the listener would simply ignore what he heard. In signal detection terms we might say that the listener raised his criterion regarding the decisions he makes in understanding the message; the higher the criterion for comprehension, the fewer comprehension responses there will be. Of course *both* sensitivity changes due to emotional reactions and reduced effort in making decisions pertinent to comprehension could occur. It should be possible to disentangle these possibilities in further research.

Dialect Variation

A second major focus in bilingualism research concerns dialect variation. Here the concern is not so much the particular language chosen by the bilingual, as the style or variety of the language spoken. For example, in the Canadian context it is relevant to consider whether a speaker of French is using Continental European French, Standard Quebec French or Familiar Quebec French. Each of the Quebec varieties is readily distinguished by Quebec Francophones and is associated with specific social contexts (Taylor and Clement, 1974).

Now, reactions to a French speaker will vary according to which variety is being used. For example, an early study by Preston (1963) (as reported in Lambert, 1967) investigated reactions of Anglophones and Francophones to speakers who spoke French with different regional accents. He found that Francophone listeners reacted to French Canadian speakers with a continental accent more positively than to speakers with a standard Quebec French accent. Anglophone listeners also tended to downgrade speakers of Quebec French more than speakers of European French, although the two groups of listeners did not show exactly the same pattern of results.

A *change* of speech style can also elicit certain reactions from a listener. Bourhis, Giles and Lambert (1975) report a study in which French Canadian subjects listened to an athlete from Quebec in two interviews. In one the athlete was interviewed by a French commentator from Quebec and in the other the commentator was from Europe. In one condition — the NO-SHIFT condition — the Quebec athlete spoke with a Quebec style French to the Quebec interviewer and maintained that style with the European interviewer. In a SHIFT-TOWARD condition, the athlete shifted to the European style French in the second interview. Finally, in a SHIFT-AWAY condition the athlete used an even broader, more popular style of Quebec French (compared to standard Quebec French) with the European interviewer. The subjects rated the athlete as being more intelligent and educated when he shifted to European French than when there was no shift, and least intelligent and educated when he shifted to the more popular style. In terms of sociableness, likeability, trustworthiness and similar traits there were no differences in the ratings across the three conditions.

A related experiment was conducted by the same authors (Bourhis *et al.*, 1975) in Wales in which interviewers used either a regional Welsh accented English, considered analogous to Quebec-style French or RP (Received Pronunciation — Standard British English), analogous in this context to European French. Unlike the Quebec example, when the Welsh athlete shifted away from RP to an even broader Welsh accent, he was rated as being more trustworthy and kindhearted than in the other conditions. Thus, although speech *shifts* elicit impressions in the listener, the exact effects may be a function of the cultural context. In Quebec, for example, a familiar style of speech may not be as favored as the more formal standard Quebec French, whereas in Wales a broad Welsh accent may be an appropriate way to express one's national identity.

The topic of speech style may have yet other implications for cross language communication when viewed in a more general socio-linguistic perspective. For example, for a number of years now linguists dealing with linguistic variation (e.g., Labov, 1970; Hymes, 1972) have demonstrated that language style differences are not only associated with differences between individuals in, say, social class or ethnic background. Rather, they have observed that every person masters several different speech styles for use in different social situations. As a consequence, in any normal communicative situation there is not only an appropriate thing to say but there is also an appropriate way to say it. Thus each communicative situation has a set of socio-linguistic demands associated with it which require the speakers to choose the appropriate style. Moreover, it appears that one of the normal "rules" of communication involves approximating some of the speech characteristics of the interlocutor. Giles and Powesland (1975) review the literature in this field and develop what they call a speech "accommodation model" in which a speaker is thought to model certain features of his speech after those of the interlocutor. The idea is that individuals will try to elicit favorable judgments about themselves from their interlocutors by reducing dissimilarities between them.

It might be, however, that modifying one's speech style according to the demands of the situation involves more than just modelling one's speech after that of the interlocutor. In some situations it may be more appropriate and desirable to maintain *different* speech styles. For example, in our culture a boss may speak very familiarly with a subordinate but usually a subordinate is expected to maintain a respectful tone. Taking these considerations into account we see that perhaps speech style reflects more than just the regional, ethnic or social class origins of the speaker. It also reflects the speaker's interpretations of — and reactions to — the social demands of the situation. The relative status of the two speakers and the quality of their social relationship will be among the important factors that influence the speech style choice.

Regarding cross linguistic communication, a second language speaker may not be able to accommodate his speech patterns appropriately. He may not be sufficiently skilled with speech styles and speech style shifts to participate in the exchange of socio-linguistic messages with the interlocutor even though he may have sufficient mastery of the basic phonology, syntax and semantics of the language to communicate the cognitive message. Thus, for example, it may be difficult for the speaker to reciprocate a change in the interlocutors' style from formal to casual speech indicating increased warmth and friendliness; in fact, the speaker may not even notice the change at all. Moreover, the speaker may wish to convey his own feelings to the interlocutor through the medium of speech style. After all, he does this all the time, and usually unconsciously, when speaking in his native language. But in cross-linguistic communication he may be cut off from this possibility because of his lack of socio-linguistic competence. This may adversely affect his feelings about how he is getting along in the situation even though logically it should not impede the communication of basic ideas (the cognitive message). If success with the interlocutor on a social level is important, and it usually is, then the lack of socio-linguistic competence may be a deterrent to people wishing to engage in cross language communication (see Segalowitz, 1976, for a study that lends support to this view).

There is also an interesting cognitive psycho-linguistic problem associated with this issue. When we talk about speech styles, speech style changes or accent, we are dealing with patterned linguistic variability. For example, in English the difference between some varieties of casual and formal speech involves changes in certain pronunciations. It is important to realize, however, that no speech style *exclusively* uses one form of pronunciation. There is variability in the speech in that at one moment the speaker may use one form while at other times he may use another; it is the predominant use of particular forms that gives the speech its general characteristics of being formal or casual. This variability is patterned or systematic in that the use of different forms will depend on the social context of the speech and the linguistic environments in which they occur.

Now, socio-linguistics are trying to incorporate an account of this *variable* aspect of language into their more general theories of language (see Dittmar, 1976 for summaries of some current proposals regarding variability). From the point of view of a cognitive psychologist, however, different linguistic solutions to the problem of variability presuppose different sorts of underlying linguistic competence. Thus the sociolinguist presents the psychologist with new puzzles, the solution to which may be relevant to our general understanding of cross language communication skills and hence second language acquisition.

Social Motivation and Language Learning

The third major focus in second language research concerns the finding that the "social" motivations of the learner can be more important than cognitive factors in determining language learning success. So-called language aptitude seems to be a relatively weak predictor of language learning success, whereas a stronger predictor seems to be the individual's motives for learning the language.

Researchers have distinguished between two major types of socially oriented motivations that an individual may possess regarding second language learning. The learner may, in one case, wish to acquire the second language because of its utility for him. Such a learner is said to be instrumentally motivated. In another case, the learner may wish to learn the language because he identifies in some way with the people who speak it and wishes to be liked by them. Such a person is said to be integratively motivated (Gardner and Lambert, 1972).

Most research on motivation in second language learning is thus formulated in terms of a relation between the learner's relatively long-term goals regarding the acquisition of a second language (e.g., "instrumental" *vs.* "integrative" goals) and his performance as measured by fairly formal scholastic measures. While such work is clearly very important from an educational point of view, perhaps there is a need for yet another type of motivational study: the study of factors affecting the second language learner's motivation in *specific* cross language encounters.

Regardless of his ultimate reasons for learning the language, a person must engage in some second language communication as part of the process of becoming a more fluent speaker. For a learner who is still a nonfluent speaker, this activity itself can be regarded as similar to any other relatively difficult activity where success is not always certain. If despite the serious possibility of failure to communicate effectively the learner makes an effort to capitalize on opportunities to practice the second language, then we can say that he has a strong motivation to acquire the language. A person's effort in using the language can thus be one indicator of his general willingness or readiness to engage in this activity. This approach allows us to raise a number of questions about cross language communication in the context of other research dealing with the determinants of performance intensity (e.g., Kukla, 1972). For example, we can inquire about the relation between the degree of effort a person makes in a given situation and the perceived difficulty of the task where the difficulty can be a function of the nature of the message being conveyed (e.g., simple *vs.* complex ideas), the socio-linguistic requirements of the situation (e.g., the need to speak tactfully) or the physical setting (e.g., quiet *vs.* noisy environments).

In addition, the importance of the communication may influence the effort made (Wortman and Brehm, 1975). This may be where instrumental and integrative motivations come into play in the specific communication situation. For instance, the socio-linguistic requirements of the task may be more important to the integratively motivated individual and hence their contribution to the difficulty of the task will be given more weight. These and perhaps other factors that affect the amount of effort a person makes to use a second language will *indirectly influence the level of skill* he attains by affecting the amount of experience he has; the more willing he is to engage in cross language communication, the more experience he will gather and the greater should be his improvement in the language.

Although a learner's readiness to speak a second language is an important variable in second language acquisition, this factor is not easy to investigate. At least one very difficult problem to be overcome is how to devise laboratory situations that allow for a suitable operationalization of the subject's performance intensity. Several ways that immediately come to mind turn out to be unacceptable after further thought. One could, for example, assume that the more quickly the subject responds in the second language or the longer he speaks, the greater must be his willingness to engage in second language communication. One could just as plausibly argue however that long latency to respond and concise statements reflect careful planning of what will be said, rather than a lack of interest in speaking. One might try asking subjects during or after the task to indicate on rating scales their readiness to speak. Unfortunately, such measures draw too much of the subject's attention to the experimenter's interest in his motivation to speak and hence are limited in their usefulness.

Social Adjustments

Lambert (1967) raises the question of the special social adjustments the bilingual has to make just because he is bilingual. It had been suggested by others that a potential source of maladjustment for the bilingual is the loosening of the bonds with his primary language culture, and the rise of inner conflict that results from having cultural experiences and values encoded in two languages: "The consequences (of bilingualism in children) is that the inner attitudes which are conditioned by language will not stand unconnected beside one another, but will enter into conflicting tensions in the child's soul . . ." (Sander, 1934, quoted in Weinreich, 1953, p. 120). The concern thus has been that bilingualism results in a certain level of anomie, a feeling of social marginality, of not belonging anywhere.

Research on this aspect of bilingualism has been relatively limited but what there is suggests that this view is false. Several authors have been led to the conclusion that the social adjustment problems facing bilinguals stem not from bilingualism *per se* but rather from other people's reactions to their bilinguality (Bossard, 1945; Soffietti, 1955; Spoerl, 1943). Moreover, Aellen and Lambert (1969) have found that in some circumstances bilingual upbringing can, if anything, lead to increased feelings of belonging and to better social adjustment.

Notwithstanding the conclusion that it is wrong to say bilingualism *necessarily* leads to social maladjustments, it is certainly possible that cross language communication can place conflicting demands on the bilingual. For example, the bilingual who is so skilled that he can pass unnoticed in the listener's group may be viewed suspiciously as an outsider, a "linguistic spy" to use Lambert's term. The bilingual who can pass as a native speaker may create more anxiety in his unilingual interlocutor then if he spoke the language with a slight accent that marked his ethnolinguistic origins more clearly. Presumably, this problem, if it arises, is a function of the ethnocentrism of the interlocutor. In other circumstances the bilingual could just as easily be admired for his linguistic prowess. Here too, however, it can perhaps be to the speaker's advantage to reveal in the way he speaks that he is indeed using a second language.

Another type of constraint on the bilingual may come from his own native language community. Because he speaks the language of another group very well, he may be perceived by members of his own group as being integratively motivated with respect to the other group and hence his ethno-linguistic loyalty may be questioned. If this is the case, then one can imagine that during cross linguistic communication in the presence of listeners of the bilingual native's language group, the bilingual will be under some pressure to modify his second language speech so that he does not appear to be too close to the other group.

There is some evidence that such pressures may exist under certain circumstances. Gatbonton (1975) presented French Canadian listeners with tape recordings of other French Canadians speaking in English with varying degrees of native-like accent. Initially the listeners heard a sample of each speaker's French language speech and hence were aware that the speakers were French Canadians. The listeners judged the speakers on a number of variables including scales related to ethnic affiliation and nationalism. The interesting, but perhaps not very surprising, finding was that increasing native-like accent in English was associated with decreasing strength of ethnic affiliation to French Canadians. This association was reflected in judgments the listeners made about the speaker's beliefs on a number of topics related to Quebecois nationalism. In the case of those listeners who were themselves nationalistic French Canadians, this association was also reflected in their decisions to choose or not to choose the speakers to be a member or leader of some hypothetical community group to which the listener also belonged. It is interesting to note, however, that the judgments the listeners made about the speaker's ethnic loyalty were probably in fact incorrect. In a related study Gatbonton (1975) found no correlation between the overall level of native-like accent in English of a large group of French Canadian speakers and their responses to the same ethnic affiliation rating scales used by the listeners in the previous study. In general, however, it appears that where language is very seriously perceived as a badge of identity, the bilingual may have to monitor carefully the way he speaks in the second language so as to avoid creating certain impressions among his listeners.

Conclusion

We have tried to convey the idea that, in recent years, research on cross language communication has moved some distance from its initial concerns with intergroup perceptions. Without minimizing the importance of that issue we suggest that the second language communicator be viewed much as we would view any individual who must perform a relatively difficult task. The nature of the communication task can, with the aid of linguistic and sociolinguistic tools, be fairly precisely specified. This in turn allows us to systematically manipulate features of the cross language communication situation to see what affects the way the speaker evaluates his experience, and what increases or reduces his readiness to continue using his second language. Viewing second language communication from this perspective allows us to broaden the domain of study by including in addition to fluent bilinguals, second language users, whatever the level of language mastery they have achieved.

References

Aellen, C. and Lambert, W.E., Ethnic identification and personality adjustments of Canadian adolescents of mixed English-French parentage, *Canadian Journal of Behavioural Science,* 1969, *1,* 123-8.

Bossard, A., The bilingual individual as a person, *American Sociological Review,* 1945, *10,* 699-709.

Bourhis, R.Y., Giles, H. and Lambert, W.E., Social consequences of accommodating one's style of speech: A cross national investigation, *International Journal of the Sociology of Language,* 1975, *6,* 55-72.

Dittmar, N., *Sociolinguistics,* London: Arnold, 1976.

Gardner, R.C. and Lambert, W.E., *Attitudes and Motivation in Second Language Learning,* Rowley, Mass.: Newbury House, 1972.

Gatbonton, E., Systematic variation in second language speech: A socio-linguistic study. Unpublished doctoral dissertation, McGill University, 1975.

Giles, H. and Powesland, P., *Speech Style and Social Evaluation,* London: Academic Press, 1975.

Hymes, D., Models of the interaction of language and social life. In J. Gumperz & D. Hymes (Eds.), *Directions in Sociolinguistics: The Ethnography of Communication,* New York: Holt, Rinehart & Winston, 1972.

Kukla, A., Foundations of an attributional theory of performance, *Psychological Review*, 1972, *79*, 454-70.

Labov, W., The study of language in its social context, *Studium Generale*, 1970, *23*, 30-87.

Lambert, W.E., A social psychology of bilingualism, *Journal of Social Issues*, 1967, *23*, 91-109.

Lambert, W.E., Gardner, R.C., Barik, H.C. and Tunstall, K., Attitudinal and cognitive aspects of intensive study of a second language, *Journal of Abnormal and Social Psychology*, 1962, *66*, 358-68.

Lambert, W.E., Hodgson, R.C., Gardner, R.C. and Fillenbaum, S., Evaluational reactions to spoken languages, *Journal of Abnormal and Social Psychology*, 1960, *60*, 44-51.

Preston, M.S., Evaluational reactions to English, Canadian French and European French voices, Unpublished MA thesis, McGill University, 1963.

Segalowitz, N., Communicative incompetence and the nonfluent bilingual, *Canadian Journal of Behavioural Science*, 1976, *8*, 122-31.

Simard, L., Taylor, D. and Giles, H., Attribution processes and interpersonal accommodation in a bilingual setting, *Language and Speech*, 1976, *19*, 374-87.

Soffietti, J.P., Bilingualism and biculturalism, *Journal of Educational Psychology*, 1955, *46*, 222-7.

Spoerl, D.T., Bilinguality and emotional adjustment, *Journal of Abnormal and Social Psychology*, 1943, *38*, 37-57.

Taylor, D.T. and Clement, R., Normative reactions to styles of Quebec French, *Anthropological Linguistics*, 1974, *16*, 202-17.

Weinreich, U., *Language in Contact*, New York: Linguistic Circle of New York, 1953.

Wortman, C. and Brehm, J., Responses to uncontrollable outcomes: an integration of reactance theory and the learned helplessness. In L. Berkowitz (Ed.), *Advances in Experimental and Social Psychology*, New York: Academic Press, 1975, pp. 277-337.

Discussion

BUEVA: Did you try to determine any changes in verbal and non-verbal communication methods when one switches from one language to the other?

SEGALOWITZ: We've done some exploratory experiments which were motivated by the idea that when you speak in a second language, if you do not have facility with speech style, you will then try to compensate for this by using your hands, your face, and so on more than you would otherwise do. We had great difficulty quantifying all these movements, and so on, and we didn't get the kind of results we'd hoped for.

BODALEV: Would you not agree that a change of the non-verbal communication pattern would have a strong influence on the interlocutor?

SEGALOWITZ: Yes, our idea was that when the speaker speaks in a second language he behaves non-verbally in a different way from when he speaks his native language. This would be another reason for the listener developing a different impression of a speaker.

BODALEV: What personality traits of the listener would determine the changed perception of a person who is speaking and changing his verbal and non-verbal patterns because of his language difficulty? I'm interested in the personality of the listener.

SEGALOWITZ: In terms of cross-language communication, one undoubtedly would be the listener's own feelings about ethnic loyalty and the relationship between language and one's identity. Secondly, the reasons for using the language that the listener imputes to the speaker will influence him.

BODALEV: You are familiar with the works of Pavlov, who divided people into first signal system and second signal system and in-between groups? It is interesting to speculate that first signal system types, for whom the physical part of the interlocutor is important, would pay great attention to the non-verbal communication. Maybe second signal system types would base their evaluations almost exclusively on verbal communication.

Memory, Cognition and Social Performance

WARREN THORNGATE

Abstract. If we are to understand the nature of cognitive processes governing performance in a social encounter, we must first understand (a) the nature of cognitive abilities and limitations, (b) the ecology or task characteristics of the social encounter, and (c) the goals of the performer. I shall try to argue (a) that it is cognitively easier to recognize than to reckon, (b) that almost all social encounters are characterized by a high degree of redundancy, and (c) that performers seek to satisfice much more often than they seek to optimize. As a result, most social performances are likely to be governed by cognitive processes rather different than those investigated in social psychology over the last 25 years. The likely processes rely heavily upon an extensive "data base" of real and imagined social encounters stored in long term memory through years of observation and experience. Stimuli from a current encounter are constantly compared to this data base in order to answer three central questions assumed to mediate social performance: (1) Is the configuration of stimuli familiar? (2) Should a response be given? and (3) Is a satisfactory response known? I shall attempt to outline some of the possible heuristics which a performer could employ to answer these questions and describe how one might proceed to investigate them. I shall also try to show how the concepts of attitude and attribution might relate to this conception of social cognition.

Memory, Cognition and Social Performance

About 45 years ago Walter Cannon proposed an insightful metaphor to help us understand the complexities of physiological processes: the body functions according to its own wisdom. I believe his metaphor is useful in helping us understand the complexities of cognitive processes as well. More specifically, I believe it is useful to assume that cognitive processes obey what I shall call the *Principle of Sagacious Allocation*: The brain tends to adapt its cognitive processes so as to exploit

289

its own strengths and avoid its own limitations.

Careful observation, introspection and experimental research indicate that there are at least six things which the brain does extremely well. (1) Because the brain is interconnected with amazingly "intelligent" receptors, it is very good at perceiving patterns and features (e.g., see Gibson, 1969); (2) it has a huge storage capacity and can commit to "long term memory" (LTM) a virtually unlimited amount of information (e.g., see Newell and Simon, `1972, or observe the recall of any experienced musician or actor); (3) it is extremely good at recognizing past events and rather good at recalling same (e.g., see Neisser, 1967); (4) it can "create" its own information by recombining stored information, then store these creations for future reference (e.g., see Newell and Simon, 1972); (5) it can monitor and remember at least some aspects of its own activity (i.e., introspect; see Newell and Simon, 1972); (6) it is quite tolerant of imprecision or "fuzziness" (e.g., see Zadeh, 1972).

But the brain is not omnipotent. At least two limitations are known to characterize the brain. First, it has a very limited span of attention (Kahneman, 1973), and second, it has a very limited short term memory (STM; see Miller, 1956).

Given these strengths and limitations, the Principle of Sagacious Allocation suggests that, whenever possible, the brain will favour cognitive processes which rely heavily on perception and long term memory to those which rely heavily on short term memory and long intervals of undivided attention. This possibility exists whenever relevant information has been previously stored in long term memory and can be recognized or recalled as such. Storage, recognition and recall of information increase with repetition of same. Thus, we should expect that the more repetitive or redundant a situation, the more one's behaviour in it will be governed by cognitive processes which feed mostly on perception and long term memory rather than by processes which feed mostly on short term memory and attention. In other words we should expect — as did James (1890, Chap. 4) and Dewey (1922, 1927) — that behaviour in familiar environments will be governed more by habit than by thought (see also Thorngate, 1976; Wertheimer, 1945).

There is now considerable research to support this expectation. Perhaps the most beautiful example is the research done by de Groot and later by Simon and his associates. de Groot (1965, 1966) was interested in what makes chess Masters better players than novices. Through a series of ingenious experiments he was able to show that Masters were not characterized by huge short term memories which enabled them to "think ahead" several more moves than novices, nor were they characterized by abnormally long attention spans which produced vastly superior powers of concentration. What did distinguish Masters was their memory for very large numbers of past games, an accumulation of their experiences in, or studies of, perhaps 3-10 games each day over a period of perhaps 15-30 years. Simon and Gilmartin (1973) were able to estimate that a Master will be able to recognize well over 10,000 distinct patterns of chess pieces on the board from past experience. Chase and Simon (1973) showed that these patterns or "chunks" are larger (i.e., contain more pieces) for Masters than for novices. A novice, for example, might recognize a pattern on the board as "black Knight three spaces to left of white King", while a Master may recognize the entire board as a pattern: "Spassky-Fisher Game 3". The Master's large repertoire of relative large patterns along with their temporal order renders more games familiar. Once a pattern is recognized, subsequent "strong" or "weak" (winning — losing) patterns can be recalled and pieces moved in the stronger direction. Of course it is always possible for a Master to revert to the usual "If I move my bishop here and he moves his queen there . . ." method of playing that characterizes novices. But for Masters such a method would run counter to the Principle of Sagacious Allocation. It would also quite likely ruin their game.

There is also considerable anecdotal evidence to suggest that individuals show a preference for cognitive processes that rely heavily on perception and long term memory over those which rely heavily on short term memory and attention. Consider, for example, the task of multiplication. The task is, of course, the formal equivalent of iterated addition, but I doubt that any of us have recently undertaken a multiplication in this formal manner. Multiplication by iterated addition places heavy demands on attention and STM. (As an illustration, try to multiply 27 x 11 by adding eleven 27's in your head, and don't use your fingers!) In order to ease the burden, we commonly learn a "times table", and in doing so sagaciously allocate much of the task of multiplication to perception and LTM. The times table allows us to do at least two things. First, it allows us to "perform" simple multiplications — say up to 12 x 12 — using a look-up procedure that minimally taxes attention and STM; if the particular multiplication is perceived/recognized as within the domain of our table, then the answer can be recalled from LTM more or less automatically. Second, it allows us to construct mental shortcuts or "heuristics" (see Newell and Simon, 1972) which can accomplish the task of multiplying numbers outside the domain of our times table with far less demand on STM and attention than those made by iterated addition. Dozens of such shortcuts exist, and we all probably know many of them. The standard multiplication method, which results in scratchings like this,

$$\begin{array}{r} 27 \\ \times\ \ 11 \\ \hline 27 \\ 27 \\ \hline 297 \end{array}$$

is one. The "lop-off-the-righthand-zeros-then-regroup-them" method (e.g., 120 x 120 = 12 x 12 and add two zeros = 14,400) is another. So too is the "big-chunk-plus-little-chunk" method (e.g., 21 x 45 = 20 x 45 + 45 = 900 + 45 = 945).

The shortcuts are diverse, but they have at least two things in common. Each attempts to partition or decompose the task at hand into components which can be "handled" by one's times table, by a corner of LTM. And each represents a stop-gap measure, a temporary method of solving a problem which is generally used only until the problem and solution can be added to that corner. Dewey said it better: "Thinking is secreted in the interstices of habits" (1927, p. 160). Once a solution is memorized, the kind of thinking to which Dewey referred — thinking characterized by fairly heavy use of attention and STM — almost always subsides. Even the now popular "turn-on-the-calculator-and-punch-in-the-numbers" method of multiplication gives way to recognition and recall when the problem and solution become known. Most people, for example, do not rush to these gadgets to compute 1000 x 1000. Nor do they start punching to determine if 2749 x 8742 is greater than 8 x 17 (they need only recognize that the former numbers are "big" and the latter are "small", and recall that the multiplication of big numbers produces a larger result than the multiplication of small ones). Such are the consequences of the Principle of Sagacious Allocation.

What does all this have to do with social performance? In the remainder of this paper I shall attempt to show that our social performances are as likely to be governed by cognitive processes obeying the Principle of Sagacious Allocation as the chess or arithmetic performances discussed above. I shall also present the rudiments of a conceptual framework for analyzing these processes, and discuss its implications for research. Finally, I shall attempt to outline the possible relationships between the framework and more traditional frameworks in which cognition and social performance (behaviour) are studied. Naturally, I am biting off more than I can chew. But if I can interest you in my approach, then I can hope that you may contribute to it much more than my capacities will allow.

Researchers in the areas of problem solving, judgement and decision making have recently converged on at least one general finding which I should like to borrow to begin my discussion. Stated as an aphorism, the finding implies something like this: In order to understand the cognitive processes underlying behaviour, we must first understand the ecology in which they operate (see Dawes, 1975; Newell and Simon, 1972; Slovic and Lichtenstein, 1971). Thus, if we are to understand the relation

294 *Warren Thorngate*

between cognition and social performance, then we must understand the nature of the environment in which the cognitions and performances occur. How do we describe the environment? What are its relevant features? The Principle of Sagacious Allocation suggests one, namely, *familiarity*. For the more familiar a social situation or segment therein is to an individual, the more the cognitive processes governing higher behaviour should exploit this familiarity.

An important research question immediately arises. Just how familiar are the everyday social situations in which one finds oneself? Familiarity, of course, is in the eye of the beholder. At very fine levels of analysis or resolution each social encounter is unique; there is no overlap. At very gross levels of analysis or resolution all social encounters are more or less the same. Most people avoid these extremes and probably judge familiarity on the basis of some fuzzy classification scheme (see Zadeh, 1968). I, for example, have been my Department's undergraduate advisor for about six years. Because of this I must engage in social intereactions with about 150 students each year. But I don't consider each interaction unique, nor do I consider all equivalent. I believe the reasons are functional. If I considered each unique, I would spend too much time, attention or STM reconstructing the answers to each student's queries from scratch. If I considered all equivalent, then I would probably embarrass myself no end by giving the same responses to each student regardless of his/her queries. (Question: Can you direct me to the bathroom? Answer: Only if you have the prerequisites.) Instead, I find myself classifying student queries into perhaps a dozen "themes" (e.g., job prospect queries, course content queries, graduate school queries) each with perhaps 20 "variations" (e.g., Can I get a job with a BA? Will a Masters Degree improve my chances of a job prospect?). The number of themes and variations have grown over the years, and I suspect that they now cover over 90% of all student queries. My responses to most theme-variation combinations have been more or less memorized. Familiarity is the rule. And like chess players with 10,000 familiar patterns, I can generate my responses without the feeling of overtaxing my attention and STM.

Yet perhaps I lead a duller life than most. Perhaps others are constantly engaged in unfamiliar and exciting social situations all the time and that they are continually filling attention and STM with information to feed much more "active" cognitive processes. This is certainly the impression I received from reading recent literature in the burgeoning area of social psychology known as the "information processing approach" (e.g. see Carroll and Payne, 1976). So it was with some trepidation that I asked two students to keep a daily log of their social interactions for a period of one month. Each was required to list with whom they interacted for longer than 3 minutes, where, when and how long each interaction occurred, and what they talked about. To my relief I discovered that both were leading almost as redundant lives as I was. For example, one student recorded 126 interactions with 40 different people, but 44 of these interactions occurred with just 2 people. The other student recorded 287 interactions with 59 people, but a mere 5 people accounted for 68% of these interactions. The latter student listed only 6 people as unfamiliar (she had not met them previously); the former student listed none. Interaction topics showed a similar pattern. For example, the first student recorded about 65 different topics (variations in her topic descriptions made a precise count impossible), but one topic — the permanent departure of her boyfriend — was repeated over 25 times.

Though these data are by no means definitive, they do suggest a high degree of familiarity with the input which individuals receive in day-to-day interactions. Perhaps this is because individuals tend to so classify the input as to render most of it familiar to them. Perhaps it is because individuals tend to avoid situations which they find or anticipate to be too unfamiliar. In either case the consequences are the same. Most segments of most interactions are probably not new. Because of this, a large proportion are likely stored in LTM along with one or more possible reactions to each, must like entries in a complex "times table" of social interactions. As a result, the Principle of Sagacious Allocation implies that current interactions will be governed more by recognizing and recalling these table entries than by involving the kind of thought — the conscious mental activity or mental calculation — which Dewey described. Social performances will likely proceed primarily from processes similar to those which Woods (1966, p. 95) argues to be characteristic of business managers:

> "In estimating the value to their company of a potential investment . . . managers . . . are preoccupied with searching for a comparable prior investment rather than identifying the relevant variables and forecasting the underlying uncertainty. Uncertainty is avoided like the plague, while the certainty of historical information is accorded such a premium that it dominates the managers' mental processes completely."

Though I believe that our everyday social ecology is full of the familiar, I do not wish to imply that it is so predictable that we can ultimately function in it from sheer recall. Obviously new things sometimes occur or, much more commonly, familiar things occur in new combinations. Appropriate responses to completely new things are hard to come by, although we can learn quickly by observing the reactions of others, asking questions, etc. Responses to new combinations of familiar things are easier to concoct. These combinations — like missing entries in our times table — force us to engage more of our attention and STM than, say, the familiar greeting "Hi! How are you?" of an old friend. It seems reasonable to assume that we develop a large set of heuristics to handle these new combinations, much like we develop our set of multiplication short cuts. But unlike these short cuts, social convention dictates that most of our social heuristics function without recourse to external aids. In addition, most interactions are relatively fast paced, and it is usually considered improper to spend more than a few seconds generating a response to input from another. These facets of our social ecology suggest that whatever social heuristics we use to generate a response from new combinations of familiar stimulus parts will be, in one sense, "simple" or (if you prefer) "crude". More specifically, the heuristics will likely rely as much as possible on perception and LTM (Thorngate, 1976).

Researchers in human judgement and decision making, as well as a few social psychologists (e.g., see Nisbett and Borgida, 1975; Slovic, 1971; Tversky and Kahneman, 1974) have recently implied that the crudeness of such heuristics is responsible for many of the errors of social judgement or of social performance, some of which can have tragic consequences. The heuristics are seen as grossly wasteful of information, and as breeding grounds of biases. Indeed, as I read their discoveries and arguments I begin to wonder how a satisfactory social interaction can ever occur. Yet satisfactory interactions occur quite often, and I think it is judicious to question seriously the social implications of their work. Many judgement and decision making heuristics (e.g., the Elimination by Aspects heuristic discussed by Tversky, 1972) are indeed wasteful of information, but in social interactions information is usually so abundant and so redundant that many of the most wasteful heuristics can do quite well in governing social performances. And even when information is scarce, great waste does not necessarily lead to great want. For example, Parsons (1975) has shown that one can correctly name each of over 14,000 popular tunes merely by noting only the ordinal pattern of the pitch of the first 16 notes. And a recent computer simulation of mine (Thorngate, 1977) has shown that some of the crudest decision heuristics can result in the same choice as the sophisticated Expected Value Rule over 90% of the time (see also Simon, 1956).

Two other attributes of social interaction mitigate the importance of errors caused by crude heuristics. First, most individuals are immensely tolerant of the social errors of others, especially if they are "little" errors produced by "nice" people, or if they are errors that favour the individual. If, for example, you make the erroneous judgement that the ideas in this paper are new and profound, I shall be more than happy to tolerate your blunder. Second, all known cultures have a wide variety of mechanisms for correcting intolerable social errors, most of which are simple and require little loss of face. The phrase "I'm sorry", for example, works wonders for relieving the minor sufferings of others which one's little errors may cause.

So too does the act of laughing at one's own foibles.

Finally, I must make one last argument in support of crude heuristics. Heuristics are rarely invoked just because appropriate stimuli are present. They are usually invoked as a means to an end. They are invoked for some purpose. What is this end or purpose *vis à vis* social interaction? Simon (1957) has forcefully argued that social man (as opposed to economic man) is much more inclined to satisfice than to maximize. In other words, we are much more likely to seek a satisfactory level of social performance in ourselves and others than to seek the optimal level of same. Obviously the dimensions on which we judge satisfaction can vary enormously across persons, situations and time. On some occasions we may perform for social acceptance, on others for status, monetary gain, revenge, etc. What is far more constant is our acceptance of a performance that is, as we often say, "good enough", of a performance that has reached a minimal level of acceptability on whatever dimensions we choose to evaluate it. Thus, even though a crude heuristic may occasionally, or even often, result in a nonoptimal performance, it may almost always meet or exceed our satisfaction level. The lower our satisfaction level — the lower our expectations — the more often a crude heuristic will generate a performance that meets or exceeds it. If a heuristic fails to result in satisfactory performances often enough, we are as free to lower our expectations (either by lowering our satisfaction level or by lowering our "often enough" criteria) to accommodate its weaknesses as we are to abandon it for a better one. Indeed, we may be forced to do this if we don't know whether better heuristics exist.

In sum, the Principle of Sagacious Allocation, the redundancy of social encounters, the relative power of many simple heuristics, the pace of social interaction, the tolerance of social errors, the availability of error correcting mechanisms, and the prevalence of satisficing reinforce and expand an old but long ignored perspective on social cognition and performance. Stated dogmatically and in modern jargon the perspective may be outlined as follows. First, as an individual engages in, watches, reads about, imagines, etc. perhaps 1000 or more social interactions each year he/she will accrue a vast data base and knowledge base of interaction segments and sequences, of responses to these, and of possible consequences of the responses. Second, during an ongoing interaction the individual will compare segments and sequences of the interaction to past ones stored in the vast data base and add the current segments to this data base whenever possible. Third, if a segment or sequence of them is recognized as demanding a response, then an attempt to generate a response will first be made by searching for an equivalent segment or sequence in the data base, recalling a satisfactory response to the equivalent segment or sequence and reproducing it (the times table method). If the search for an equivalent segment or sequence is unsuccessful, or if a satisfactory response to it cannot be recalled, then an attempt will be made to decompose the segment or sequence into its largest familiar components, search the data base for segments or sequences with equivalent components, recall satisfactory responses to these segments or sequences, and either select one of these responses or combine two or more of them for reproduction. If a decomposition of segments or sequences into large components does not result in the recall of a satisfactory response, then decompositions into increasingly smaller components will be attempted (much like the decomposition of a multiplication problem). This will continue until a satisfactory response is recalled, until a point of intolerable confusion is reached, or until attention is interrupted or exhausted. If intolerable confusion (overflow of STM?) results, attempts will be made to seek further information about or clarification of the segment or sequence from the person or persons generating it. If attention is interrupted or exhausted, a "punt" will be initiated (punts include such honourable responses as "I don't know", "I give up", "What do you think?", "You don't say!", "Well I'll be. . .", "Right"), or an attempt to leave the interaction will be undertaken.

If you feel that this perspective is vague, sketchy, oversimplified or even naive, you are right. There are great gaps in it which need to be filled, and it must be tightened considerably before one could even hope to test it as a theory. But as perspectives go I think it is more realistic, more elegant, and more suggestive of fruitful research than the other perspectives on social cognition and performance which currently vie for our attention (e.g., the balance perspective, the Bayesian perspective, the regression perspective). In case you are unconvinced, permit me to list some of the interesting questions which I believe this perspective stimulates, to report some of the research and thinking relevant to each question, and to suggest some directions for further enquiry.

How are social interactions represented in memory? Unfortunately this question is only slightly easier to answer than "What is the meaning of life?" To the best of my knowledge no answer has yet been found. But a growing number of researchers are engaged in the search, and are at least providing us with some promising leads. Extensive research by Jenkins (1974), for example, suggests that there is no invariant representation of all interaction segments or sequences; what is represented and how it is represented depend on a number of factors (e.g., the goals of the individual, the nature of the interaction, perceptual set). Thus, it is futile to look for any one representation. Instead we must first develop a syntax in which many different representations can be classified and related. Then we can embark on the horrific task of assessing the relative popularity of these representations and how this popularity shifts with persons, situations and time (see Thorngate, 1975b).

There are at least three syntaxes available for representing representations. One, the overworked General Linear Model, is a Procrustean Bed: it forces us to consider stimuli only as points in some *n*-dimensional space, and though it can handle configural representations, it does so in one of the most cumbersome ways imaginable. I do not wish to discuss the plethora of disadvantages of the GLM here (for a brief discussion see Boyd, 1972). Suffice it to say that our use of the GLM has done more to retard the progress of cognitive social psychology than all our other foibles combined. The sooner we abandon it, the better.

A second syntax shows considerable promise, but it is quite new and I don't believe it has yet been sufficiently developed to serve as a ready-made grammar for models of memory. I refer to Fuzzy Set Theory (Zadeh, 1965, 1968, 1972), a generalization of classical set theory which allows for degrees of membership in a set. If you read Zadeh, I think you will find that his theory is very "psychological" (for example, compare it to the work of Rosch and Mervis, 1975) and that it can easily handle many of the imprecise concepts in psychology — for example, the perception of features such as "tall", "roundish", "somewhat funny", etc. — which classical mathematics can treat only by adding awkward fudge factors (random variables being the most common). This has had one unfortunate consequence: many have taken his theory as a general model of the mind as a homomorphism of brain function (see Gaines, 1976 for a review). Of course, it is no more a general model of the mind than was George Boole's rendition of classical set theory, a rendition published under the grossly misleading title, *Laws of Thought*. Fortunately, not all fuzzy set theorists have become lost in this cul-de-sac, and I am hopeful that those who pursue the theory as a syntax alone will soon develop it to the point where social psychologists will adopt it as their own (for some promising developments, see Bezdek, 1974; Zadeh, 1976).

In the meantime a third syntax seems quite useful for classifying and relating representations of social encounters, namely, Graph Theory. Researchers in memory, linguistics and artificial intelligence have relied quite heavily on this syntax in the last decade and in doing so have produced some rather intriguing models of memory organization. These models commonly treat memory as a network of features or concepts connected by relations (e.g., see Anderson and Bower, 1973; Winograd, and Franks, 1971; Schank, 1973; Tulving, 1972; Winograd, 1972). The models vary widely in their assumptions about what features or concepts are stored and of how they are related. But all assume, either explicitly or implicitly, that stimuli are normally represented as a configuration of elements rather than as a mere list of elements or as some dimensional representation. Recent research strongly supports this assumption (e.g., Lockhead, 1972; Thorngate, 1971).

It seems to me the most realistic of these models are those which assume that all kinds of features and concepts are stored in a configuration and are linked by all sorts of relations (e.g., see Craik and Lockhart, 1972; Schank and Abelson, 1977; Winograd, 1972). I need only look at my bookshelves to realize that I have configured part of this stored information by topic, part by author, part by date, part by height, part by thickness, part by time of storage, and part by sheer caprice. In addition, I seem to remember which parts are stored which way: statistics books by topic, social psychology books by topic and degree of use, history and philosophy books by random access, and so forth. In one sense this multi-faceted organization (that's the euphemism for sloppiness) is terribly inefficient. But in another sense it is quite wise. If I were to adopt one method of organization, select only one feature of the books (e g., author's last name) and configure them with only one relation (e.g., alphabetical), then I would be quick on the draw only when I was selecting a book on the basis of that feature and relation. Otherwise I would flail at my shelves in frustration. But if I adopted several methods of organization, several features and relations, and stuffed my memory with all the appropriate cross-references, then my chances of quickly finding a book from several different starting points would increase immensely. Since my time and level of frustration are far more limited than my capacity to remember trivia (e.g., that Shaver's Attribution book is a fairly thin, brownish-covered, new-looking paperback which I either shoved on top of my lower row of social psychology texts or squeezed in the paperback side of my cognitive processes shelf), and since I never can be sure how I will want to reference a book when next needed, I am quite satisfied with my haphazardness. For a more theoretical treatment of the advantages of such diversity and redundancy, see Ashby (1956).

We should expect that most social interactions are stored in a multifarious network of features, concepts and relations as well. If an interaction "gets in" long term memory, it is likely to retain many of the following kinds of information: who was involved, what was discussed, where, when and why it occurred, and how it affected people. In addition, it may well contain a good deal of reflective information, that is, information about one's cognitions during the interaction or second thoughts about the interaction after it occurred. The information may be stored partly as ideas, partly as images, partly as verbal synopses. And, of course, the sheer amount of information stored may vary widely from interaction to interaction.

Schank and Abelson's Script Theory (1977; see also Abelson, 1976) is based on the same multifarious assumption. Interactions are assumed to be stored as "scripts", as sequences of "vignettes", much like a well annotated script of a play. Since this part of their theory bears a close resemblance to my own hunches, I am disposed to believe that it is all true. But the validity of their theory has yet to be assessed, and in all fairness I must admit to a strong suspicion that it never could be. The problems of validation are part methodological and part conceptual (see Frijda, 1967). The conceptual problems derive from the non-committal nature of their Theory, and my corresponding hunches. Stripped bare of examples and anecdotes, all we are saying is that memory is rich, complex and variable. The alternatives — memory is rich, but simply organized and static, impoverished and variable, etc. — appear senseless, so we are really not committing ourselves to much more than a cliché. The theory needs more substance, for example, statements about the conditions under which certain kinds of information will be stored or ignored. It is not difficult to make such statements. We could, for example, get good mileage out of the possible relations between the structure and content of memory and the von Restorff effect. But it is massively difficult to test such statements. At present we have no elegant methodology for extracting graph theoretic representations of our would-be dependent variables (structure and content) from individuals. The methodologies which are currently available (for example, content analyses of introspections, information seeking paradigms, computer simulations) are terribly cumbersome and full of artifacts.

Perhaps elegant methods will be developed, or perhaps we will find that a switch to the Fuzzy Set Theoretic syntax will make our Methodological problems more tractable (see Kokowa, Nakamura and Oda, 1975). Until then we can at least console ourselves with the observation that many of our brightest colleagues in learning, perception and psycholinguistics are currently at the same impasse (e.g., see Derwing and Baker, 1976). Of course, many of them have been there longer; Tolman, as I recall, found it easier to demonstrate the existence of "cognitive maps" (an earlier term for something like a script) than to draw them. In any event, we have arrived.

Where do these representations of social interactions come from? Somehow this question seems much easier to answer than the previous one. There are likely three general ways in which interactions, or fragments thereof, can be added to LTM: direct experience, indirect experience, and imagination. When we interact directly with others we make available to LTM a plethora of information, a good deal of which is probably retained. If you doubt this, try the following sometime: write down the names of everyone you ever recall meeting; or if you can't recall the name of someone, write down as much about the physical features of that person as you can recall. Tom Storm, a very clever social psychologist of British Columbia, tried this one time, but gave up after about 500 names-descriptions; he proceeded in roughly chronological order and stopped at around age 15! I'm not sure what proportion of people that Tom met by this tender age made his list, nor obviously is he. But if you accept his list or generate your own, I'm sure you will come to appreciate just how much information about others can be tucked away in your memory through direct experience. There is no reason to believe that other aspects of interactions are remembered in lesser amounts. I presume, for example, that we can all recall something of the situations in which we interacted with these people, something of our behaviours and feelings towards them, something of their mannerisms, etc. Certainly, many interactions are entirely forgotten. But enough remain to provide us with a very rich data base for use in current and future encounters.

Many of the representations of social interactions which we store in LTM come from indirect experience, from "observational learning" or "modelling" to use more recent terms. There are of course several forms of indirect experience: watching live interactions, watching television, listening to radio, reading novels, hearing gossip, etc. Many of these forms provide us with relatively little information about social encounters. Yet we often represent them with elaborate embellishments. When reading a novel, for example, it is common to create rather detailed visual and auditory images of the locale and of the characters (their appearance, mannerisms, etc.), and to create intricate causal explanations for the characters' behaviour (Heider, 1958). It is not clear why this is done, and it presents a fascinating problem for research.

Finally, we seem to be as adept at storing representations of imagined interactions in LTM as we are at storing directly or indirectly experienced ones. Anyone who has engaged in a frustrating social encounter and afterwards has rehearsed it *ad nauseam* while imagining how he/she should have acted has at once provided another candidate for LTM. The fact that most of the imagining takes place after encounters, or when there is nothing else to do, suggests that the activity places heavy demands on STM and attention, demands which normally cannot be met when the encounter itself is using these limited facilities. The environmental demands on STM and attention are usually at a minimum during sleep — a time when our imaginations can run wild. The result is dreaming, and though I may be doing just that as I write these words, I see no reason to deny the possibility that our dreamed interactions may be stored right along with our directly and indirectly experienced ones, and provide the same sort of reference points in governing social performance.

Attempts to trace the etiology of particular stored interaction representations have yet to be done, but I think they should be. The task may not be too difficult, for most individuals commonly store the source of their information along with the information itself. Most Canadians, for example, can tell you that they learned how Trudeau acts in a press conference from watching television, or that they have some idea of how to respond to a Sasquatch by imagining the interaction. A much more difficult task is to discover just why 'this extra information ever gets stored in the first place.

How do we "find" representations of interactions that are equivalent to the one in which we are currently engaged? This question quickly reduces to the venerable research problem of memory retrieval. We know a good deal about the retrieval of information from STM, but we know very little about the retrieval of information from LTM (Posner, 1973). It is likely that we do not "search" 'LTM in any way that researchers propose STM is searched; there is no little genie in our heads looking around for relevant past experiences (Pylyshyn, 1973). Perhaps the process can instead be described by a tuning fork analogy: each interaction representation acts as a complex tuning fork which may vibrate sympathetically when the fundamental tones or the "overtones" of the current interaction reach it. Since this is hard speculation, I might as well go on to say that these tones and overtones may be "broadcast" to very many representations at once in a manner we detect as the noise in brainwaves. The closer the match between the current interaction and a past one, the more sympathetically the latter will vibrate — an effect much like that obtained by plucking one string on a harpsichord, then stopping it noting the other strings that vibrate either from the fundamental, an overtone, or an overtone of a string vibrating sympathetically, and the strings which don't vibrate at all. Plucking middle C, for example, will set all C strings into active motion, and all F and G strings into somewhat less active motion, while all C # strings will remain almost still. The relative activity will, of course, depend on the relative amplitude of the overtones of the plucked string. By analogy, a current social encounter may include, say, someone asking the question: "What do you think of Trudeau?" which may shake (activate) representations that include Trudeau information, opinion giving information, political philosophy information, question answering procedure information, etc., but which may not shake representations filled with restaurant information, drain cleaning procedures, and the Dewey Decimal System.

To round out the tuning fork analogy we need only relate the extent of the sympathetic vibrations of stored representations to recognition and recall. I have no idea how to do this, indeed I suspect that it is here the analogy breaks down. It could be that all activated representations compete for one's attention and that only those that are activated the longest will win. It could also be that the activated representations produce some unique composite − a "new chord", if you will − which captures one's attention on its own. Research on binocular rivalry suggests that both resolutions might occur (e.g., see Woodworth and Schlosberg, 1954, Chap. 13).

Each mode of resolution may have functional advantages and disadvantages for the individual. Consider, for example, what might happen if the competition-for-attention mode were operating. If there were little attention to compete for, relatively few representations might "get through"; only the ones that vibrate the most sympathetically with the ongoing encounter − the virtually identical ones − might be recognized or recalled. A similar state of affairs would occur if one were overly discriminating, if one allowed only closest matches to be equivalent. The result would be to increase the chances that the current encounter would not match any previous ones, and hence increase the chances that one could recall nothing to do. People under great and immediate stress often show this "blocking out" syndrome − perhaps because none of their attention can be spared for the computation of recognition and recall. So do some philosophers, who are occasionally so overly discriminating, so prone to making the finest of distinction, that nothing remains equivalent and all past experiences are rendered useless.

At the other extreme, consider what would happen if a large chunk of attention were opened to sympathetically vibrating representations, or if one were more or less indiscriminate in their matches. In both cases, a great number of representations would likely succeed in capturing some part of attention or STM and the individual may have difficulty knowing what to do with them all. Those who see a thousand analogies in the smallest of encounters may well be reminded of a hundred possible reactions to it. Selecting one reaction from the multitude may so overtax STM (see the next section below) that no reaction will occur. If the mythical indecisive poet does exist, this hypothesis may explain why.

Thus, the compete-for-attention mode of retrieval should only function smoothly between the extremes of hypo- and hyper-attention (or standards of acceptance). This is another way of saying that the mode is subject to Yerkes-Dodson Law (see Walley and Weiden, 1973). The composite mode of retrieval is more difficult for me to fathom. I suspect that most composites, like mutants, are stillborn and serve no useful purpose. But some composites may result in what we call insight, or in what we call humour, or what we call creative problem solving. In these cases they may be very useful indeed.

Though I do not wish to push the tuning fork analogy too far, I should note that several models of neural mechanisms of perception, attention and memory are at least superficially compatible with it. Hebb's (1949) theory of learning, for example, rests heavily on the notion of reverberating circuits: Barlow's (1972) neural doctrine stresses the sensitivity of neurons to varying frequencies (pitches) of firing. Walley and Weiden's (1973) model of arousal emphasizes neural activation and inhibition of several levels of abstraction, as does Craik and Lockhart's (1972) model of memory. These levels strike me as analogous to fundamentals and overtones. I should also note that several musical metaphors occur in social psychological and everyday parlance: cognitive dissonance, rhythms of dialogue, harmonious relations, good vibes, ominous overtones, themes of conversation and so forth. This may mean nothing. But at least it reminds us that we don't model all of our thinking on the physical sciences.

How do we select an appropriate response? In the simplest of cases, a current social interaction will remind each participant of only one well learned previous interaction. Responses in the LTM representation will look like a chain, each link will comprise a part of someone's social performance, there will be no branches, no alternatives to consider; response "selection" will occur from pure habit. Reproductions of these interactions we call rituals; actors reproduce them in plays, musicians reproduce them in recitals, priests reproduce them in mass.

Fortunately, most interactions are not quite as dull as this. Most interactions, or interaction segments, probably activate several scripts or representations. When only one of these captures some attention, and when it contains only one satisfactory response appropriate to the moment and no unsatisfactory responses, then a decision to reproduce that response will likely be made by fiat. But when two or more responses are recalled, something must be done with them. The doing demands STM, attention and time which — I am sure you are now convinced — are generally in short supply. It is thus likely that we develop over years of direct, indirect and imaginary experience an impressive array of clever heuristics for getting the job done quickly, easily and most often satisfactorily. Here are some of the more common ones:

(1) *Ask for clarification.* Since the existence of alternative responses is often the result of alternative representations of a current encounter, and since much of this encounter is generated by others, it is often useful to employ the clarification heuristic as a means of decision making. One simply asks others to be more specific, restate their position, expand on their ideas, etc. With luck, their response will eliminate all but one of the alternative representations and thus will probably reduce the number of alternative reactions from which to choose to a very manageable size.

(2) *Stall.* If the choice of a response cannot be made at the moment, one may attempt to maneuver for extra time. At parties this is often accomplished by lighting cigarettes, sipping drinks, or by temporarily excusing oneself. Small amounts of time can be gained with phrases such as "Hmmm" or "Let me see now", larger amounts with phrases such as "Give me some time to think it over". Tabling works wonders in Faculty Meetings, while conveniently forgetting the stimulus works wonders almost everywhere.

(3) *Copy.* Many social interactions require responses of several individuals. If one is undecided about a response, it may be possible to observe the responses of others first, then mimic one of the satisfactory or at least popular ones. Once known as the "herd instinct", this heuristic is very effective in resolving trivial inner conflicts between alternative responses — providing, of course, that everyone else isn't using it at the same time.

(4) *Publicize the dilemma and seek advice.* If one is at loose ends about the choice of a response, it is often advantageous to admit it and ask for help. Mouthing such phrases as "I don't know what to do", "I'm not sure how to respond to that", "I'm of two minds", followed by a question such as "What do you think?", "What would you do?" will usually lighten the STM and attentional burden that vascillation brings. It will also have at least two side benefits. First, it will flatter those on whom you inflict it, generally raising you in their eyes. Second, if you take their advice, it will give you the opportunity to blame them for any undesirable consequences.

(5) *Advance and (possibly) retreat.* If the pressure is on to choose an alternative response at once, it may be possible to make a tentative response or "feeler", then pursue it or withdraw it (with apologies, if necessary) depending upon early public reaction. Politicians find this heuristic much to their liking, as do a wide assortment of other wishy-washy individuals.

(6) *Synthesize.* Alternative responses may not be completely incompatible, and the cognitive pain of a decision between them can be avoided by reproducing them all. This is especially easy when the alternative responses are verbal, and one can talk one's

way around the problem. In this regard, generalities work wonders, as do long discourses filled with those marvellous phrases "but", "in contrast", and "on the other hand". Many academics couldn't survive without this heuristic. I, for example, have found it invaluable in writing this paper.

We do, of course, occasionally find ourselves in situations where only one alternative response can be selected and where we must firmly commit ourselves to a decision between them. In such situations the above heuristics will lose their utility and we will be forced to apply other heuristics to get the job done. Many of these other heuristics have been delineated by decision making researchers. They include the minimax and maximax heuristics (see Thorngate and Ferguson, 1977), the paired comparison heuristic (Russo and Rosen, 1975), the intra-dimensional comparison and elimination by aspects heuristic (Tversky, 1969, 1972), the unit weighting heuristic (Dawes, 1976), and several variants of the satisficing principle (Simon, 1957). The heuristic selected seems to depend on several factors of which only one: the complexity of the decision, has been studied in great detail (Payne, 1976; Thorngate and Maki, 1976). Research on problem solving set suggests that decision heuristics, like problem solving methods, will vary according to the judged similarity of the situation to ones for which a useful heuristic is recalled (see Luchins, 1942). And casual observation of gamblers suggests that heuristics for making social decisions, like those for gambling decisions, will vary according to personality as well. These suggestions are worthy of further enquiry. So too is the question of how all these heuristics get into our heads.

How is whole system controlled? It is a major miracle that all of the mental activities discussed above manage to coordinate themselves in the production of what are usually smooth, flexible and highly adaptive social performances. This coordination suggests that something is doing the coordinating, and it is perhaps the ultimate goal of social psychology to determine just what this "thing" is. Schank and Abelson (1977) have suggested that it is a Master script, a script for selecting scripts appropriate to the occasion. However, they have so far done little more than give the thing a name. Newell (1973) has progressed somewhat farther, primarily because he has restricted himself to a far smaller domain of enquiry than that of Schank and Abelson. But Newell readily admits that his models of "control structures" are nascent (pp. 515-24) and no one would deny that there is simply not enough knowledge of these things to do much more than wave our hands at them. For now it is sufficiently rewarding to know that at least a few very sharp cookies are thinking about the problem. And it is rather frightening to know that sooner or later someone will have to develop research methodologies to test the goodness-of-fit of their thoughts. I am currently very much obsessed with this methodological challenge, and am working on a simple-minded goodness-of-fit procedure (Ordinal Pattern Analysis) which may prove useful as an alternative to traditional statistical analyses in testing the predictions of very complex models. But the procedure will never be more useful than the data that feed it, and the real trick will be to develop the tools which will reap a nutritious harvest.

Perhaps you have noticed that throughout this paper I have failed to use two words which have come to dominate most traditional discussions of social cognition and behaviour, to wit: attitudes and attributions. I feel a wee bit guilty about this, because some discussions of attitudes and attributions have much in common with the present perspective, and I do not wish to put their old wine in my new bottles. So to assuage my conscience I must mention that Abelson's (1973) discussion of the structure of belief systems and Kelley's (1972) discussion of causal schemata and the attribution process both demonstrate that there is some continuity between the terms employed in traditional discussions of social cognition and the terms I have chosen herein. However, these particular works of Abelson and Kelley do not dominate the literature and they have yet to inspire much research. I have not, for example, found many journal articles which have attempted to assess or measure actual belief systems or causal schemata, much less relate them empirically to social performances. What I have found instead is an odd congeries of articles which appear to have little, if anything, to say about the kinds of questions I have outlined above. In this respect I feel no guilt whatsoever in avoiding the use of the terms "attitude" and "attribution", and see no merit whatsoever in attempting to relate them to the present perspective.

At the same time I am curious about why the present perspective — which, again, is in no way new — has not been pursued by social psychologists before. Perhaps it is too grandiose, too full of big problems that require too much time and effort to solve (if, indeed, they could be). Perhaps it is because social psychologists too often mold their theoretical perspectives around their research methods (Kelley's (1967) ANOVA model of attribution is a classic example) and that only now are methods appropriate to the present perspective being considered. Perhaps the reasons are more sociological, more geared to the chances of academic survival and the safety of pedantic research. Or perhaps the reasons are entirely logical: the present perspective may simply be wrong.

References

Abelson, R., The structure of belief systems. In .R. Schank & K. Colby (Eds.), *Computer Models of Thought and Language,* San Francisco: Freeman, 1973.

Abelson, R., Script processing in attitude formation and decision making. In J. Carroll & J. Payne (Eds.), *Cognition and Social Behavior,* Hillsdale, New Jersey: Erlbaum, 1976.

Anderson, J.R. and Bower, G., *Human Associative Memory,* Washington, D.C.: H.C. Winston, 1973.

Ashby, R., *An Introduction to Cybernetics,* London: Chapman & Hall, 1956.

Barlow, H., Single units and sensation: A neuron doctrine for perceptual psychology? *Perception,* 1972, *1,* 371-94.

Bezdek, J., Numerical taxonomy with fuzzy sets, *Journal of Mathematical Biology,* 1974, *1,* 57-71.

Boyd, J., Information distance for discrete structure. In R. Shepard, A.K. Romney & S. Nerlove (Eds.), *Multidimensional Scaling* (Vol. I), New York: Seminar Press, 1972.

Bransford, J. and Franks, V., The abstraction of linguistic ideas, *Cognitive Psychology,* 1971, *2,* 331-50.

Cannon, W.B., *The Wisdom of the Body,* New York: Norton, 1932.

314 *Warren Thorngate*

Carroll, J. & Payne, J. (Eds.), *Cognition and Social Behavior,* Hillsdale, New Jersey: Erlbaum, 1976.

Chase, W. and Simon, H., The mind's eye in chess. In W. Chase (Ed.), *Visual Information Processing,* New York: Academic Press, 1973.

Craik, F. and Lockhart, R., Levels of processing: A framework for memory research, *Journal of Verbal Learning and Verbal Behavior,* 1972, *11,* 671-84.

Dawes, R., The mind, the model and the task. In F. Restle, R. Shiffrin, J. Castellan, H. Lindman & D. Pison (Eds.), *Cognitive Theory* (Vol. 1), Hillsdale, New Jersey: Erlbaum, 1975.

Dawes, R., Shallow psychology. In J. Carroll & J. Payne (Eds.), *Cognition and Social Behavior,* New York: Erlbaum, 1976.

de Groot, A., *Thought and Choice in Chess,* The Hague: Mouton, 1965.

de Groot, A., Perception and memory versus thought: Some old issues and recent findings. In B. Kleinmuntz (Ed.), *Problem Solving,* New York: Wiley, 1966.

Derwing, B. and Baker, W., On the re-integration of linguistics and psychology. Paper presented at the Psychology of Language Conference, University of Stirling, Scotland, June, 1976.

Dewey, J., *Human Nature and Conduct,* New York: Holt, 1922.

Dewey, J., *The Public and its Problems,* London: Unwin, 1927.

Frijda, N., Problems of computer simulation, *Behavioral Science,* 1967, *12,* 59-67.

Gaines, B.R., Foundations of fuzzy reasoning, *International Journal of Man-Machine Studies,* 1976, *8,* 623-68.

Gibson, E., *Principles of Perceptual Learning and Development,* New York: Appleton-Century-Crofts, 1969.

Hebb, D., *Organization of Behavior,* New York: Wiley, 1949.

Heider, F., *The Psychology of Interpersonal Relations,* New York: Wiley, 1958.

James, W., *The Principles of Psychology,* New York: Holt, 1890.

Jenkins, J., Remember that old theory of memory? Well, forget it! *American Psychologist,* 1974, *29,* 785-95.

Kahneman, D., *Attention and Effort,* New York: Prentice-Hall, 1973.

Kelley, H., Attribution theory in social psychology. In D. Levine (Ed.), *Nebraska Symposium on Motivation,* University of Nebraska Press, 1967.

Kelley, H., *Causal Schemata and the Attribution Process,* Morristown, N.J.: General Learning Press, 1972.

Kokowa, M., Nakamura, K. and Oda, M., Experimental approach to fuzzy simulation of memorizing, forgetting and inference process. In L. Zadeh, K. Fu, K. Tanaka & M. Shimura (Eds.), *Fuzzy Sets and their Application to Cognitive and Decision Processes,* New York: Academic Press, 1975.

Lockhead, G.R., Processing dimensional stimuli, *Psychological Review,* 1972, *79,* 410-19.

Luchins, A.S., Mechanization of problem solving: The effect of Einstellung, *Psychological Monographs,* 1942, *54,* No. 248.

Miller, G., The magical number seven, plus or minus two: Some limits on our capacity for processing information, *Psychological Review,* 1956, *63,* 81-97.

Neisser, U., *Cognitive Psychology,* New York: Appleton-Century-Crofts, 1967.

Newell, A., Production systems: Models of control structures. In W. Chase (Ed.), *Visual Information Processing,* New York: Academic Press, 1973.

Newell, A. and Simon, H. *Human Problem Solving,* Englewood Cliffs, N.J.: Prentice-Hall, 1972.

Nisbett, R. and Borgida, E., Attribution and the psychology of prediction, *Journal of Personality and Social Psychology*, 1975, *32*, 932-43.

Parsons, D., *Dictionary of Popular Tunes*, London: Spencer Brown, 1975.

Payne, J., Task complexity and contingent processing in decision making: An information search and protocol analysis, *Organizational Behavior and Human Performance*, 1976, *16*, 366-87.

Posner, M., *Cognition: An introduction*, Glenview, Illinois: Scott-Foresman, 1973.

Pylyshyn, Z., What the mind's eye tells the mind's brain: A critique of mental imagery, *Psychological Bulletin*, 1973, *80*, 1-24.

Rosch, E. and Mervis, C., Family resemblances: Studies in the internal structure of categories, *Cognitive Psychology*, 1975, *7*, 573-605.

Russo, J.E. and Rosen, L.D., An eye fixation analysis of multialternative choice, *Memory and Cognition*, 1975, *3*, 267-76.

Schank, R., Identification of conceptualizations underlying natural language. In R. Schank & K. Colby (Eds.), *Computer Models of Thought and Language*, San Francisco: Freeman, 1973.

Schank, R. and Abelson, R., *Scripts, Plans, Goals, and Understanding*, Hillsdale, New Jersey: Erlbaum, 1977.

Simon, H.A., Rational choice and the structure of the environment, *Psychological Review*, 1956, *63*, 129-38.

Simon, H.A., *Models of Man*, New York: Wiley, 1957.

Simon, H.A. and Gilmartin, K., A simulation of memory for chess positions, *Cognitive Psychology*, 1973, 29-46.

Slovic, P., Limitations of the mind of man: Implications for decision making in the Nuclear Age, *Oregon Research Institute Research Bulletin*, 1971, *11*, 41-9.

Slovic, P. and Lichtenstein, S., Comparison of Bayesian and regression approaches to the study of information processing in judgment, *Organizational Behavior and Human Performance*, 1971, *6*, 649-744.

Thorngate, W., *On the Learning and Transfer of Multi-cue Judgment Processes*, Report 71-3, Social Psychology Labs., Department of Psychology, University of Alberta, 1971.

Thorngate, W., Process invariance: Another red herring, *Personality and Social Psychology Bulletin*, 1975, *1*, 485-8 (a).

Thorngate, W., *Research Strategies and the Analysis of Process Variability*, Report 75-3, Social Psychology Labs., Department of Psychology, University of Alberta, 1975 (b).

Thorngate, W., Must we always think before we act? *Personality and Social Psychology Bulletin*, 1976, *2*, 31-5.

Thorngate, W., *Comparisons of the Power and Efficiency of Several Decision Heuristics*. Manuscript submitted for publication, 1977.

Thorngate, W. and Ferguson, T., Behind the eyeball: Some popular misuses of information in human decision making, *Canadian Journal of Information Science*, 1977, *2*, 1-11.

Thorngate, W. and Maki, J., *Decision Heuristics and the Choice of Political Candidates*. Unpublished manuscript, 1976.

Tulving, E., Episodic and semantic memory. In E. Tulving & W. Donaldson (Eds.), *Organization of Memory*, New York: Academic Press, 1972.

Tversky, A., Intransitivity of preferences, *Psychological Review*, 1969, *76*, 31-48.

Tversky, A., Elimination by aspects: A theory of choice, *Psychological Review*, 1972, *79*, 281-95.

Tversky, A. and Kahneman, D., Judgment under uncertainty: Heuristics and biases, *Science,* 1974, *185,* 1124-31.

Walley, R. and Weiden, T., Lateral inhibition and cognitive masking: A neuropsychological theory of attention, *Psychological Review,* 1973, *80,* 284-302.

Wertheimer, M., *Productive Thinking,* New York: Harper & Row, 1945.

Winograd, T., *Understanding Natural Language,* New York: Academic Press, 1972.

Woods, D., Improving estimates that involve uncertainty, *Harvard Business Review,* 1966, *44,* 91-8.

Woodworth, R. and Schlosberg, H., *Experimental Psychology (Revised),* New York: Holt, 1954.

Zadeh, L., Fuzzy sets, *Information and Control,* 1965, *8,* 338-53.

Zadeh, L., Fuzzy algorithms, *Information and Control,* 1968, *12,* 99-102.

Zadeh, L., Fuzzy languages and their relation to human intelligence, *Proceedings of the International Conference on Man and Computer,* Bordeaux, France, Basel: Karger, 1972, 130-65.

Zadeh, L., A fuzzy-algorithmic approach to the definition of complex or imprecise concepts, *International Journal of Man-Machine Studies,* 1976, *8,* 249-91.

PART IV

Assessment

Soviet and Western Social Psychology: Reflections [1]

LLOYD H. STRICKLAND

An editor of a symposium volume should normally attempt to end the book with a critical assessment and a coherent overview of the contributions, supplying clues to the reader of the possible future value of the collection. I have tried to meet these obligations in different ways, in an attempt to deal with both the unique advantages and disadvantages of the conference.

To the first purpose, I have attempted to preserve throughout the book the current of criticism that pervaded the conference, by presenting edited transcripts of the discussions that followed most papers. The criticism, voiced either through questions or assertions, both of and by representatives of the East and West, often "reads" more harshly than it "plays", to borrow a description from the theatre; those occasions which a reader might sense as being most tense were often marked with good humour and laughter. But this does not imply that the antagonists were any less earnest.

Regarding an editor's second task, I have concluded that it would be presumptuous to try to provide here an overview of Russian or (chiefly) Canadian social psychology. With respect to the former, an informed reader will already be familiar with the many well-known Russian voices that were *not* heard at the conference, and the newer reader will have learned

(1) Portions of the following are taken from an Invited Talk at the Meetings of the British Psychological Society, University of York, April 1978.

from this book the names of many important but absent Soviet scholars, from the references of those present. The formal papers of the Soviet participants are too few to be construed as being completely representative, and hence it would seem inappropriately premature to premise a global assessment, either positive or negative, of Soviet social psychology on the basis of the collection herein presented.

For different reasons, it does not seem greatly useful to try to force an appearance of coherence on the Canadian contributions. These are as varied as the country they represent; some reflect interest in problems important to most Western social psychologies, while others represent interests ranging from a concern with "universal" to more "local" issues (e.g., communication between English- and French-Canadians). Just as the Soviet efforts, whatever their immediate focus, reflect a preoccupation with building a unified, Marxist social psychological study of man, the Canadian contributions reflect the varied and vigorous nature of the social and/or intellectual communities in that country.

So, if we are limited in making useful generalizations about the separate social psychologies of the two countries mainly represented, of what use can such a juxtaposition of two views of the field serve, presented as they are with evaluative criticism by the participants from West Germany and the United States? Answers to this question will vary with the sophistication and intent of the reader, so I can only describe the ways in which they have enlightened me, meanwhile risking the assumption that I am typical of North American social psychologists.

I have begun to see a different route to a solution of social psychology's so-called "paradigm problems". Perhaps our task should not be to decide what paradigm to use — old or new — but to decide what problems to study — what phenomena to try to understand. I see more clearly that Western social psychology's major mistake has been to use methods to determine problems, when we really should have been working the other way around.

When I review our own development, I speculate that we, to a great extent, have stopped asking *basic* social psychological questions. Perhaps this is better put by saying that we stopped asking *socio*-psychological questions. In America, this came about when group membership, and conformity, and a concern for a "silent generation" stopped being important in the 1950s, to be replaced by a folk-philosophy which said, in brief, "Do your own thing". This, of course, has been reflected in our development of an individual-oriented experimental social psychology.

Kurt Lewin knew what the basic questions were; he even tried to develop a new language for stating and understanding them. I refer here to his topological and vector psychology. This paradigm, or "template", was practically laughed out of existence, in part because mathematicians told us it was naive topology — it was mathematically weak. What techniques were substituted for it in social psychology, as it was taught in psychology departments? They were statistical designs and analyses gleaned largely from scholars who were concerned with agricultural experiments; these agricultural statistics and designs were the tools that became more important than the problems. Possibly another reason that topology was not given a real try was that it was too difficult, or perhaps novel, that department chairmen couldn't find anyone to teach it. I leave these questions to the historians, and I look forward to what they may supply as answers. But the basic social psychological questions stopped being heard.

I do not mean to imply that there is a set of "legitimate" social psychological questions — if anything, I tend to argue, as did some of Chelpanov's colleagues (see Andreeva's paper, pp. 57-68), that almost *all* of our most important psychological questions are social psychological questions; as we are reminded in this volume, even our psychophysical judgements are appropriately construed as being social phenomena. Yet I continue to entertain the possibility that there remains a set of *basic* questions that are primarily socio-psychological. These are the sort of individual-group questions which seem to have figured so

322   *Lloyd H. Strickland*

prominently in the Soviets' preoccupation with the "collective".
These are questions that we in the West started with, too; these
are the ones that have to a great extent dropped out of sight.

When searching for support for this conjecture, I discovered
an excellent but too rarely acknowledged paper by Kurt Back
(1963), in which he built a strong case for social psychology as
an "interstitial science covering the situations where the actions
of the individual and the forces of organized society interact"
(p. 368). I offer a few selections from his thoughts:

> It seems that the general course of social science has been an escape from the
> searching questions which originally motivated its inception, and a substi-
> tution of more exactly measurable problems. Probably the original questions
> were badly phrased and unanswerable as stated. Much has been gained by the
> introduction of operationally defined concepts and empirically verifiable
> problems. However, if a shift occurs and the subject matter changes, the price
> of scientific precision may be a loss of importance [p. 368].

> We cannot lose sight of the fact that individuals and societies occur together
> and do so in varied forms of interrelationship. There can be interactions between
> systems, there can be conflicts, there can be areas of action which are not
> covered by either system. Social psychology is the science which deals with
> these conditions; it is an interstitial. science between systems of different
> levels, as biochemistry or psychophysiology [p. 372].

> If there is a coincidence between the needs of the individual and society, there
> is no social psychological problem. Social psychology enters if there is a
> conflict between the two, or if there is a no man's land which is covered by
> neither individual nor society.

> What is meant, then, by a social psychological question? It concerns itself
> with situations in which a human being asserts a particular representation
> simultaneously in the social and individual field. He can be defined in the
> social and in the individual system, and it is a meaningful definition in either.
> In the social psychological problems, human beings are defined (or define
> themselves) in both systems simultaneously, although they may not be defined
> in the same way. If the question is asked in this way, it is naturally one which
> cannot be dealt with purely by sociological or psychological methods and
> theories [p. 372].

> The advancement of theory in social psychology lies more in the approach to
> the issue, in the way of asking the questions, than in the specific form of theory
> formulation itself. The latter alternative, the language of the theory, whether
> it is to be mathematical or not, or deductive or descriptive, becomes a later
> decision whose outcome will depend on the appropriateness of a particular
> theoretical technique to a problem as stated" [p. 374].

I close, reasserting that Western social psychologists who
are wondering *how* to do what we want to do should go back
and decide *what* questions we really want to ask. If we want

to study individual information processing and decision making with, say, social stimuli of varying degrees of physical attractiveness (and this certainly seems to be a "legitimate" social psychological question), we should probably do it in the laboratory in the best tradition of experimental psychology, while reminding ourselves of the social context of our research. We shall probably learn of a great deal that isn't obvious. If we are interested, alternatively, in contagion of violence, and the norms governing its expression, then we will do better to make our unobtrusive measures at football matches, and our theories about why brawling occurs will probably be non-elusive refinements of what everybody knows (see discussions and examples of ethnogenic social psychology in Marsh, Rosser and Harré, 1978). But this is alright; as Thorngate (1976) has pointed out, we are expecting too much of *any* theory when we ask that it be general, simple, *and* accurate.

However, if we choose to go back to our socio-psychological questions, we may just have to develop a new conceptual scheme in which to try to frame and answer them. And why not? Why should we be so arrogant as to suppose that social psychological phenomena *must* be best phrased with the language mathematical statistics on the one hand, or on the other with the verbal language that we all share, and with which we communicate? The new conceptual scheme might not be topology — but maybe it could be given a second chance. It might be a form of symbolic logic, it might be graph theory, it might be catastrophe theory. There is much interest now in developing mathematical and statistical tools for "evaluation research". There is plenty of space for the adventurous to move about in — in social psychology's house there are many mansions.

I, however, have our Russian colleagues to thank for reminding me of social psychology's original concerns and how these should have shaped methodologies. Before flooding their literature with studies, they have debated at length on what methods are best suited to what problems. They have wrestled with these questions just as they have begun to do good empirical research. From reading their work, and from talking with them, I have come to think they, too, *must* develop a new conceptual or methodological paradigm, or they will very probably repeat all our mistakes. We in the West are, I feel, beginning to back into the same conclusion after three decades of careful empirical research. Possibly Soviet and Western social psychologists can begin to develop together the paradigms to fit the questions. If not, in another five to ten years, there are going to be some very interesting comparisons to make.

References

Back, K.W., The proper scope of social psychology, *Social Forces*, 1963, *41*, 368-75.

Marsh, P., Rosser, S. and Harre, R., *The Rules of Disorder*, London: Routledge & Kegan Paul, 1978.

Thorngate, W., Possible limits on a science of social behaviour. In L. Strickland, K. Gergen & F. Aboud (Eds.), *Social Psychology in Transition*, New York: Plenum, 1976.

Name Index

Page numbers in *italics* indicate names appearing in reference lists on those pages

330 *Name Index*

Subject Index

Academy of Sciences of the USSR
6, 19, 225
Activity
definition — as *dyeyatelnost* 116–18
joint, requiring communication
211–23
principle of, as special methodology
60, 67
regulative role of 211–23
and self-concept or sense 17, 254
and social relations (unity with)
11, 113–16
American Psychological Association 4
Animal social behaviour *see* Non-human behaviour

Bilingualism 273–85

Canada Council 19, 20
Canadian social psychology 3, 43, 72
Canadian social science and US domination 10
Carleton University 19
Cognition
and communication 12, 143–7
as context for experimental study
147–8
and memory and social performance
289–313
processes of, in social psychology
12, 143–50
significance of 147
as social perception 12, 143–50

Cognitive norms 35, 36
Cohesion (or cohesiveness)
and conflict 152–3, 164–6
definition 166
and reaction to threat 154, 166
Collective
and the individual 5
and the personality 13–14
place in Soviet social psychology
65–7
and social perception 149
Communication
"in the broad sense" 62, 63
and cognitive processes 211–25
cross-language 18, 273–85
and decision-making 17, 211–25
and information processing 17,
211–25
and memory processes 218–23
non-verbal 18, 148, 276
as *obshcheniye* 62, 63
and policing 258
and sensory judgement 17, 227–33
as subject matter of Soviet social
psychology 16, 50
Community psychology
and the police 17
and social psychology 17
Conflict
as controversies in social science
35–40
intergroup
and cohesiveness 13, 151
and hostility 13, 151
and theories of 104, 151–62
research (European vs. N. American)
37, 38, 39

333

Crisis in social psychology   2, 25, 26,
    27, 35, 55, 61, 93, 184
Crowding   125—35, 138—41

Decision-making
    vs. attitudes and attributions   19,
        312—13
    and communication   17, 211—25
    and information processing   17, 19
Dialectical materialism as general metho-
        dological principle   15, 59,
        202—3, 207
Dialectics
    and psychology   30
    scientific   30
Differentiation, intergroup   156—62
Dyeyatelnost as activity   116—18

Elites
    evidence for   42, 43
    in science and social science   40, 41,
        42
Emic approach vs. etic   76, 90
Equivalence, types of, in data   79—81
Ethics in research   14, 15, 181, 182,
        188—97, 199—200
Ethnocentrism
    as a bias in social psychology   46,
        47, 73
    and social conflict   151
Etic
    approach vs. emic   76—8
    derived   77
    imposed   77, 90
    pseudo-   77
    and theorics   78

Groups
    in Soviet social psychology   58, 59,
        64—7
    in Western social psychology   101—
        6, 322
    see also Intergroup behaviour

Historical/cultural conditioning, principle
        of, as special methodology
        60

History
    of science   44
        in the USSR   45
    of social psychology   44—7

Ideology
    as cognitive norms   36
    Marxist   4, 57
    and social psychology   4, 26, 34
Information processing
    vs. attitudes and attributions   19,
        312—13
    and communication   17
    and decision-making   17, 19
    and "levels of methodology"   205—
        6
Interaction and obshcheniye   63
Intergroup behaviour
    vs. interindividual   104—6
    and social perception   149

Laboratory experiments, role of, in
        Soviet social psychology   61

Marxism
    approach to personality   167—76
    approach to social psychology   3, 4,
        57—8
    -Leninism   5
Matter, levels of motion of   15, 202—5,
        206
Memory
    cognition and social performance
        19, 289—313
    joint (under conditions of communi-
        cation)   218—22
Methodology
    and dialectical materialism   15
    in different sciences   201—5
    and ethics   181
    ethogenic   98
    general vs. special vs. methodics
        58—60
    inadequate, in social psychology
        56
    levels of   9, 201—5
    problems of   2, 15